W9-ARJ-412

Conventional Wisdom
and American Elections

WITHDRAWN

6/08

I.C.C. LIBRARY

Conventional Wisdom and American Elections

Exploding Myths, Exploring Misconceptions

Jody C. Baumgartner
and
Peter L. Francia

I.C.C. LIBRARY

ROWMAN & LITTLEFIELD PUBLISHERS, INC.
Lanham • Boulder • New York • Toronto • Plymouth, UK

JK
1976
.B34
2008

ROWMAN & LITTLEFIELD PUBLISHERS, INC.

Published in the United States of America
by Rowman & Littlefield Publishers, Inc.
A wholly owned subsidiary of The Rowman & Littlefield Publishing Group, Inc.
4501 Forbes Boulevard, Suite 200, Lanham, Maryland 20706
www.rowmanlittlefield.com

Estover Road, Plymouth PL6 7PY, United Kingdom

Copyright © 2008 by Rowman & Littlefield Publishers, Inc.

All rights reserved. No part of this publication may be reproduced, stored in a retrieval system, or transmitted in any form or by any means, electronic, mechanical, photocopying, recording, or otherwise, without the prior permission of the publisher.

British Library Cataloguing in Publication Information Available

Library of Congress Cataloging-in-Publication Data

Baumgartner, Jody C., 1958–
  Conventional wisdom and American elections : exploding myths, exploring misconceptions / Jody C. Baumgartner and Peter L. Francia.
    p.   cm.
  Includes bibliographical references and index.
  ISBN-13: 978-0-7425-4737-7 (cloth : alk. paper)
  ISBN-10: 0-7425-4737-X (cloth : alk. paper)
  ISBN-13: 978-0-7425-4738-4 (pbk. : alk. paper)
  ISBN-10: 0-7425-4738-8 (pbk. : alk. paper)
  1. Elections—United States.   2. Politics, Practical—United States.   3. United States—Politics and government.   I. Francia, Peter L.   II. Title.
  JK1976.B34 2008
  324.70973—dc22
                                                    2007006370

Printed in the United States of America

♾ ™ The paper used in this publication meets the minimum requirements of American National Standard for Information Sciences—Permanence of Paper for Printed Library Materials, ANSI/NISO Z39.48-1992.

5/08 B&T 24.95

For Lei and Kali

Contents

Part III: Understanding Election Outcomes

Illustrations

BOXES

FIGURES

TABLES

Preface

Elections are the foundation of a democracy, yet they are often misunderstood. Popular accounts of American elections sometimes oversimplify complex subjects or overhype the latest political fads. In an age of cable television, talk radio, and Internet blogs, this occurs all too frequently. The result is that exaggerated assertions and other misinformation can become a part of the conventional wisdom of American elections.

During the 2004 election, for example, many commentators made a point to emphasize the negative tactics and practices of the Bush and Kerry campaigns. One political observer went so far as to call the 2004 election "the ugliest" presidential election in American history.[1] Such claims reflect a deep misunderstanding about the pervasive role that negative campaign tactics have always played in U.S. elections. For instance, critics of Thomas Jefferson stated that his election in 1800 would bring about legal prostitution and the burning of the Bible. Opponents of Andrew Jackson charged that he was a murderer and that his wife was a bigamist. Perhaps most scurrilous of all, Jackson's opponents even accused his dead mother of being a prostitute.

As these examples and others that we will profile in this book demonstrate, there are several myths and misconceptions about American elections that require more reflection and deeper analysis than they typically receive in the popular press. The conclusions that we draw are based largely on the most current political science research. In some instances, the literature is clear in debunking popular myths about American elections. On other issues, the research is more mixed. In either instance, we attempt to make the findings in the literature as clear as possible so that

readers can decipher between the issues that scholars have largely re-
solved and those in which honest debate remains.

To be clear, our intent in this book is not to attack the press, which we
believe generally does a very good job of reporting on politics and American elections. Likewise, it is not our intent to criticize any talk radio or
cable television hosts, many of whom we find to be both entertaining and
engaging. Indeed, we confess to being political junkies who enjoy and
routinely tune in to various radio and cable political programs, such as
Hardball, The O'Reilly Factor, and *Real Time with Bill Maher.*

Nevertheless, with the ever-increasing venues for people to exchange
political ideas, it has become virtually inevitable that some information
will be less than accurate. The myths and misconceptions that we identify
in this book come from these less-than-accurate accounts of American
elections and campaigns as well as other sources that we reference in various chapters. Those who are politically knowledgeable and informed will
probably find some of the information presented in this book to be quite
familiar. In chapter 9, for example, we discuss the popular notion (reinforced in books such as *The Selling of the President* and movies such as *The
Candidate*)[2] that success in presidential elections ultimately boils down to
clever marketing and the ability of campaign specialists to "sell" their candidate to the public. While political scientists and other astute political
observers understand that there are other important factors involved in a
winning presidential campaign, the public often has a more distorted picture of the process.[3] Certainly, the less glamorous details of presidential
campaigns, notably the importance of volunteers and the grassroots work
that they perform on the ground level of a campaign often receive considerably less attention.

Our intent in this book is therefore to bring some clarity to issues and
topics in American elections that are sometimes misunderstood or only
partially understood by the general public, especially those who only passively follow politics and interpret the half-truths perpetuated in the
information age as something more. More specifically, we wrote *Conventional Wisdom and American Elections* for instructors to assign to beginning
college and university students to help clarify much of the misinformation
that surrounds American elections. Our hope is that *Conventional Wisdom
and American Elections* will provide students with an interesting and accessible supplement to their traditional American government texts.

Before we begin, we wish to share with the reader a quick history of how
this project originated. On the night before Election Day in 2004, Peter
Francia, who had just joined the faculty at East Carolina University, presented a talk to the Rotary Club in Greenville, North Carolina, about "popular misconceptions and misunderstandings" in American elections. By
coincidence, Jody Baumgartner was contemplating a book project about

the "ten myths of American presidential elections" around the same time. When we learned of our shared interests, the two of us quickly agreed to write this book together. Not only did the subject material appeal to us but we both believed (and still do) that this project was a worthwhile endeavor. With the book now complete, we hope that readers will agree.

In the course of writing and preparing the manuscript, we benefited from the assistance of others who deserve recognition. First, we owe thanks to our research assistant Michael Shaw. His careful work on this project was immensely helpful. Second, we wish to thank our colleagues in the political science department at East Carolina University (ECU) for their constant support. Professor Jonathan Morris offered useful advice to us when we confronted difficulties during the project. Our senior colleagues at ECU also were exceptionally generous in encouraging our research efforts. Many of our senior colleagues teach an additional course during each academic year to help junior faculty members with their research. Those sacrifices certainly helped make this book possible.

In addition to the support we received from our colleagues at ECU, we benefited from the assistance of other scholars as well. Nathan Bigelow of Austin College and Renan Levine of the University of Toronto read an initial draft of this manuscript. Their suggestions helped improve the overall clarity and quality of this book.

We owe a special debt of gratitude to the many people at Rowman & Littlefield Publishers, especially our editor, Niels Aaboe, for his helpful suggestions and assistance with this project. Our copy editor, Naomi Burns, also deserves acknowledgment for her very thorough reading of the manuscript. Her attention to detail proved to be extremely valuable.

Finally, we leave our last and warmest appreciation to our wives, Lei Baumgartner and Kali Francia. As is the case with virtually all book projects, authors must sacrifice a significant amount of personal time to complete their manuscript in a timely fashion. Lei and Kali tolerated numerous inconveniences to allow us to finish this book. We are both grateful and thankful for their support and patience.

I

VOTERS

1

The Big Year
for the Youth Vote
Myth and Reality

Heading into the 2004 presidential election, several polls indicated that young Americans (eighteen- to twenty-four-year-olds) would vote in near-record numbers.[1] A May 2003 survey conducted by Harvard University's Institute of Politics reported that an estimated 59 percent of eighteen- to twenty-four-year-olds claimed that they would "definitely be voting" and that an additional 27 percent would "probably be voting" in the 2004 election.[2] Many Americans also believed that young voters might play a decisive role in deciding the 2004 election. Some 70 percent of Americans believed that youth voters potentially could be "very important" in defeating George W. Bush in 2004.[3] Several prominent celebrities further added to these high expectations by making special efforts to increase turnout among young voters. Sean "P. Diddy" Combs and his "Vote or Die!" campaign drew perhaps the most attention and led Combs to predict boldly that young voters were "gonna come out in numbers you've never seen before."[4]

By virtually any measure, young voters did turn out in near-record numbers in the 2004 presidential election, accounting for 20.9 million votes—an increase from 16.2 million in 2000.[5] Massive efforts to register young voters and get them out to vote aided this result. These efforts included those by independent groups (Citizen Change, MTV's "Choose or Lose: 20 Million Loud," Rock the Vote, Vote for Change, Music for America, and more), political parties (the Republicans' "Reggie the Registration Rig" and Democrat John Kerry's "Change Starts with U: Kerry Campus Tour 2004"), and others working to get out the vote for their candidates (e.g., Internet sites MoveOn.org and Punkvoter.com). Rock the

Vote, for example, almost tripled the number of youth voters they registered from the 2000 to the 2004 election cycle.[6]

In the end, however, the increase in the number of young voters accompanied an overall increase in turnout among voters from all age groups. Turnout rates remained the lowest for those between the ages of eighteen to twenty-four.[7] And despite predictions that the eighteen- to twenty-four-year-old vote would play an especially significant role in the 2004 election, young voters comprised the same percentage of the electorate as they did in 2000.[8] In the words of gonzo journalist Hunter Thompson, young voters "betrayed us again."[9]

Of course, the 2004 election was only one of many recent elections in which there were high expectations for young voters. In 1996, some speculated that the passage of the "motor-voter" law (which allows citizens to register to vote at motor vehicle agencies), the rise of the Internet, and a growing number of youth organizations would lead to a larger-than-usual youth turnout.[10] Despite those developments, a dismal 39 percent of young voters turned out to the polls in 1996.[11] Even the 1992 election, which many consider a benchmark for youth participation, witnessed only a 51 percent turnout among eighteen- to twenty-four-year-olds. This same story line of high expectations for the youth vote followed by disappointing results seems to repeat itself in each election. Like Samuel Beckett's play *Waiting for Godot*, the big year for the youth vote never seems to arrive.

Why is it then that young voters consistently turn out at the polls in numbers that consistently rank below those in other age categories? In this chapter we explore that question, looking first at the history of the passage of the Twenty-sixth Amendment, which lowered the voting age from twenty-one to eighteen. We then turn our focus to why more Americans, in general, do not vote, why youth do not vote, why it matters, and what, if anything, can be done about it.

THE HISTORY OF THE YOUTH VOTE

In 1941, Representative Jennings Randolph from West Virginia introduced a constitutional amendment that would lower the voting age to eighteen. He, like many others at the time, thought it was appropriate that, if the country asked eighteen-year-olds to serve in the armed forces during wartime, then the country should also grant eighteen-year-olds the right to vote. In virtually every year afterward, some legislator offered a similar measure. The idea also had the backing of Presidents Dwight Eisenhower (1953–1961) and Lyndon Johnson (1963–1969). Johnson asked Congress to pass a constitutional amendment lowering the voting age to eighteen in 1968. During the 1960s, several states passed laws that gave citizens under the age of twenty-one the right to vote, although the law applied only to state and local elections (twenty-one remained the voting age for federal elections in all states). Georgia and Kentucky lowered their voting age to eighteen, Alaska to nineteen, and Hawaii and New Hampshire to twenty.

Nationally, proposals to lower the voting age gathered serious momentum in the late 1960s. During this period there were widespread protests on college campuses across the country aimed at, among other things, ending the war in Vietnam. After 1969, when the military instituted a lottery-style draft, young people mobilized around the slogan "old enough to fight, old enough to vote."[12]

In response, Congress considered amending the Voting Rights Act of 1965 to extend the franchise to eighteen-year-olds. There was concern, however, that such an amendment would violate the Constitution. In their review of the Voting Rights Act in 1970, Congress included a provision that lowered the voting age to eighteen in all federal, state, and local elections. President Richard Nixon signed this bill into law on June 22, 1970. Later that year, however, the provision was challenged in the Supreme Court, and the Court ruled that although Congress was empowered to set the voting age for federal elections, it could not do so for state and local elections.[13] This meant that most states would have to maintain separate voter registration lists, one for federal elections and one for state and local elections. Because of this, Jennings Randolph (now a senator) reintroduced his constitutional amendment in January of 1971. The amendment passed in both the House and the Senate in March. By June, the requisite three-fourths of the state legislatures ratified the amendment. On July 1, 1971, less than seven months after its introduction, President Nixon formally certified the Twenty-sixth Amendment, lowering the voting age to eighteen. Never had a constitutional amendment been proposed, passed, and ratified so quickly.

Unfortunately, after this auspicious beginning, many young voters have since failed to take advantage of their newfound right to vote. In 1972, the first election following the ratification of the Twenty-sixth Amendment, the turnout rate for eighteen- to twenty-four-year olds was 54.6 percent.[14] This percentage represents the high mark for youth voting, although it needs to be placed in context of its time. During the early 1970s, young voters were mobilized because of the Vietnam War and a law-and-order president who was extremely unpopular with increasing numbers of countercultural youth. There was a significant upturn in the turnout rate of young voters in 1992 (from 42.4 percent in 1988 to 51.3 percent in 1992), which might have been due to Bill Clinton's active courting of the youth vote through appearances on networks such as MTV. However, in the next election (1996), turnout fell to a low of 39.5 percent. The election of 2000 saw a minor recovery, and in 2004, as many pundits expected, turnout almost reached the high mark of 1972 (see figure 1.1).

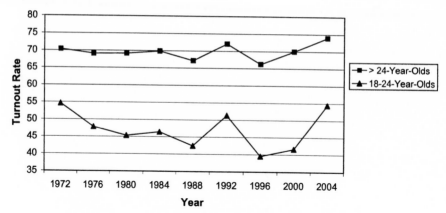

Figure 1.1.   Voter Turnout in Presidential Elections, 1972–2004
Source: The Center for Information and Research on Civic Learning and Engagement (CIRCLE).

Two other trends are evident from figure 1.1. First, the two trend lines representing under-twenty-four- and over-twenty-four-year-old voter turnout rates seem to move in concert. With only a few exceptions, when turnout increases or decreases for one group, there is a similar change for the other group. Indeed, people of all ages are more apt to vote if they believe their vote might make a difference in deciding the contest. Not surprisingly, the data confirm that voter turnout was higher during the competitive presidential elections of 1992 and 2004 than it was during less competitive elections, such as in 1996 when few experts gave Senator Robert Dole a serious chance to defeat Bill Clinton. Second, a higher percentage of older Americans (those over the age of twenty-four) go to the polls than younger Americans. The difference between under-twenty-four- and over-twenty-four-year-old voter turnout rates was 15.8 percent in 1972 and increased to 28.4 percent in 2000. In 2004, the difference dropped to 19.6 percent, an encouraging sign, but this number is still greater than the 1972 differential. The picture is similar when examining the turnout rates for midterm elections (congressional elections held in nonpresidential election years). Although participation of older Americans is lower in these elections than in presidential elections, the difference between under-twenty-four- and over-twenty-four-year-old voter turnout rates here is greater, averaging about 30 percent (see figure 1.2).

Thus, in both presidential and midterm elections, turnout rates among young voters are consistently lower than they are among older Americans. Given this history, it is hard to imagine why there are consistently such high expectations for a strong turnout from young Americans. So, why is it that more youth do not vote?

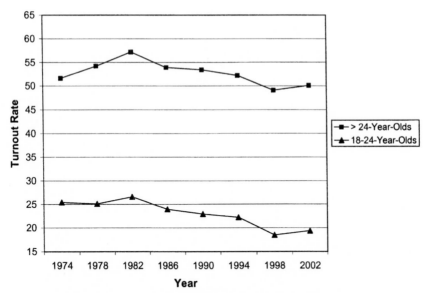

Figure 1.2.   Voter Turnout in Midterm Elections, 1974–2002
Source: The Center for Information and Research on Civic Learning and Engagement (CIRCLE).

WHY YOUNG PEOPLE DO NOT VOTE

Many political observers point to apathy to explain why young adults do not vote. However, some critics counter that apathy is not the problem. They note that a large segment of young Americans are involved in community service projects and express interest in serving the public.[15] There are certainly several other and perhaps better explanations to understand why young Americans vote less frequently than others. One prominently mentioned argument is that voting is an act of habit: the more a person does it, the more likely he or she is to keep doing it.[16] Because young voters have not had the time to develop the habit of voting, older voters who have developed the habit are more likely to vote.[17]

There are also barriers to voting that seem to have an especially significant effect on the turnout of young voters. A first broad category of explanations deals with the rules governing the administration of elections. The act of voting in the United States is more difficult than it is in other democracies. Borrowing from economists, some political scientists hold that individuals are "rational actors" who weigh the *costs* of voting against its perceived *benefits*.[18] For example, traveling long distances to reach a polling place might be too much of a cost when compared with the difference (benefit) one vote might make. A second set of explanations deals with various social-psychological factors, such as how much people trust government, how attached they are to political parties, and more.[19] This line of thinking focuses on the idea that Americans—and especially youth—might be less connected to politics than they were a half century ago. Because of this, young adults might feel that voting simply does not matter.

The Rules: Legal Barriers

Several aspects of election law in the United States are important to understanding why people do not vote.[20] Many studies confirm that restrictive laws, such as registration laws, or deadlines that force citizens to register early in the election season, result in decreased levels of voter turnout. In all but one state (North Dakota), registration is necessary to vote. This is not the case in most established democracies, where voter registration is the responsibility of the government. Each state determines voter registration laws, and voters must register in the local precinct where they live. Moreover, in most states, people are required to register to vote before Election Day. The length of time varies from state to state, but it is usually at least a few weeks prior to the election. Some people, even the best intentioned, simply forget to register until it is too late. In addition, in most states, if someone forgets to register—or reregister after moving—he or she cannot vote. This probably disproportionately affects young people, many of whom move frequently and know less about the process than do citizens who vote on a regular basis.

Another election law that probably depresses voter turnout is the fact that Election Day is on a Tuesday. This is significant simply because most people work (or go to class) on a Tuesday. In order to vote, there are several inconvenient options. One is to rise early in the morning to arrive at the polls before work. A second option is to schedule voting during a lunch break. A third possibility is to vote after work. And a fourth option is to ask the boss to vote during work. By comparison, most other democracies in the world permit voting to take place on weekends or on special holidays dedicated to voting. While Tuesday voting in the United States drives turnout down for all voters, young voters may be the ones most affected. One reason for this is that young voters often fail to realize that they can register to vote at their college or university and are often unaware of how the absentee voting process operates.[21] Young voters might opt not to vote, given that the election occurs a considerable distance away while also taking place during the middle of the workweek when traveling a long distance is most difficult to schedule. These additional costs to voting, as rational choice theory would suggest, reduce the likelihood of voting.

There are also more elections in which to vote in the United States than in any other nation. In most European nations, there are only three or so elections (representative in Parliament, representative to the European Union, and a scattering of local offices) during a four-year period. By comparison, there are many more elections in the United States. Americans have the option to vote in primary and general elections for the U.S. House of Representatives every two years (during all even-numbered years). In some states and cities, citizens also vote in a primary and general election for governor or mayor during odd-numbered years. Other states might hold elections for voters to decide on ballot propositions, which might occur at different times of the year. In some rare instances, citizens might even have to vote in a recall election. Again, these demands can be especially problematic for young adults, especially students who attend college.

Finally, with respect to the rules governing elections, voting in the United States is more complicated than in other countries and, thus, more difficult to understand. In most democracies, citizens might be asked to cast a vote for a political party and maybe a single member of Parliament from their district, and perhaps a few other offices. Our system of federalism and separated government means there are a multiplicity of offices that voters must select, from president down to county commissioner, local sheriff, circuit court judges, and more. In total, there are over one million elective offices in the United States, and ballots rarely give voters the option of voting a straight-party ticket.[22] It is the rare individual who has taken the time to research each candidate running for each office. The array of choices citizens face at the voting booth can be especially intimidating to first-time voters, who are inexperienced and more likely to be lacking in information about the process and the choices facing them. It might, in fact, be so intimidating that they do not bother to vote.

Social-Psychological Factors: Connections to the Political World

Other reasons that more youth do not vote has to do with their connections to the social and political world around them. Like the factors above, this affects all Americans. However, it might be that youth are disproportionately disadvantaged for a few reasons. First, many young adults have less of a sense of community than their older counterparts. This is partly a function of the fact that they have had less time to develop various community ties (career, home, marriage, etc.). They are in college, starting careers, and often moving to different locales within the same area or to other areas. In addition, youth engage in more solitary activities (watching television, playing video games, listening to iPods) and are less likely than earlier generations to join face-to-face organizations.[23] This contributes to nonvoting. People who feel connected in their communities are more likely to vote, if only because they have something to protect or advocate (e.g., lower property taxes for homeowners).

Second, young people are more cynical about government and politicians. This is generally true of all Americans, if one compares data from several decades ago. However, young people are more likely than older Americans to think that politicians are corrupt and that money plays too large a role in politics. A survey from the Harvard University Institute of Politics reported that roughly two-thirds of college students do not trust the federal government to do the right thing most of the time.[24] Many others complain that campaigns are too long, are too negative, and focus too much on personality rather than on the issues. This is significant because these negative perceptions lead to skepticism about campaign politics and the belief that voting has little impact in affecting change. These feelings are important because an individual's sense of political efficacy (the idea that what each individual does has an effect), trust in government, and sense of duty associated with citizenship are often significant predictors of voting.[25]

Third, young voters have weaker party attachments than older voters. This is important because people who feel attached to a political party are more apt to vote than people who claim they are independents.[26] Youth are also much more likely to support third parties and independent candidates than their older counterparts[27] and are less likely to perceive differences between the two parties. There are major substantive differences between the policy platforms of the two parties, but in the midst of an election campaign, these differences can become blurred as candidates attempt to capture the attention and votes of the large numbers of citizens who see themselves as moderates. The choice that one must make on Election Day is less clear and, thus, more difficult.

Youth also report that parties and politicians do not address the issues they think are important. One survey reported that nearly three-fourths of college students believe that "political candidates, campaigns, and institutions do not seem concerned with what students think about major political issues."[28] In short, young voters believe that they are being ignored, and research confirms the fact that they typically are.[29] This failure on the part of political parties and candidates to speak to young Americans depresses their motivation to vote.

Finally, young voters are often less politically knowledgeable, which can affect the decision to vote. For example, young voters often do not understand the absentee ballot process.[30] Some 87 percent of college students claim they would become more involved in politics if they had more practical information about politics.[31] The same is probably true for young voters not in college. Of course, in the information age, citing a lack of "practical information about politics" seems like a questionable if not dubious reason for not participating in the political process.

WHAT, IF ANYTHING, CAN BE DONE
TO INCREASE YOUTH TURNOUT?

In addition to the factors already noted, other barriers exist for young voters to overcome. This is not to suggest that it is impossible, or even difficult, to vote in the United States. However, various rules make the act of voting both complicated and burdensome. Beyond the rules, various other aspects of society and politics in the United States make it less likely that people of all ages, especially youth, will be able or willing to jump over the hurdles these rules set up in order to vote.

Is nonvoting—in general, and in particular by young adults—a cause for concern? Many maintain that it is not. Some argue that non-voting is an indication that people are content with their government and that most citizens desire to be less involved in political decision making.[32] Others make the case that only people who care enough to learn about the candidates and issues during the campaign and make the effort to vote should have their voices heard. This argument suggests that good government and good policy depends on informed choices.[33] Countering this argument is the idea that democratic citizenship is in many ways an acquired skill. People learn more and, importantly, appreciate the value of participation, by voting.[34] Another perspective suggests that voting is a choice and citizens thus have the right not to vote. Countering this is the argument that democracy requires participation by its citizens, and as a result, all citizens have a duty to vote.[35]

The fact that young people vote less frequently has important consequences. Voting *does* matter, if only because it is the most fundamental aspect of democratic citizenship. Elections put people into office who will determine policies that will affect people's lives. For young voters, issues such as rising college tuition costs and affordable student loans might have an effect on young Americans' current and future financial burdens. Other issues concerning equality, the environment, balancing the budget, and making sure social security is solvent when *they* retire are all potentially important to young voters' future. In short, young voters have a stake in any number of political decisions that will have long-term consequences in their everyday lives.

Those who believe that low youth turnout is a problem suggest any variety of reforms. For example, making voting mandatory is one such proposal. Several studies have shown that, in countries where voting is mandatory, turnout rates are close to 15 percent higher than in countries where voting is optional.[36] Another suggestion is to move Election Day from a Tuesday to a weekend or to make it a holiday. Of course, the government is unlikely to adopt any of these reforms.

Several successful efforts have eased the burden on citizens to vote. The most prominent was the National Voter Registration Act of 1993 (the Motor Voter Bill) that requires motor vehicle offices to accept voter registration applications and allows other government agencies and programs to do so as well. Mail-in voter registration has also become more common in most states. In addition, several states (Idaho, Minnesota, Maine, New Hampshire, Wisconsin, and Wyoming) allow Election Day registration. Indeed, the surprise victory of independent gubernatorial candidate Jesse "The Body" Ventura in Minnesota during the 1998 election was widely attributed to a high turnout from young voters who took advantage of Election Day registration.[37] However, it is not clear that these registration reforms have significantly boosted overall turnout rates.

Perhaps the easiest problem to correct would be the lack of information that young voters have about obtaining absentee ballots. All states have absentee ballots that allow individuals to vote from a location other than their designated polling place and at a time that is convenient to them. Many states now allow voters to request absentee ballots for any variety of reasons ("no-excuse" absentee voting), including when voting would require a long commute. In addition, as many as thirty states allowed early voting in 2004 (in person or by mail).[38] Some reformers have suggested that a public service campaign about how to obtain absentee ballots would be a logical step to increase youth voting, especially among college students.[39]

Young voters have further expressed a lack of enjoyment from the political process. For a generation used to fast food, instant messaging, and other time-saving conveniences, waiting in long lines to vote is an activity that most young voters are not predisposed to enjoy. Internet voting, which promises a faster and more convenient method of voting, is one option, although security concerns would need to be carefully addressed before considering this method. Early voting and satellite voting might alleviate long lines and make the process more convenient, although there were wide reports that early voting locations also experienced long lines during the 2004 election.[40]

However, reform measures have only raised youth voter turnout slightly.[41] Part of the reason might be that, even in the case of same-day registration, early voting, or absentee voting, the voter must still make some effort. This is not to suggest that institutional reforms are unnecessary or that states should not consider experimenting with some. It is to say that reformers hoping to boost turnout among the young should be realistic about the limited potential of institutional reforms.

Politicians could play a role in stimulating the political interest of young voters. In 1992, Bill Clinton made a concerted effort to address issues that matter to youth, and it resulted in one of the higher youth voter turnout rates in thirty years. Candidates could make additional appearances at college campuses. Students who meet a candidate are more than twice as likely to get involved in politics as are those who have never met an elected official.[42] Unfortunately, there appears to be little incentive for candidates to engage with youth. After all, it makes little sense for a campaign to invest its resources into courting a segment of the electorate that historically is not likely to vote. This becomes a vicious cycle: candidates ignore young voters and their issues because they do not vote, and young Americans ignore politics and elections because the candidates do not speak to their interests and concerns. This cycle seems unlikely to end any time in the near future.

One especially interesting finding from the past few years is that personalized messages and appeals can be a particularly effective method to generate increased turnout, especially among young adults.[43] The same is true for person-to-person contact, which can be extremely effective in getting people out to vote. This is especially true if there is peer group contact. Thus, increasing voter turnout among youth—or any age group—does not necessarily require complex rule changes. One person can make a difference by simply talking to friends, to family, to co-workers, or to associates.[44] This too, however, is not likely to happen among less socially connected and politically uninterested youth, but it is something that one person could do. Perhaps this is the bright spot in our otherwise somewhat dismal portrait of youth voting. Systemic changes might not make much difference, but individuals can.

CONCLUSION

There will undoubtedly continue to be predictions of the big year for young voters. While there are certainly some reforms that might improve the turnout of young Americans, we would caution that any changes are likely to bring only modest results. This is not to suggest that mobilization efforts, such as those of P. Diddy, are a waste of time. Many recent get-out-the-vote campaigns helped encourage many young adults to participate in the democratic process for the first time, which is a laudable accomplishment. Nevertheless, political observers must also be realistic. Given the obstacles to voting for young Americans, the cynicism of young adults toward the political process, and three decades of unfulfilled promise since the passage of the Twenty-sixth Amendment, it seems clear that young voters hitting the polls in numbers equal to their older counterparts is unlikely to occur.

FOR MORE READING

Cultice, Wendell W. *Youth's Battle for the Ballot: A History of Voting Age in America.* New York: Greenwood Press, 1992.

Lopez, Mark Hugo, Emily Kirby, and Jared Sagoff. "The Youth Vote 2004, with a Historical Look at Youth Voting Patterns, 1972–2004." Working Paper 35, Center for Information and Research on Civic Learning and Engagement, July 2005.

Piven, Frances Fox, and Richard A. Cloward. *Why Americans Still Don't Vote: And Why Politicians Want It That Way.* Boston: Beacon Press, 2000.

Shea, Daniel M., and John C. Green, eds. *Fountain of Youth: Strategies and Tactics for Mobilizing America's Young Voters.* Lanham, Md.: Rowman & Littlefield, 2007.

Wolfinger, Raymond E., and Steven J. Rosenstone. *Who Votes?* New Haven, Conn.: Yale University Press, 1980.

2

The "America Divided" Myth

Red States, Blue States, and Other Gaps

The 2000 and 2004 presidential elections were two of the most closely contested races for the White House in American history. In 2000, Republican George W. Bush captured the state of Florida by a mere 537 votes, giving him an electoral college majority over Democrat Al Gore of 271 to 266, despite losing the popular vote to Gore by roughly a half-million votes. Four years later, Bush earned 286 votes in the electoral college to 251 for his opponent, Democrat John Kerry. Bush also won the majority of popular votes in 2004, earning 51 percent to Kerry's 48 percent.

In the aftermath of these two highly contested presidential elections, many in the news media began discussing how politically polarized the electorate had become, with some labeling the United States a "fifty-fifty nation" deeply divided along "red" and "blue" state lines (a shorthand reference for states that gave their electoral votes to Bush or Gore respectively). Many journalists followed these stories with claims that the nation was divided at the polls because there is a "culture war" in the United States in which there are deep and fundamental divisions in American society on issues ranging from abortion to gay marriage to gun control.[1] In the words of one analyst, "There is . . . a political and cultural divide that has turned America into a 50–50 nation . . . a seething cauldron of 'red' and 'blue' states, in the color-coded maps of network television analysts."[2]

Some political observers exaggerated the cultural divide to the point of being humorous. One account described the stereotypes of red state voters who supported George W. Bush as "ignorant, racist, fascist, knuckle-dragging, NASCAR-obsessed, cousin-marrying, road-kill-eating, tobacco-juice-dribbling, gun-fondling, religious fanatic, rednecks."[3] Another

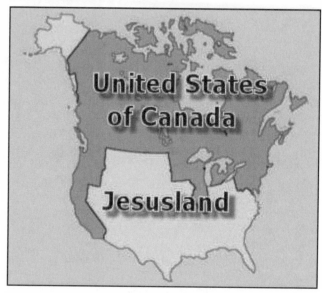

Figure 2.1.   Satirical "Jesusland" Map of Red and Blue States
Source: Wikipedia, at en.wikipedia.org/wiki/Jesusland_map.

summary described Democratic voters' perceptions of Republicans as "a collection of pampered rich people who selfishly seek to cut their own taxes, allied with religious fundamentalists who want to use government power to impose a narrow brand of Christianity on everyone else."[4]

Stereotypes of blue state voters who supported John Kerry were no more flattering. One account summarized them as "godless, unpatriotic, pierced-nose, Volvo-driving, France-loving, leftwing Communist, latte-sucking, tofu-chomping, holistic-wacko, neurotic vegan, weenie perverts."[5] Another added that Republicans view Democrats as little more than "godless, overeducated elitists who sip lattes as they look down their noses at the moral values of 'real Americans' in 'the heartland' and ally themselves with 'special interest groups' that benefit from 'big government.'"[6] Not surprisingly, there were even popular graphic representations of this divide on the Internet immediately following the 2004 election (see figure 2.1), with the red states being represented as "Jesusland" and blue states comprising part of the "United States of Canada."

Again, these extreme characterizations underscore a belief that Americans have grown polarized in the electoral and political arena. Not everyone, however, accepts the premise that the culture war has been the dominating source of conflict in American elections. Indeed, significant controversy and various different perspectives surround this subject. In this chapter, we attempt to make some sense of the various issues surrounding the culture war debate and its effect on American elections. While there is no uniform agreement among social scientists about the importance of cultural issues and the extent of polarization among the electorate, there is consensus on a few points.

First, there are significant gaps in recent voting behavior that are reflective of at least some degree of polarization in the electorate. One is the so-called gender gap, although the differences in voting behavior between men and women narrowed considerably in 2004.[7] Other gaps, however, have remained considerable. First, the religion gap has widened in recent years and has obvious implications for any discussions about cultural politics in the United States. Second, there is increased partisanship with respect to voting behavior. Third, there is a growing gap between the voting behavior of urban and rural residents. However, to begin to understand the debate that surrounds the so-called culture war, some background and perspective is in order.

THE ORIGINS OF THE CULTURE WAR

The term *culture war* gained prominent attention in academic circles following the publication of sociologist James Davison Hunter's 1991 book, *Culture Wars: The Struggle to Define America*. Hunter argued that Americans are deeply split by two competing world views: progressivism and orthodoxy. Those adhering to progressivism believe in policies that will bring about social change. In contrast, those adhering to orthodoxy oppose social change and are deeply committed to maintaining existing traditions. According to Hunter, these values are the source of fundamental divisions among Americans on a range of social and cultural issues including abortion, school prayer, and homosexual rights.[8]

According to some, these divisions trace back to the social movements of the 1960s. One reporter described the period as the "big bang" in bringing about the social and cultural schisms of today.[9] The major political issues of that time involved protests over civil rights and the Vietnam War. However, the unrest of the 1960s transcended politics. It also saw a rebellion against mainstream culture. Perhaps the best illustration of this was the "counterculture" movement, which came to describe a generation of young Americans (referred to as "hippies") who snubbed traditional values. The counterculture movement with its popular slogan to "turn on, tune in, and drop out" encouraged a generation to reject traditional sexual mores such as monogamy, to experiment with illicit drug use such as LSD, and to disengage from mainstream society.

Other social movements further challenged traditional social norms such as the role of women in society. Betty Friedan's best-selling book, *The*

Feminine Mystique, published in 1963, challenged the prevailing gender stereotypes that women could only discover true happiness in their role as a wife, mother, and homemaker. Feminists also pushed for reproductive freedom, campaigning to have state laws stricken that restricted access to birth control methods or that prohibited abortion.

These events, according to some experts, played a significant role in shaping contemporary cultural divisions. According to political scientist Larry Sabato, "Since the 1960s, the society and the culture have moved to the left, almost consistently, over the years, and as a result, Americans who have traditional views on social values have become increasingly alienated and even angry. That has now fully manifested itself in our politics."[10] (For a complete timeline of events related to the culture war since the 1960s, see box 2.1.)

However, tensions over various contemporary cultural issues date back much earlier than the 1960s. The roots of the women's rights movement trace as far back as 1848 to the Seneca Falls convention and the ensuing women's suffrage movement. The debate over whether to teach evolution or creationism—known by some today as "intelligent design"—in public schools was a source of controversy in the nineteenth century and early twentieth century. In 1844, for example, the city of Philadelphia experienced a series of violent protests and riots. Known as the Philadelphia Nativist Riots or the Philadelphia Prayer Riots, Protestants and Catholic immigrants violently clashed over which version of the Bible should be taught in public schools.[11] Perhaps the best-known example is the "Scopes" or "Great Monkey" trial in which the state of Tennessee brought charges against John Scopes for teaching evolution in his science class in 1925. The issue remains salient today. In 1999, the Kansas Board of Education created a national stir by voting to eliminate the teaching of evolution from the state's science curriculum.[12]

Similarly, the modern abortion movement found its roots in the century-old battle to reform birth control laws. In 1916, Margaret Sanger opened the first birth control clinic in the United States and shortly after formed the National Committee for Federal Legislation for Birth Control. She led the effort to legalize various forms of contraceptives and organized Planned Parenthood in 1942.[13] Partly as the result of these efforts, the Supreme Court overturned a Connecticut law banning contraception in 1965 in the landmark case *Griswold v. Connecticut.* The Court's decision in the case of *Roe v. Wade,* which legalized most abortions, was based in large part on the right to privacy established in *Griswold.*

In short, there have long been social and cultural divisions in the United States. In fact, the counterculture movement of the 1960s traces its roots to an earlier period, drawing its inspiration from the "beat" movement of the 1950s. Referred to as "beatniks," members of the beat movement were

---

BOX 2.1

SOME SIGNIFICANT EVENTS
IN THE "CULTURE WARS," 1965–2005

1965   *Griswold v. Connecticut* invalidates Connecticut law prohibiting use
        of contraception by married couples, establishing constitutionally
        protected "right to privacy."

1967   Colorado passes first law allowing abortion in cases involving rape,
        incest, severe defects, or threats to health of mother. Also, *Loving v.
        Virginia* overturns state laws banning interracial marriage.

1968   Pope Paul VI issues *Humanae Vitae*, condemning use of artificial
        birth control. The case of *Epperson v. Arkansas* declares any law
        forbidding teaching of evolution to be unconstitutional. Also, *Hair*,
        the first Broadway musical to depict nudity, premieres.

1969   Stonewall riots in New York City kick off the modern American gay-
        rights movement, the Woodstock music festival is held, and the X-
        rated *Midnight Cowboy* wins best picture award.

1970   New York passes law allowing abortion up to twenty-fourth week of
        pregnancy.

1971   *United States v. Vuitch*, the first Supreme Court decision on
        abortion, upholds D.C. law allowing abortion when necessary for
        mother's physical and psychological health. Also, *All in the Family*,
        a popular television sitcom, premieres.

1972   The first issue of *Ms. Magazine*, cofounded by Gloria Steinem,
        appears on newsstands; *The Joy of Sex*, by Alex Comfort, is
        published; and *Deep Throat* premieres.

1973   The case of *Roe v. Wade* invalidates all state bans on abortion
        before third trimester, and *Miller v. California* holds that material can
        be banned for obscenity only if they "depict or describe patently
        offensive 'hard core' sexual conduct specifically defined." Also,
        George Carlin's "Seven Dirty Words" monologue airs.

1974   Larry Flynt founds *Hustler* magazine.

1975   U.S. television networks establish a nightly "family hour" free of sex
        and violence.

1976   Episcopal Church permits female priests, and the New Jersey
        Supreme Court rules that parents of Karen Ann Quinlan, a woman
        in persistent vegetative state, may remove her respirator.

(continued)

BOX 2.1 *(continued)*

1978	Harvey Milk, first openly gay elected official in America, assassinated in San Francisco.
1979	Moral Majority founded under leadership of Jerry Falwell.
1980	Ronald Reagan elected on Republican platform that calls for *Roe v. Wade* to be overturned.
1981	The first test-tube baby born in the United States, and the debut of MTV.
1984	Nude photos surface of Miss America Vanessa Williams (she abdicates her throne).
1985	Debut of *Silent Scream*, controversial video of an abortion produced by abortion-provider turned pro-lifer Dr. Bernard Nathanson. Tipper Gore and other congressional wives found Parents Music Resource Center to combat "alarming trends" in popular music.
1986	*Bowers v. Hardwick* holds that sodomy is not protected under right to privacy.
1987	*Edwards v. Aguillard* holds that teaching creationism in public schools violates separation of church and state.
1988	The Senate rejects Robert Bork's nomination to the Supreme Court, televangelist Jimmy Swaggart is caught with a prostitute, and Pat Robertson shocks the GOP by placing second in the Iowa caucuses.
1989	Pat Robertson founds the Christian Coalition, and *The Simpsons* premieres.
1990	*Cruzan v. Director* upholds right to reject medical treatment, sparking interest in living wills.
1991	"Summer of Mercy" in Wichita, Kansas: Pro-life activists launch an effort to shut down abortion clinics. Also, *LA Law* airs first lesbian kiss on network television.
1992	The case of *Planned Parenthood v. Casey* reaffirms right to abortion but accepts certain limitations. Dan Quayle attacks the television character Murphy Brown for glamorizing unwed motherhood. At the Republican National Convention, Pat Buchanan declares that the Cold War has given way to a "cultural war."
1993	Abortion doctor David Gunn shot to death by Michael Griffin in Pensacola, Florida. After failed attempt to allow homosexuals into military, Bill Clinton announces the "Don't Ask, Don't Tell" compromise. Also, the Hawaii Supreme Court rules that prohibiting same-sex marriage might violate the state constitution.

BOX 2.1 (continued)

1994 John Salvi shoots and kills workers at two abortion clinics in Brookline, Massachusetts, and Paula Jones files suit against Bill Clinton for sexual harassment.

1996 *Romer v. Evans* bars states from excluding gays from antidiscrimination laws, and Bill Clinton signs the Defense of Marriage Act, defining marriage as a "legal union between one man and one woman."

1997 The case of *Washington et al. v. Harold Glucksberg et al.* finds no right to assisted suicide in Constitution. The "Death with Dignity" law, allowing physician-assisted suicide, goes into effect in Oregon. Ellen DeGeneres "comes out" on her sitcom, *Ellen*, and *South Park* premieres.

1998 The Monica Lewinsky scandal erupts, and Matthew Shepard, a gay college student, is murdered in Laramie, Wyoming.

1999 Vermont passes a law permitting civil unions between homosexual couples, and the Kansas Board of Education votes to delete any reference to evolution from state's science curriculum.

2000 *Stenberg v. Carhart* invalidates state bans on partial-birth abortion.

2001 George W. Bush restricts federal funding for stem-cell research.

2003 The Episcopal Church consecrates its first openly gay bishop, in New Hampshire. George W. Bush signs a national partial-birth-abortion ban into law. The case of *Lawrence v. Texas* rules that bans on homosexual sodomy are unconstitutional, and the Massachusetts Supreme Court rules gays have right to marry under state constitution. Finally, Alabama chief justice Roy Moore is relieved of office for refusing to remove Ten Commandments monument from state Supreme Court building.

2004 George W. Bush calls for constitutional ban on gay marriage, and gay-marriage bans pass by referendum in eleven states. *The Passion of the Christ* is released, and Janet Jackson suffers a "wardrobe malfunction" at Super Bowl.

2005 The Supreme Court allows Ten Commandments exhibit in Texas courthouse but bans two such displays in Kentucky, and Teri Schiavo's feeding tube is removed.

Source: Adapted from E. J. Dionne Jr., "Why the Culture War Is the Wrong War," *Atlantic Monthly* (January/February 2006): 132–35.

sharply critical of traditional American values, especially what they perceived to be mainstream society's preoccupation with materialistic concerns and other elements of the dominant culture, such as Christianity.
Politically, they supported desegregation and civil rights for African Americans during a time when many white Americans did not.[14] As E. J. Dionne
summarizes,

> There is a hidden assumption that we were once a happy, homogenous na-
> tion that came apart only when hippies preached free love, the religious right
> rose, secularists became more assertive, the Supreme Court began issuing lib-
> eral decisions, talk-show hosts began yelling, and intelligent designers began
> lobbying school boards. . . . So we forget that the seeds of modern feminism
> were planted in Ozzie and Harriet's day. . . . We forget that the hippies of the
> 1960s were preceded by the Beats of the 1950s. . . . Before the battles in the
> 1960s and 1970s to legalize abortion there were fights in the late 1940s to le-
> galize birth control.[15]

THE CULTURE WAR TODAY:
GROWING GAPS IN THE ELECTORATE

While it is clear that cultural battles have a long history in the United States,
less obvious is how deep cultural divisions in American society are today.
As mentioned earlier, some political observers believe that the United States
is a deeply polarized nation, divided along red state and blue state lines.
Several political observers as well as some prominent politicians believe
that cultural divisions have polarized a large segment of the American public. Many cite a speech made by conservative commentator and presidential
candidate Patrick Buchanan during the 1992 Republican National Convention as the start of the contemporary culture war. In it, Buchanan told a
national audience: "My friends, this election is about much more than who
gets what. It is about who we are. It is about what we believe. It is about
what we stand for as Americans. There is a great religious war going on in
our country for the soul of America. It is a cultural war, as critical to the kind
of nation we will one day be as was the Cold War itself."[16]

Some suggest that Buchanan's rhetoric was consistent with changes that
had been occurring in the Republican Party. According to one account, the
1992 presidential election saw evangelical Christians emerge as the "base
of the Republican vote."[17] Others concluded that voter positions on abortion were a major determinant of vote choice in 1992.[18] As the 1990s progressed, according to some, the "values divide" widened. President Bill
Clinton's sex scandal involving intern Monica Lewinsky sharply split
Americans along party lines. Similarly, President George W. Bush has been
a polarizing figure.[19]

Indeed, many political observers believe that Bush's electoral success resulted in part from his campaign's ability to mobilize those sharing traditional values.[20] In addition, there is some survey research that supports the idea that culture matters. In a 2003 poll, approximately 45 percent of adults reported that "moral or cultural issues" outweighed economic conditions in selecting a president.[21] One election expert concludes, "The last three elections (2000, 2002, 2004) have all had strong 'culture war' components that have severely depressed white working class support for Democrats."[22] In a recent book, *What's the Matter with Kansas?* author Thomas Frank argues that low-income Americans in rural areas vote against their own class interests because of their strongly held positions on moral issues, such as abortion and gay rights. As one account summarizes,

> Much recent commentary has characterized the United States as a polity deeply driven by a clash of culture and values between conservative, red state Republicans and liberal, blue state Democrats. Many appear to believe that Samuel Huntington's "clash of civilizations" has sunk roots in American soil. And it must be said that evidence to support this perspective has been ready at hand, especially in the aftermath of the 2000 election. A cliff-hanging presidential election, a Senate divided in half, a narrow Republican majority in the House of Representatives—these electoral outcomes fit within a pattern of narrow partisan division of both the electorate and the government that has prevailed for a decade.[23]

Still, not all scholars accept the premise that a culture war has been the dominating source of conflict in American politics. A few suggest that economic issues, such as taxation, government assistance programs for the needy, unemployment, and inflation consistently outweigh values issues for the majority of voters.[24] One study suggests that "the electorate is indeed pulled in two directions . . . but the pull of economic issues is so much stronger that the role of moral issues is clearly of secondary importance."[25]

Some even dispute the notion that most Americans are divided on cultural issues. One prominent study reports that most Americans are not polarized but rather share moderate positions on most issues and are generally ambivalent in their political attitudes.[26] The authors suggest that the misunderstanding about polarization derives from selective media coverage that tends to exaggerate differences between red and blue state voters. The study adds that the "myth" of a culture war also comes from confusing politicians and other elites with the average American. The authors note that political candidates have become increasingly partisan in an attempt to "rally the base" with extremist language and overheated rhetoric.[27] Indeed, the evidence suggests that the "base" of the major parties, notably elites such as convention delegates, party activists, and campaign donors, are extremely ideological and polarized.[28] This pushes candidates away from moderate positions, making compromise in governing more difficult. The latest research empirically supports this, as roll-call data indicate that congressional Democrats vote with other congressional Democrats in unity more than ever before, while congressional Republicans vote with other congressional Republicans in unity more than ever before as well.[29]

Such different perspectives make it clear that there is significant debate surrounding the subject of polarization and the culture war. However, there is much greater agreement that there are growing gaps among the American electorate with respect to voting behavior. Sharper and more consistent partisan divisions, religious differences, and a growing gap between the political attitudes of urban and rural voters have increased in recent years.

Partisanship

Recent data from the 2004 American National Election Study show that partisan polarization has increased over the past several decades. Democrats and Republicans hold significantly different opinions on numerous political issues, including jobs and living standards, health insurance, and presidential approval. Indeed, President George W. Bush has been particularly polarizing. According to one account,

> Evaluations of presidential performance have become much more divided along party lines since the 1970s and evaluations of George W. Bush in 2004 were sharply divided along party lines. Ninety-two percent of Republican voters approved of Bush's performance and 70 percent strongly approved; in contrast, 86 percent of Democratic voters disapproved of Bush's performance and 69 percent strongly disapproved. Evaluations of George W. Bush were more divided along party lines than those of any president since the NES began asking the presidential approval question in 1972.[30]

The preferences of Democrats and Republicans voters also differ significantly on a number of issues, with Democratic voters expressing quite liberal views and Republicans quite conservative views. Perhaps most important, evidence indicates that these differences are not driven by a small group of party activists. As one study reports, "Active participants are not a small group of left-wing and right-wing extremists. They are a large minority of both parties' primary voters."[31] Perhaps not surprisingly, Democrats and Republicans are sharply divided on cultural issues. Democrats are significantly more likely than Republicans are to support the legalization of abortion, gay rights, and an equal role for women in society.

The dominant explanation for this development is the partisan realignment of the South. Conservative southerners, once a dominant bloc in the Democratic Party, began to drift to the Republican Party. Issues related to race (notably the passage of the 1964 Civil Rights Act, the 1965 Voting Rights Act, and the 1967 Open Housing Act) contributed to realignment, although some recent evidence attributes the change to rising incomes in the region.[32] As the South transformed, there began a steady decline in conservative southern Democrats in Congress. As southern conservatives moved into their more natural home in the Republican Party, another significant change also occurred in the South. Democrats gained African American voters in the South, who gained the vote following reforms, such as the Voting Rights Act of 1965. These changes fundamentally altered the base of the two parties. The Republican base became more conservative, and the Democratic base became more liberal.

Religion

There are significant religious differences across party lines. Since the 1980 presidential election, the Republican Party has become increasingly associated with religious conservatism and "moral traditionalism."[33] White Americans who attend church regularly or identify themselves as a born-again or evangelical Christian are strongly correlated with Republican party identification and presidential voting. Indeed, religious factors are more strongly correlated with party identification and voting behavior than income, education, gender, marital status, and union membership.[34] As two prominent religious scholars declare, "The fact of the matter is that there is a religious gap in American voting behavior."[35]

Religious political divisions were once rooted in denominational differences. Catholics and Jews voted primarily for Democrats, while Protestants voted Republican. However, by the 1980s, this began to change. Divisions within respective traditions between religious conservatives and religious liberals became a greater source of conflict.[36] Religious scholars Steven Waldman and John Green have divided the electorate into what they call the "12 tribes." One tribe is the "Republican Right," which consists of white evangelical Protestants. This group constitutes 12.6 percent of the electorate. They are the heart of the so-called values voters of the 2004 election. They are the most conservative on virtually all issues, especially those that would fall under the moral values category. Almost 90 percent of these voters supported George W. Bush in 2004.[37]

Another important group to the Republican Party is what Waldman and Green refer to as "Heartland Culture Warriors." This bloc is very conservative on moral issues, such as same-sex marriage, although it is outside of the evangelical community. They are a healthy 11.4 percent of the electorate, and more than seven out of ten supported Bush in 2004. There are also "Moderate Evangelicals" who comprise 10.8 percent of the electorate. This group is culturally conservative but moderate on economic issues. As Waldman and Green summarize, "The three red tribes make up about 35 percent of the electorate, and although their members don't vote exclusively on the basis of cultural issues, values are certainly a key ingredient in the glue that holds the three together."[38]

The religious shades of the Democratic electorate are less well understood. The common stereotype perpetuated by conservative commentators, such as Ann Coulter, is that Democrats and liberals do not worship and are even hostile to religion. As she writes in her book *Godless*, "Democrats revile religion but insist on faking a belief in God in front of the voters claiming to be 'spiritual.'" She adds, "Everything liberals believe is in elegant opposition to basic Biblical principles . . . let us not flinch from identifying liberalism as the opposition party to God."[39]

Yet, the Waldman and Green research suggests that Coulter's assessments of the religious attitudes of Democrats are too simplistic, if not wholly inaccurate. They write,

> A deep-blue religious left is almost exactly the same size as the religious right but receives much less attention. . . . Members of the religious left espouse a progressive theology (agreeing, for instance, that "all the world's great religions are equally true") and are very liberal on cultural issues such as abortion and gay marriage. About one-quarter attend church weekly. The religious left is somewhat liberal on economic policy and decidedly to the left on foreign policy.[40]

It is also worth noting that black Protestants, Jews, and Muslims disproportionately identify themselves as Democrats. While religious seculars are disproportionately Democratic, they comprise just 10.7 percent of the electorate. Moreover, Democratic voters are not even remotely monolithic in their views on cultural issues. As Waldman and Green explain, "Indeed, while [Democrats] are fairly well united on economic and foreign-policy issues, they're all over the map on cultural issues. Because the Democratic coalition includes highly religious tribes, non-religious tribes, and everything in between, talking about values can be perilous."[41]

Of course, the debate over how moderate Americans really are misses an important point. Americans who are active in the political process and are the best organized almost always have an amplified voice in a democracy. Thus, a small minority, such as the Religious Right, can have a significant influence in American politics. Indeed, during the 1980s and beyond, the Republican Party has successfully mobilized Christian conservatives to support its candidates. In the process, this has heightened party differences on social and cultural issues.[42] As Linda Feldman explains, "But even if most Americans are moderates, it's the so-called religious right—a highly motivated coalition of Evangelical Protestants, conservative Catholics, and Orthodox Jews—that is feeling the momentum. . . . Of all the factions in the

Table 2.1.   Church Attendance and Presidential Vote

Frequency	Percent Voting for Bush	Percent Voting for Kerry
More than once a week	64.7	35.3
Once a week	58.9	41.1
A few times a month	50.7	49.3
A few times a year	45.2	54.8
Never	36.6	63.4

Source: Laura R. Olson and John C. Green, "The Religion Gap," *PS: Political Science and Politics* (July 2006): 457, table 1.

Republicans' winning coalition, religious conservatives were the most organized and energized."[43]

Of course, whether the religion gap translates into polarization is perhaps a matter of how one defines the term polarization. On the one hand, both parties include religious voters. On the other hand, church attendance and the religious "tribe" that one belongs to are significant predictors of one's political positions. In many instances, these tribes can be quite polarized on a number of cultural issues, suggesting that at least on some level, deep divisions on cultural issues exist. At a minimum, these differences translated into a significant religious gap in presidential voting in 2004 (see table 2.1).

Geography

Some scholars have challenged the use of the red state–blue state map as an inaccurate illustration of political divisions in the United States.[44] Certainly, the red state–blue state model is useful for understanding electoral college outcomes, but it is a rather shallow way of understanding voting behavior. There are many red counties in blue state California, just as there are solid blue counties in red state Texas.

While the red state–blue state map might not be an accurate way to describe the American electorate, there are geographic divisions that reflect significant political differences. In 2004, for example, George W. Bush drew his strength from rural areas, whereas Kerry drew his from urban areas. In fact, Republican presidential candidates are generally more successful than Democrats are in rural areas, at least during most elections of the past few decades (see figure 2.2).

This can also be seen quite clearly in figures 2.3 and 2.4, which are replications (and enhancements) of maps that have been available on the Internet since the election. To standardize the figures for comparability, we rendered highly populated areas in gray/black (see figure 2.3), and blue (Democratic) counties in black (see figure 2.4). While the black

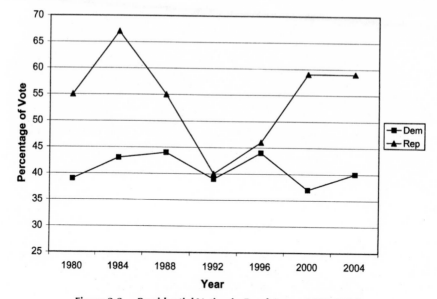

Figure 2.2. Presidential Voting in Rural Areas, 1980–2004
Source: W. K. Kellogg Foundation, "The Message from Rural America: The Rural Vote in 2004," March 22, 2005, at www.wkkf.org.

areas of each map do not perfectly coincide, there is clearly a fair amount of congruence.

As the figures illustrate, there is clearly a difference in the voting behavior of residents in rural and urban areas. One possible explanation for this is that different value orientations develop in these regions based on lifestyle differences. For example, rural residents are more likely to be married than urban residents. This has political implications because those who are married exhibit different political attitudes and behavior than those who are single.[45] In addition, rural residents are more likely to be homeowners than urban residents, which can direct their political interests toward issues such as property taxes—an issue that is less important to most urban residents who are more likely to rent property.[46] Rural residents are also more likely to be gun owners and, as a consequence, are less likely than others to support gun-control policies.[47] Table 2.2 illustrates some of the differences in lifestyle characteristics between urban and rural Americans.

While the connections between lifestyle differences and political attitudes might not always be straightforward, the fact is that rural residents are more likely to vote Republican in presidential elections. As table 2.3 indicates, the differences between rural and urban residents' vote for Republican presidential candidates have grown over the past four election

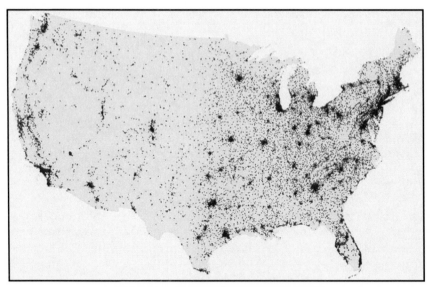

Figure 2.3.   U.S. Population Density, 2000
Source: U.S. Census Bureau.

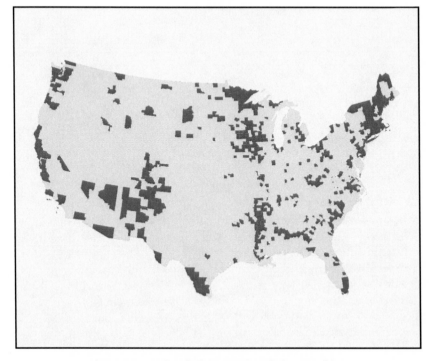

Figure 2.4.   Red and Blue Counties (dark gray = blue)
Source: U.S. Census Bureau.

Table 2.2.   Lifestyle Characteristics of Urban and Rural America (in percentages)

	Rural	Urban
Religion		
Church attendance (every week)	39.4	33.5
Religion provides a great deal of guidance in everyday living	47.9	31.8
Prayer several times a day	37.3	29.8
Bible is the actual word of God	48.9	34.9
Home Life		
Never married	8.4	24.9
Own a gun	68.5	30.5
Own a home	84.9	66.5
Lived in community fifteen years or less	29.6	43.6

Source: Peter L. Francia and Jody C. Baumgartner, "Victim or Victor of the 'Culture War'? How Cultural Issues Affect Support for George W. Bush in Rural America," *American Review of Politics* 26 (Fall/Winter 2005–2006): 356, table 3.

Table 2.3.   Republican Presidential Vote, 1992–2004 (in percentages)

Year	Rural Residents	Urban Residents	Difference
1992	37	26	11
1996	39	32	7
2000	53	29	24
2004	57	35	22

Source: Peter L. Francia and Jody C. Baumgartner, "Victim or Victor of the 'Culture War'? How Cultural Issues Affect Support for George W. Bush in Rural America," *American Review of Politics* 26 (Fall/Winter 2005–2006): 355, table 2.

cycles. These trends suggest that, at least at the polls, there is a growing gap between urban and rural residents.

CONCLUSION

Significant debate has emerged about whether a culture war rages in the United States. Certainly, as history suggests, cultural issues have long divided the nation and continue to divide at least some Americans today, particularly those who are active in politics. Whether these differences translate into a "war" involving most Americans is less clear. Certainly as Morris Fiorina observes, the United States is not remotely close to resembling a nation in which the political battleground is dominated by "Maoist guerilla and right-wing death squads [that] shoot at each other."[48] On the other hand, there are some clear gaps in voting behavior that divide large segments of the American population. Partisan and religious gaps have grown over time as have the gaps in presidential voting behavior that separate urban and rural residents.

FOR MORE READING

Brewer, Mark D., and Jeffrey M. Stonecash. *Split: Class and Cultural Divides in American Politics*. Washington, D.C.: CQ Press, 2007.

Fiorina, Morris P., Samuel J. Abrams, and Jeremy C. Pope. *Culture War? The Myth of a Polarized America*. New York: Longman, 2005.

Frank, Thomas. *What's the Matter with Kansas? How Conservatives Won the Heart of America*. New York: Metropolitan Books, 2004.

Hunter, James Davison. *Culture Wars: The Struggle to Define America*. New York: Basic Books, 1991.

3

The Myth of the Vanishing Voters and the Rise of the Independent Voter

Voting behavior is one of the most thoroughly studied subjects in political science. One could literally fill entire rooms with the amount of scholarship that has been devoted to understanding how and why voters and potential voters exercise their most fundamental of democratic freedoms. Nevertheless, despite decades of voluminous research, many commonly held assumptions about voting behavior are not as simple as some political observers portray them to be.

First, conventional wisdom, as well as several academic studies, have long held that American voter turnout is in decline and, second, that political parties have become weak and less important to voters, as evidenced by the increasing number of Americans who have become independents. While there is some truth in both assertions, the overall picture is more complex. As this chapter will discuss, recent research suggests that American voter turnout might not be in decline, and partisanship within the electorate has actually increased in the past decade or so, reversing a forty-year trend.[1]

AMERICAN VOTER TURNOUT

Discussions about voting behavior in the United States often begin with the premise that Americans do not vote in numbers equal to the past or that they do not vote in numbers proportionate to citizens in other democracies. Most American government textbooks frame the discussion of voting in the United States in terms of "low voter turnout," noting correctly that the United States ranks near the bottom of the world in voter turnout and offering explanations for the decline.[2] During the campaign of 2000, a number of stories covered subjects such as "why Americans don't vote," or predicted that "voter turnout may slip again."[3] The picture these accounts present, at least implicitly, is that our democracy is in decline.[4]

Many scholars echo similar sentiments. Works such as *The Disappearing American Voter, Why Americans Don't Vote, Why Americans* Still *Don't Vote* (emphasis added), *Why America Stopped Voting,* and *Where Have All the Voters Gone?* all reveal in their titles the basic assumption that American turnout is in decline.[5] Other less suggestive titles focus on the problem of American voter turnout as well, in one case referring to "Democracy's Unresolved Dilemma."[6] As one account summarizes, "In ever larger numbers over the past three decades, Americans have been tuning out campaigns and staying home on Election Day. Turnout has fallen in virtually every type of American election."[7]

Some of the prominent explanations for the decline in voter turnout include voter apathy, alienation from the political process, the effects of lower socioeconomic status (lack of education, lower income, racial minority status), onerous voter registration laws, Tuesday voting, the number of elections, a single-member district as opposed to proportional representation electoral system, and the demobilizing effect of weakened political parties.[8] While all of these factors undoubtedly contribute to lower voter turnout, the extent of the decline in American voter turnout is less clear. Moreover, the problem of nonvoting is not even uniformly viewed as a problem.[9]

In the section that follows, we discuss some of the problems with the frequently made claim that the American voter is disappearing or vanishing. In doing so, we highlight two major arguments. First, most accounts of voter turnout rely on somewhat questionable methods in computing turnout statistics. Second, voter turnout trends in the United States are not unique to the rest of the world. Other established democracies have also experienced slight declines in voter turnout.

VOTER TURNOUT: A STATISTIC IN SEARCH OF A STANDARD

Determining voter turnout is a fairly straightforward calculation. One counts the number of votes cast and then divides it by the number of people eligible to vote. Mathematically, the equation looks like this: number of votes cast divided by number of potential voters. It is relatively easy to tabulate the number of votes counted in any given election. Tabulating the number of potential voters, on the other hand, is not as simple to do as one might think. Voter turnout statistics typically utilize census data, with the denominator representing the number of those living in the United States who are age eighteen or older (also referred to as the voting age population or VAP). The VAP measure, until recently, was the accepted standard in calculating voter turnout rates. However, political scientists Michael McDonald and Samuel Popkin have noted that the VAP measure is problematic in that it fails to tabulate precisely the number of eligible voters. Age, they note, is not the only criterion to be eligible to vote. Noncitizens are ineligible to vote, as are prisoners and convicted felons in many states. Even after completing a criminal sentence, several states prohibit ex-felons from voting for life. The rationale for this is that those who do not follow the law should not have a voice in making the law. Most accounts of voter turnout throughout American history fail to consider the eligible population. As a result, increases in the noncitizen and felon population, which have occurred over the last several decades, would seem to account for some of the recent decline in voter turnout.

Early History

In the early days of the republic, there were numerous restrictions to voting that left very few people eligible to vote. The Constitution originally left the matter of the franchise, or the right to vote, to the states.[10] Most states limited the right to vote to white males who owned land. In some states, there were also religious requirements. By some estimates (there are no exact figures), as few as 6 percent of the adult white male population was actually eligible to vote. The elimination of property and religious requirements, accelerated during the presidency of Andrew Jackson, gradually expanded the voting eligible population (VEP). By the 1850s, the pool of eligible voters included virtually all adult white males.

The next formal expansion of the electorate occurred in 1870 with the passage of the Fifteenth Amendment to the Constitution. According to the provisions of this amendment, states could no longer deny the right to vote to any person based on their "race, color, or previous condition of servitude." The amendment theoretically extended the right to vote to former slaves. In practice, however, most southern states enacted various laws designed to deny blacks the right to vote. These "Jim Crow" laws included levying a poll tax on voters, which many poor blacks could not afford. They also included literacy tests that registrars administered in discriminating fashion, meaning that blacks almost always failed. Most southern states further adopted so-called grandfather clauses, which exempted those who had voted before 1867 (almost all of whom were white) from the various restrictions the state placed on the right to vote.

Most statistics showing the difference between turnout rates in the South and the rest of the country throughout the century following 1870

Chapter 3

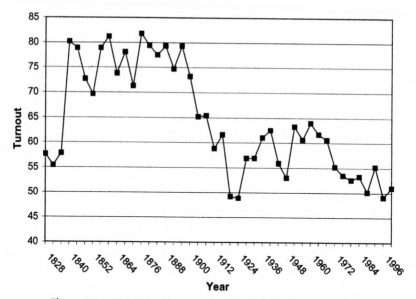

Figure 3.1.   U.S. Voter Turnout, Presidential Elections, 1828–2000
Source: Lyn Ragsdale, *Vital Statistics on the Presidency* (Washington, D.C.: Congressional Quarterly Press, 1998), 132–38; 2000 data from FairVote: The Center for Voting and Democracy, www.fairvote.org/turnout/ preturn.htm. Figures are based on voting age population.

illustrate one of the problems in trying to understand voter turnout. The best estimates show turnout in the South plummeting relative to the non-South by the 1880s. By the turn of the century, the difference was as high as fifty percentage points.[11] This decline is attributable to the fact that the turnout statistics calculated the potential voters based on the number of white *and black* male southerners age twenty-one or older. Of course in practice, nearly all blacks were not allowed to vote. The number of potential voters in the South during this period was thus artificially inflated, leading to lower turnout rate statistics both in the South and nationwide (see figure 3.1).

The next major expansion of the electorate occurred in 1920 with the passage of the Nineteenth Amendment granting women the right to vote. Although several western states already allowed women to vote, this amendment had the effect of virtually doubling the number of people eligible to vote. As it happened, women did not immediately flock to the polls, and as a result, national voter turnout statistics begin to show a sharp decline between 1916 and 1924. Yet another decline, albeit a smaller one, is attributable to the lowering of the voting age from twenty-one to eighteen with the passage of the Twenty-sixth Amendment in 1971 (see also chapter 1). In short, from 1870 to 1971, the expansion of the electorate was responsible for a decline in the percentage of those who turned out to vote, relative to figures given for the latter half of the 1800s—the high point in American history.[12]

VAP versus VEP

As noted earlier, research from McDonald and Popkin suggests that the decline in voter turnout in the past fifty to sixty years has been systematically overestimated because of the growth in the number of those eighteen years of age or older who are noncitizens or felons. In addition to the above, some states do not allow the mentally incompetent to vote, although this is only a tiny fraction of the population (perhaps one-tenth of 1 percent). McDonald and Popkin also estimate the residency requirements still in place in various states, which they contend disenfranchises approximately 1 percent of the voting age population in any given election.[13] Finally, they note that the census has become more accurate over the past half century. In 1940, the Census Bureau estimated that their count missed approximately 5.8 percent of the population. (Many of these "missed" citizens were likely to be poor and less educated, and therefore less likely to vote, resulting in potentially biased turnout statistics.) This number shrank to 1.8 percent in 1990. This means, all other things being equal, that the number of people counted as part of the voting age population has grown relative to those who have reported voting. Because the voting age population is typically part of the turnout calculation, these discrepancies have created a situation whereby the statistics have *over*estimated the number of people eligible to vote, thus *under*estimating voter turnout.

Counting Votes

To this point, we have discussed only one-half of the voter turnout equation—the number of eligible voters. A final aspect of our discussion centers around the calculation of the number of votes cast. Many experts believe that one of the reasons voter turnout was so high in the late 1800s is that there was a good deal of voter fraud in various states and localities.[14] For example, some research suggests that in certain areas of the country corrupt election officials "stuffed" ballot boxes or deliberately reported false returns, often inflating the vote totals for the candidate of the party machine.[15] This would, of course, lead to inflated rates of voter turnout. Unfortunately, no complete data are available to estimate the effects of vote fraud on voter turnout.

McDonald and Popkin's research points to another fact worth considering. The numerator in the voter turnout equation relies on the number of votes cast for president (during presidential election years) or the number

Table 3.1.   VAP vs. VEP: Voter Turnout Rates in U.S. Elections, 1972–2000

Year	Turnout Rate (VAP %)	Turnout Rate (VEP %)	Difference (%)
1972	55.2	57.2	2.0
1974	38.2	40.8	2.6
1976	53.5	56.4	2.9
1978	37.9	40.7	2.8
1980	52.8	56.2	3.4
1982	40.6	44.8	4.2
1984	53.3	58.6	5.3
1986	36.5	40.4	3.9
1988	50.3	55.5	5.2
1990	36.5	41.2	4.7
1992	55.0	61.7	6.7
1994	38.9	43.2	4.3
1996	48.9	53.9	5.0
1998	36.1	40.5	4.4
2000	51.2	57.1	5.9

Source: Michael P. McDonald and Samuel Popkin, "The Myth of the Vanishing Voter," *American Political Science Review* 95 (2001): 966.

of votes cast for Congress (during midterm election years). However, this method systematically *undercounts* votes cast because some citizens, albeit a small percentage (2 percent), show up to the polls to vote for ballot propositions or local offices but abstain from casting votes for higher office.[16] This would not have been possible until the widespread adoption of the Australian ballot in the 1890s, a period that corresponds with yet another fairly sharp decline in turnout.[17]

In table 3.1, we present data from McDonald and Popkin's seminal article on this subject. It shows the turnout rate using the voting age population (VAP) as well as their corrected version of voting eligible population (VEP). Importantly, they only correct for felons and noncitizens who are ineligible, not for the mentally incompetent, those disenfranchised by residency requirements, or census undercounting. In other words, their corrections are conservative. In the final column, the results indicate a fairly significant difference using these two methods to calculate the turnout rate.

FRAMING THE ISSUE: REPORTING AND DISCUSSING TURNOUT RATES

Regardless of whether one calculates voter turnout using VAP or VEP, turnout in the United States has declined over the past century and remains lower when compared with turnout in other established democracies. However, the way in which some political observers present this

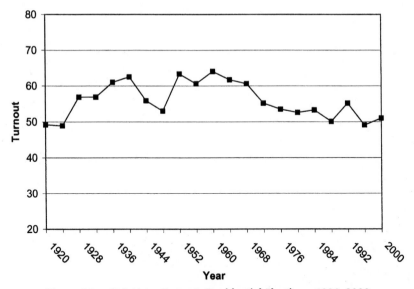

Figure 3.2.   U.S. Voter Turnout, Presidential Elections, 1920–2000
Source: Lyn Ragsdale, *Vital Statistics on the Presidency* (Washington, D.C.: Congressional Quarterly Press, 1998), 132–38; 2000 data from FairVote: The Center for Voting and Democracy, at www.fairvote.org/turnout/preturn.htm. Figures are based on voting age population.

fact often makes the situation appear bleaker than it actually is. For example, figure 3.2 presents turnout rates in the United States from 1920 (when the size of the electorate effectively doubled) forward. The results show that turnout has remained relatively consistent, at an average of about 55.9 percent. While we certainly share some of the concerns that various observers have voiced over the decline in turnout, figure 3.2 suggests that the decline might be less serious than some portray it to be. In fact, since 1976, when turnout was 53.5 percent (using VAP statistics), it has hovered consistently in the low 50 percent range. In 2004, the U.S. Election Project tracked the turnout rate at 55.3 percent (using VAP statistics). This only reinforces the point that voters do not appear to be vanishing.

While turnout has dropped only modestly over time, U.S. rates are consistently lower when measured against turnout in other established democracies. However, it is also true that turnout has been declining modestly in other nations over the past fifty years.[18] As figure 3.3 indicates, the average voter turnout rate has declined in six established democracies from 1950 to 2000. There is a fairly significant decline in all six cases. In fact, while U.S. voter turnout is lower than all of the others, the *decline* in the United States during this period in less than in any of these countries except the United Kingdom (see table 3.2).

To be clear, Americans are voting at lower rates than one hundred years ago or when compared with citizens of other countries. However, to suggest

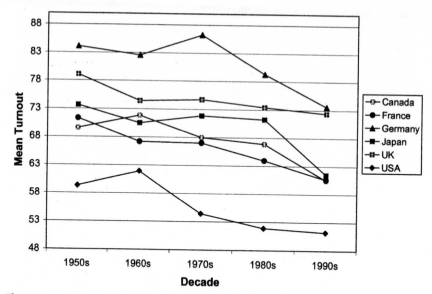

Figure 3.3. Mean Voter Turnout for Six Established Democracies, 1950–2000
Source: International Institute for Democracy and Electoral Assistance, at www.idea.int/index.cfm.

Table 3.2. Decline in Voter Turnout for Six Established Democracies, 1950–2000 (in percentages)

	Canada	France	Germany	Japan	U.K.	U.S.
Mean, 1950s	69.6	71.3	84.1	73.7	79.1	59.3
Mean, 1990s	60.5	60.6	73.6	61.5	72.4	51.2
Decline	9.1	10.7	10.5	12.2	6.6	8.1

Source: International Institute for Democracy and Electoral Assistance, at www.idea.int/index.cfm.

that voters in the United States are vanishing appears to overstate the case. Turnout has remained relatively constant over the past few decades, and any decline in voter turnout in the United States is quite consistent with developments in other countries. Whether or not this is a problem is certainly debatable. One could make a good case that it is. But, at a minimum, it is difficult to argue that voter turnout in the United States is in crisis.

THE INDEPENDENT AMERICAN VOTER

The vaunted independent voter has been the subject of numerous press reports and stories over the years. These so-called independents are those who have eschewed attachments to either of the two major parties. Popular accounts often portray these voters in a favorable light for shunning party labels and for making their voting decisions based on a thorough examination of the issues of the day and the candidates' stands on them. The independent voter is virtuous for choosing the best candidate—a criterion consistent with the civics course model of a good citizen.

A widely held tenet of American politics is that since the 1950s the numbers of independent voters are growing. News accounts of the partisan preferences of American voters routinely reflect this belief. Headlines proclaim that the number of "independent voters [is] burgeoning" and that "more voters are steering away from party labels."[19] Because they are growing in number they quite naturally are becoming the most important bloc of voters in any given election. One recent headline sums up the conventional wisdom: "Independent voters hold [the] key."[20]

Not surprisingly, those who cover or study American politics frequently equate the increased numbers of independent voters with the decline of political parties. One well-known American government textbook is explicit, referring to the "*decline of both parties and resultant upsurge of independents.*"[21] A book from the early 1970s sounded the alarmist note that "the party's over."[22] One of the leading texts on party politics is a bit less dramatic but still suggests that "the American electorate is somewhat less partisan now than it was prior to" the 1960s.[23]

To be fair, the number of people registering as independent has been increasing in the past fifty years.[24] If we examine the traditional measurement of partisan identification, there *has* been a rise in independents since the 1950s. This is consistent with a trend toward what some refer to as partisan dealignment.[25] A good deal of research exists that suggests that political parties are increasingly seen as being less central to government and the political system. It is difficult for many people to see how political parties are relevant. Many, in other words, are not *non*partisans as much as they are *a*partisans.[26]

There is, however, more to the story. In 1952, the Survey Research Center and the Center for Political Studies of the Institute for Social Research at the University of Michigan conducted a wide-ranging national survey related to the presidential and congressional elections. They subsequently conducted similar surveys in the following thirteen presidential and midterm elections, until 1976. In 1977, the National Science Foundation began funding the surveys and, in the process, established the National Election Studies (NES).[27] The stated mission of the NES "is to inform explanations of election outcomes by providing data that support rich hypothesis testing, maximize methodological excellence, measure many variables, and promote comparisons across people, contexts, and time."[28]

One of the many questions that the NES has asked over the years concerns partisan identification. The interviewer asks respondents, "Generally speaking, do you usually think of yourself as a Republican, a Democrat, an Independent, or what?" Other choices include "other" and, starting in 1966, "no preference." If the respondent answers either "Republican" or "Democrat," there is a follow-up question: "Would you call yourself a strong (Republican/Democrat) or a not very strong (Republican/Democrat)?" On the other hand, if the respondent answers "independent," "other," or "no preference" to the first question, the second question that follows is "Do you think of yourself as closer to the Republican or Democratic party?"[29]

The significance of the NES surveys on the study of voting behavior would be difficult to overstate. After an initial study produced in 1954, the research team in 1960 produced what is arguably the most important work in the study of American voting behavior, *The American Voter*.[30] This book alone has spawned a veritable mountain of research since its publication, produced by several generations of scholars. It is, in short, impossible to study American voting behavior without coming face-to-face with its theories and conclusions.

One of the primary findings of the book is that the majority of voters cast their ballots based on their partisan identification. Although others have challenged the centrality of partisan identification in vote choice,[31] over time political science research has clearly demonstrated its powerful influence. This identification develops primarily during childhood under the powerful influence of one's parents.[32] While some have questioned the validity of the NES partisan identification measure,[33] it has stood the test of time and is now a standard component of how political behavioralists model the study of voting. It is therefore quite understandable that some associate the use of this measure with the claim that independent voters are growing in number and importance.

As already mentioned, the number of people answering "independent" to the first party identification question has increased, and fairly significantly, since 1952. The number of independents has risen from 22.6 to 38.9 percent—almost double—in the past half century (see table 3.3). This statistic is the one that most political observers typically use to suggest that there are increasing numbers of independent voters.

However, when one includes responses to the second party identification question, the number of people who claim to be closer to *neither* party is rather small. This fits with an intuitive understanding of what an independent actually is. Table 3.4 presents the data again but this time divides the independents into three categories: those who claim to lean toward either party, as well as the "pure" independents. Although the percentage of these pure independents has fluctuated over the past fifty years, it has never constituted more than 14.6 percent (in 1976) of the electorate and currently

Table 3.3. Democratic, Republican, and Independent Identification, 1952–2004 (in percentages)

Year	Democrats	Independents	Republicans
1952	47.2	22.6	27.2
1956	43.6	23.4	29.1
1960	45.3	22.8	29.4
1964	51.7	22.8	24.5
1968	45.4	29.1	24.2
1972	40.4	34.7	23.4
1976	39.7	36.1	23.2
1980	40.8	34.5	22.5
1984	37.0	34.2	27.1
1988	35.2	35.7	27.5
1992	35.5	38.3	25.2
1996	37.8	34.7	26.4
2000	34.3	40.4	23.9
2004	32.1	38.9	29.0

Source: Herbert F. Weisberg and Dino P. Christenson, "Changing Horses in Wartime? The 2004 Presidential Election," prepared for presentation at the annual meeting of the American Political Science Association, Washington, D.C., September 1–4, 2005, table 1.

Table 3.4. Partisans and Leaners, 1952–2004 (in percentages)

Year	Democrats	Democrats and Leaners	Pure Independents	Republicans and Leaners	Republicans
1952	47.2	56.8	5.8	34.3	27.2
1956	43.6	49.9	8.8	37.5	29.1
1960	45.3	51.6	9.8	36.1	29.4
1964	51.7	61.0	7.8	30.3	24.5
1968	45.4	55.2	10.5	32.8	24.2
1972	40.4	51.5	13.1	33.9	23.4
1976	39.7	51.5	14.6	33.0	23.2
1980	40.8	52.2	12.9	32.7	22.5
1984	37.0	47.9	11.0	39.5	27.1
1988	35.2	46.9	10.6	40.8	27.5
1992	35.5	49.8	11.6	37.5	25.2
1996	37.8	51.8	9.1	38.1	26.4
2000	34.3	49.6	12.3	36.7	23.9
2004	32.1	49.6	9.7	40.7	29.0

Source: Herbert F. Weisberg and Dino P. Christenson, "Changing Horses in Wartime? The 2004 Presidential Election," prepared for presentation at the annual meeting of the American Political Science Association, Washington, D.C., September 1–4, 2005, table 1.

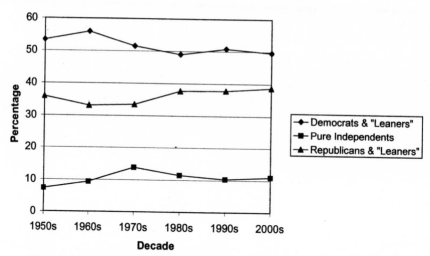

Figure 3.4. Mean Percentages of Partisans, Leaners, and Pure Independents
Source: See International Institute for Democracy and Electoral Assistance, at www.idea.int/index.cfm.

hovers near 10 percent. Figure 3.4 shows the mean percentage of partisans and leaners, and pure independents, by decade. Again, while there is an increase in the number of independents, the rise is hardly dramatic.

One conclusion to draw from these data is relatively straightforward: It is not necessarily the measure of partisan identification that is the culprit in propagating the myth of the independent voter but rather how some have used the data from this measurement. A second problem is that an understanding of how leaners and independents behave politically receives short shrift. For example, most leaners are actually partisans in their voting behavior. And as suggested earlier, partisans tend to be loyal to candidates from their own party. Table 3.5 shows that Democratic leaners increased their partisan loyalty in presidential and House elections from 1952 to 2004, with better than 70 percent voting with their party. Although Republican leaners showed a decrease for the same period, they are far from independent, given that three-quarters vote Republican.

In fact, there is a larger trend of greater partisan voting behavior overall.[34] One illustration of this is in table 3.6, which shows the percentage of partisans in each of the past six decades who decided earlier as well as later in the campaign to vote with their party. While the percentage of Republicans who remained loyal has stayed relatively constant, Democrats have begun to display similar levels of loyalty. In both cases (for both early and late deciders), partisanship clearly matters when it comes to voting.

Table 3.5. Party Loyalty in Presidential (and House) Voting, 1952–2000, by Party Identification* (in percentages)

Year	Strong Democrat	Weak Democrat	Leaning Democrat	Leaning Republican	Weak Republican	Strong Republican
1952	84 (90)	62 (78)	60 (64)	93 (81)	94 (90)	99 (95)
1956	85 (94)	63 (86)	68 (83)	94 (83)	93 (88)	100 (95)
1960	88 (92)	69 (82)	88 (82)	87 (79)	82 (83)	99 (94)
1964	95 (94)	82 (84)	90 (79)	75 (72)	56 (64)	90 (92)
1968	85 (88)	56 (73)	52 (63)	82 (82)	82 (78)	96 (92)
1972	73 (92)	48 (81)	60 (80)	86 (73)	90 (76)	97 (85)
1976	90 (89)	74 (78)	72 (79)	83 (68)	78 (72)	96 (86)
1980	86 (85)	60 (69)	45 (70)	76 (68)	86 (74)	92 (78)
1984	88 (89)	67 (70)	79 (78)	93 (61)	93 (66)	96 (85)
1988	93 (88)	70 (82)	88 (87)	84 (64)	83 (70)	98 (77)
1992	93 (88)	69 (82)	70 (77)	63 (65)	62 (65)	86 (81)
1996	96 (88)	82 (71)	76 (69)	68 (79)	70 (79)	94 (97)
2000	97 (90)	89 (74)	72 (73)	79 (75)	85 (82)	97 (88)
Average	89 (90)	69 (78)	71 (76)	82 (73)	81 (76)	95 (88)

*House vote percentages are in parentheses.
Source: Joel David Bloom, "Independent Leaners and Party Loyalty: Cause or Effect?" Paper prepared for presentation at the 2002 Annual Meeting of the Western Political Science Association, Long Beach, Calif., March 21–24, 2002, tables 2 and 3.

Table 3.6. Partisan Loyalty in Presidential Elections (in percentages)

Decade	Democrats, Early Deciders	Democrats, Late Deciders	Republicans, Early Deciders	Republicans, Late Deciders
1950s	81.6	61.1	98.5	82.9
1960s	88.7	72.6	91.9	77.6
1970s	72.0	70.4	96.2	74.8
1980s	86.9	69.1	96.7	84.8
1990s	95.3	84.5	94.5	76.9
2000s	94.6	81.1	97.3	83.2

Source: James E. Campbell, *The American Campaign: U.S. Presidential Campaigns and the National Vote*, updates of text and tables for the 2004 presidential election from www.tamu.edu/upress/BOOKS/2000/table5.1.pdf (College Station: Texas A&M Press, 2000), table 7.6.

As for the true independents, there are significantly fewer of them than popular accounts typically portray. Moreover, the lessons of *The American Voter*, as well as subsequent analyses (e.g., Keith et al.'s, *Myth of the Independent Voter*) need to be remembered. Research strongly suggests that many independent voters are neither attentive to nor involved in politics. While they might be independent, many are not politically active, and they vote at much lower rates than do partisans.[35]

CONCLUSION

The conventional wisdom that American voter turnout is in decline and that independent voters are a growing segment of the electorate oversimplifies the more complex reality of the American electorate. As this chapter has shown, American voter turnout has declined only modestly and even less so when one applies McDonald and Popkin's more precise measure that relies on the voting eligible population (VEP) rather than the voting age population (VAP) in the denominator of the voter turnout statistic. In addition, despite increases in the percentage of self-identified independents, independent leaners have proven to be quite partisan at the polls, casting some legitimate doubts on whether independents are truly increasing in number and importance. In short, two of the most widely discussed subjects about the American electorate—the decline in voter turnout and the rise of the independent voter—require several caveats and a more nuanced discussion than popular accounts typically provide.

FOR MORE READING

Bennett, Stephen Earl, and David Resnick. "The Implications of Nonvoting for Democracy in the United States." *American Journal of Political Science* 34 (1990): 771–802.

McDonald, Michael P. "State Turnout Rates among Those Eligible to Vote." *State Politics and Policy Quarterly* 2 (2002): 199–212.

———. "Up, Up and Away! Voter Participation in the 2004 Presidential Election." *Forum* 2(4) (2004): article 4.

Piven, Frances Fox, and Richard A. Cloward. *Why Americans Still Don't Vote: And Why Politicians Want It That Way.* Boston: Beacon Press, 2000.

II

FOLLOWING CAMPAIGNS

4

Misconceptions about the E-Campaign

What the Internet Can and Cannot Do for Political Campaigns

The Internet was the subject of numerous stories during the presidential election of 2004. Reporters and political pundits inundated the public with information about online fund-raising, blogs (web logs) filled with fact checks, rumor and innuendo, speculation about online voting in the future, and much more. Indeed, during the past decade there has been a considerable amount of hype about how the Internet, and in particular, the World Wide Web, was going to revolutionize political campaigns.[1]

Although many in the academic community were skeptical about the power of the Internet, some asked provocative questions about whether Internet technology could save or invigorate democracy. Former Clinton adviser and political consultant Dick Morris went further, suggesting that people bound together with new online technologies would fundamentally alter the balance of power in the United States. Morris referred to this as the "fifth estate." Headlines during the presidential campaign of 2004 routinely talked about the "buzz" that Internet campaigns were generating. Some went so far as to speak of campaign revolutions in examining the online success of Howard Dean in 2003. One journalist boldly asked, "What will happen when a national political machine can fit on a laptop?" suggesting that Dean's online success spelled the death knell for the established political parties.[2]

Of course, like most hype, there is some truth to these claims, however exaggerated. The Internet has proven to be quite useful for some aspects of electioneering but, in other respects, considerably less so. In this chapter, we review the past decade or so of Internet campaigns, focusing on what does and what does not seem to work. The focus of the chapter will be on how candidates use the Internet in their electioneering activities. First, however, a short history of Internet campaigning is in order.

BRIEF HISTORY OF INTERNET CAMPAIGNING

The Internet is actually a collection, or network, of smaller networks that connect computers around the world. The impetus for its creation was to help the military ensure that it could maintain its command and communication functions in the event of a nuclear attack. Begun in 1969, it originally linked computers in four American universities. Throughout the 1970s and 1980s, the military and those in the academic professions were the primary users of the Internet. By the early 1990s, the use of home computers and commercial access to the Internet connected a small but growing segment of the population. As a result, more and more people began to use e-mail, although the Internet remained a rather esoteric communications medium.

The transformation of the Internet dates back to 1991. Tim Berners-Lee, a computer engineer working with the European Particle Physics Laboratory (CERN) in Geneva, Switzerland, developed and implemented a system to link large numbers of documents on computers all over the world together. The system involved embedding "hyperlinks" into documents, so-called because these words, phrases, or objects linked to other files or objects. Clicking on one of these hyperlinks allows users to access the linked file. Although computer users were able to "browse" the Internet before this, the advent of this system, known as the World Wide Web, made browsing more convenient. It also displayed documents with formatting, pictures, audio, and more. With the spread of home computer ownership and faster Internet connection technology in the early to mid-1990s, the Internet became a mainstream communications medium.[3]

In 1993, the regional "Baby Bell" companies (those spawned by the breakup of AT&T, or "Ma Bell") contracted to have a website built advocating telecommunications policy.[4] The first website created for a political campaign is credited to California senator Dianne Feinstein, for her successful 1994 campaign. That same year, an organization called Minnesota E-Democracy hosted online candidate debates.[5] The following year, Ted Kennedy became the first sitting senator to build a website, and Phil Graham and Lamar Alexander became the first presidential candidates to build and maintain websites for their campaigns.

The Republican Party registered their primary domain name, RNC.org, in March of 1995, and the Democrats followed (DNC.org) in April of that same year.[6] Both national party organizations as well as many state and local party organizations had websites in place for the 1996 campaign.[7] At the end of the first presidential debate of 1996, Republican candidate Bob Dole brought online campaigning to the general public by giving out the (incorrect, as it happened) address to his website. The site received more than two million visitors in the following twenty-four hours.[8] Early campaign websites were little more than brochures placed online and offered little by way of two-way interaction. Users could not do much more than view the candidates' web pages.

By 1998, more than two-thirds of congressional candidates established and used websites in their campaigns for office. Candidates and their consultants also had become adept at e-mail, using it to communicate with others in the campaign and with the press. Former professional wrestler Jesse Ventura relied heavily on the Internet in his third-party (the Reform Party) bid for governor of Minnesota. Although his website was rather amateurish, Ventura built an e-mail network of over three thousand supporters as well as drawing on existing networks of professional wrestling fans and Reform Party activists. Individuals associated with the campaign were able to communicate quickly and efficiently with each other, to urge supporters to register and vote, and to coordinate and encourage supporters to attend campaign rallies.[9]

In 1999, the race for mayor of San Francisco again demonstrated the potential for campaigns to use the Internet for more than simple, one-way communication. A member of the San Francisco Board of Supervisors, Tom Ammiano, entered an already crowded race after supporters built a website to collect signatures on a petition drive to have him placed on the ballot. Ammiano spent a mere twenty-five thousand dollars on his campaign but finished a surprising second in a field of four, placing him in a runoff election. While Ammiano would lose the runoff election, his campaign reinforced the idea—and for many, the hope—that the Internet could add to the democratic process by leveling the playing field for outsiders.[10]

Just a year earlier, a group known as MoveOn created a website titled "Censure and Move On." The group advocated censure rather than impeachment of President Clinton for his involvement with White House intern Monica Lewinsky. By the end of its first week online, the group had collected more than one hundred thousand signatures for a censure petition. Three months later, when the House of Representatives voted on impeachment, the group had over 450,000 signatures. The next day, the group collected five million dollars in pledges in an effort to raise early funds for the 2000 election to defeat Republican candidates who voted for impeachment. MoveOn more than doubled the amount of money it raised by the time the Senate voted on whether to remove Clinton from office.[11]

The first highly visible and successful use of the Internet in a national election came in the Republican presidential primaries in 2000. By this time, all major-party presidential candidates had Internet campaign professionals—so-called dot-pols—who specialized in the development and maintenance of websites. One Internet campaign milestone occurred when New Jersey senator Bill Bradley, a candidate for the Democratic Party presidential nomination, became the first political candidate to raise one million dollars online. What really caught the notice of the press, however, was when John McCain, contender for the Republican Party nomination, raised over five hundred thousand dollars online in a single day. Both of these candidates eventually lost their bids for their party's nomination but clearly demonstrated the potential of the Internet for fund-raising.[12]

This brief history ends with the 2004 candidacy of Howard Dean for the Democratic Party presidential nomination. Early in 2003, the former governor of Vermont was a long-shot candidate for the nomination. However, Dean's Internet savvy campaign manager, Joe Trippi, saw the potential for building support through the Internet site Meetup.com, a site that helps like-minded individuals arrange local meetings wherever there are enough people to warrant it. After Dean attended one of the meetings of his Meetup supporters, he also recognized its potential and, from that point forward, took Meetup seriously. The campaign updated its blogs several times a day with journal entries, photos, and sound from the campaign trail, and sent targeted e-mail messages to supporters from the meetings. Perhaps most important, Dean's online fund-raising significantly eclipsed the efforts of any previous candidate. By the end of the year, Dean had become the presumed front-runner for the nomination.[13]

In the next two sections, we summarize what experience suggests seems to work or not work with respect to electioneering activities on the Internet. Our focus will be primarily on presidential candidate websites, mainly because presidential races attract the most attention. The national scope of a presidential race effectively demands that presidential campaigns develop technologically sophisticated websites.

POLITICAL ADVERTISING ON THE INTERNET

To understand what types of electioneering activities can and cannot be effectively conducted via the Internet, it is important to remember that a political campaign is an exercise in communication (see box 4.1). While a candidate or party might target a message through the Internet to a citizen or group of citizens, it is possible that the intended recipient never receives the message. All other things being equal, fewer potential receivers of a political message translate into a less effective message. In the case of Internet communication, this can be the result of a few factors.

For starters, not all Americans use the Internet. While the online universe is still expanding and estimates vary, approximately two-thirds of

---

BOX 4.1

A COMMUNICATIONS MODEL
OF POLITICAL CAMPAIGNS

Sender: Candidate, party, or group

sends a

Message: "Vote for me," "don't vote for her"

through a

Medium: Television, newspaper, radio, the Internet

to a

Receiver: Citizen or group of citizens

in hopes of creating an

Effect: Citizen or citizens vote for candidate or party

---

the adult population used the Internet during the 2004 campaign. This leaves one-third of the voting public unable to receive Internet campaign messages because they are not online. According to one survey, 61 percent of the online population (37 percent of all adults) used the Internet for various political purposes (e-mail, news, debates, volunteering, contributing) during the campaign. As one might expect, this represents a rather dramatic increase from the 1996 to the 2000 presidential campaign cycles. However, it remains the case that most adults do not make use of the Internet for political activity.[14]

One could argue that television advertising faces similar challenges, but virtually every household owns at least one television, and even with the advent of cable and satellite television, there are still significantly fewer television channels than there are websites. In most cases, it makes little sense to develop an advertising strategy that relies wholly, or even primarily, on the Internet. The exception to this rule would apply to candidates, political parties, or political organizations with very little money. Professional website construction and maintenance expenses (i.e., a salary paid to a full-time webmaster) are a fraction of the cost of television advertising. In 2004, for example, money spent on political advertising in the presidential campaign on the Internet accounted for less than 1 percent of all television advertising.[15] But it is important to remember that a website is "a passive publicity device," meaning that "it cannot attract attention in and of itself."[16] People must actually visit a candidate's website to be persuaded to support the candidate, and this requires some effort on the part of the individual. This selective exposure limits the reach and impact of internet advertising. In short, campaign material on the Internet "cannot be dropped on doorsteps, glimpsed from cars, or handed out in churches."[17] In fact, only about one-third of respondents in a recent poll claimed they had visited a candidate's website for information about the campaign.[18] This is one reason why most web campaigns also rely on traditional media (television, radio, and printed materials) to advertise on their websites.

Not surprisingly, political candidates have adapted advertising strategies to the web. In the first place, a candidate's website is in a very real sense a political ad.[19] But other strategies are available as well. By spring of 2004, the Republican National Committee placed ads on more than one thousand websites that attacked Democratic presidential nominee John Kerry's war record. In response, Kerry placed ads on more than one hundred sites by late May. Both Kerry and Bush made use of their websites to display ads originally developed for print and television. In addition, Bush took at least one ad, titled "Weapons," and adapted it to the web by adding interactive features that distinguished it from the original. The campaigns also produced and distributed original ads for the web, many of which are the so-called banner ads so familiar to Internet users.[20]

Both candidates focused most of their Internet ad buys on local markets. By the end of September, one analysis showed that local news organizations (television, radio, newspaper) featured almost 70 percent of Bush's ads and 60 percent of Kerry's ads on their websites. Print and online national periodicals were also popular venues. Both candidates made use of blogs, but of course, virtually all blogs preach to the converted given that their respective audiences are comprised almost exclusively of supporters. A recent survey suggests that only about one-quarter of all adults relied on a blog to obtain information about candidates and the campaign. However, few (7 percent) believed blogs to be an accurate source of information.[21] In terms of geographic targeting, Bush focused almost half of his Internet ads in fifteen battleground states. Kerry, though, aired only one-fifth of his ads in these states; he targeted metropolitan areas more heavily than Bush, by a six to one margin (21.2 percent to 3.3 percent).[22]

The content of web advertising generally reflects the priorities of the campaign. More than three-quarters of the advertisements that Kerry and the Democratic National Committee placed during the 2004 campaign had fund-raising as their primary purpose. Bush and the Republican National Committee attempted to recruit supporters to the campaign effort and to persuade potential voters. Most Internet ads, according to one report, were positive rather than negative. In fact, 98 percent of Bush's

Internet ad placements were devoted to a single two-and-a-half minute ad featuring First Lady Laura Bush discussing education. Almost no ads featured endorsements by celebrities or political notables, a common practice in e-mail, telephone call, and direct mail voter outreach.

The main point, however, with respect to political advertising on the Internet, is that neither the candidates nor the party committees spent more than a fraction of their budget on this medium. Of course, advertising on the Internet is still considerably less expensive than on television. By the end of September 2004, Kerry spent approximately three times the amount that Bush did on Internet advertising ($1.3 million to $419,000).[23] Despite Howard Dean's campaign manager and Internet campaign advisor Joe Trippi's proclamation in his recent book that "the revolution will not be televised," it seems entirely too early to write television off as the medium of choice for political advertising. The relative ease with which one can reach target audiences on television as opposed to the Internet suggests that this might hold true for the immediate future. This is especially likely given that, in the past few years, the rate of increase in households with Internet access has slowed. In addition, television remains the medium of choice for news, significantly outpacing the Internet.[24]

WHAT *CAN* THE INTERNET DO FOR POLITICAL CAMPAIGNS?

To this point, we have focused on some of the Internet's limitations with respect to political advertising. There are, however, distinct advantages to incorporating an Internet component into a candidate's overall campaign strategy. Here we will distinguish between two main types of Internet communication: websites and e-mail. Within each, we will discuss various activities that have proven to be effective.

Websites

At relatively low cost, a candidate, party, or interest group can construct a website. This is now standard practice, at least at the level of national campaign politics. According to one comprehensive survey conducted in 2004, the overwhelming majority of congressional and gubernatorial candidates, including both incumbents and challengers, maintained websites during the campaign (see table 4.1).

While websites themselves have become standard for campaigns, their content includes some common features. First, most campaign websites provide information in a format similar to an online campaign brochure. Standard practice is to post the candidate's personal and professional biographies as well as information about the candidate's family. In 2000,

Table 4.1. Use of Candidate Websites during 2004

Type of Candidate	Percentage with Website(s)
Major Party Candidates for U.S. Senate	
Incumbents	100
Challengers	88
Total, Competitive Races	81
Total	92
Major Party Candidates for U.S. House	
Incumbents	76
Challengers	86
Total, Competitive Races	91
Total	81
Major Party Candidates for Governor	
Incumbents	78
Challengers	100
Total, Competitive Races	68
Total	91

Source: Philip N. Howard, *New Media Campaigns and the Managed Citizen* (Cambridge, UK: Cambridge University Press, 2006), 26–28, tables 1.2A–C.

the Gore-Lieberman website (algore.com) had four small photos of the candidates and their wives under a "Get to Know Us" heading, each linked to their respective biographies.[25] Second, most campaign websites have contact information, including toll-free telephone numbers and e-mail addresses, a site search feature, and a feature to send the link or page to someone. The site will also have photos, statements of issue positions, rebuttals of charges from the opposition, and so on. Often, it will further include downloadable documents or pamphlets that are analogous to the campaign books of previous eras. One such example was Howard Dean's *Common Sense for America*. Presidential candidate websites further provide links to campaign organizations within each state.

Typically, the site will include itineraries of where the campaign will be in the coming days or weeks. The campaign site offers materials, including campaign trail diaries, videos, and speeches (either as text or as an audio file). It also has become standard practice for presidential candidates to post web versions of their television advertisements on their websites. In addition, it is common to include a section about why voters should *not* vote for the opposition candidate. In Kerry's case, his website had a section entitled "Bush-Cheney: Wrong for America" and linked it to the Rapid Response Center. Bush's Kerry Media Center was similar and contained rebuttals to the opposition candidate's position.

In 2004, both Kerry and Bush had information about voter registration and early voting in all fifty states, as well as information about the campaign in each state. There is usually a section of the website devoted to news stories and press releases by the campaign organization. The Bush-Cheney site labeled this area "Newsroom." Both major-party presidential candidates in 2000 and 2004 had Spanish versions of their sites as well. Also, both campaigns had special sections of their sites devoted to the specific demographic groups whose support they were attempting to swing or fortify. For Kerry, these were what he called "Communities," while Bush labeled them "Coalitions." These included the following:

- African Americans
- Asian Pacific Americans
- Catholics
- Conservative values voters
- Democrats
- Educators
- Farmers and ranchers
- First responders
- Health professionals
- Hispanics
- Jewish team leaders
- Seniors
- Small business owners
- Sportsmen
- Students
- Veterans
- Women

Kerry and Gore both sold campaign materials online in sections called "Kerry Gear" and "Gore Stores," respectively. Bush had his online campaign materials store in a section that he labeled "Wstuff." This section included a reading list, opportunities to create a campaign poster, the ability to create a campaign newsfeed to visitors' websites, and downloadable screen savers and wallpapers for home computers (see box 4.2).

The fact is that, since 2000, campaign websites of candidates for national office usually include all of the features that any sophisticated commercial site would offer. For example, the Gore-Lieberman website invited visitors to join their Instant MessageNet, a forum to chat online with other supporters. Bush invited visitors to do the same in 2004 in his Chat Center and allowed visitors to pose real-time questions to campaign staff in a State of the Race section. In 2000, Gore offered personal digital assistant (PDA) campaign updates. Both candidates in 2004 also had links to their official blogs.

In addition, campaign websites have begun to include interactive features that resemble games. Bush's site in 2004 included a Kerry Gas Tax

---

BOX 4.2

"WSTUFF" SECTION
OF BUSH 2004 WEBSITE

- Suggested reading list
- Create a poster
- Get a newsfeed for your site
- Screen savers and wallpapers
- George W. Bush online store

Calculator. The calculator allowed visitors to estimate how much Kerry's proposed fifty-cent-per-gallon gas tax would cost them personally.

Perhaps the most sophisticated use of campaign websites thus far is the feature that invites visitors to enter their zip code in order to find local campaign events, volunteer, and otherwise become involved. Kerry, for example, had a Get Local section where visitors selected a state and, based on that entry, received information with various ways to get involved in the campaign. In a similar way, Al Gore called his section "Take Action," which did not ask for a zip code but instead invited visitors to select a state and a coalition. The website then made suggestions about how one could assist or help the campaign. In 2004, Bush had something very similar with a section on his website called "Grassroots." The Gore campaign also invited supporters to build their own pro-Gore web page—albeit a simple one—by joining the Gore I-Team. Kerry's Core did something similar, although it was more advanced, allowing visitors to build a web page, send e-mails, and organize various campaign activities.[26]

In short, presidential candidate websites give visitors a myriad of convenient ways to become involved in campaigns. Candidate websites, however, also provided the means for visitors to recruit friends and send voting reminders to friends, family, and others (see box 4.3, which replicates sections of Bush and Kerry's websites). One of the most ballyhooed advances the Internet has brought to political campaigns at all levels is the ability to allow donors to contribute money in a convenient way. This is especially true with respect to smaller donations and those made to cash-strapped campaigns that need money quickly. This was the lesson

BOX 4.3

VOLUNTEERING FOR KERRY AND BUSH, 2004

"Take Action" (Kerry)

- Contribute
- Be a volunteer
- Volunteer center
- Recruit friends
- Send voting reminders
- Contact media
- Raise money
- Plan/attend events
- Vote early

"Join the Team" (Bush)

- Be a volunteer
- Donate to GELAC*
- Action center
- Party for president
- Calendar
- Vote early
- Register to vote
- Wstuff

*Refers to the general election legal and accounting compliance fund, allowed by federal election law in order to offset the costs of compliance with campaign finance laws.

from the insurgent campaigns of Bill Bradley and John McCain in the 2000 presidential primaries. McCain, for example, was virtually out of money by the time New Hampshire held its primary on February 1. At least partly as the result of the publicity generated from his surprise win, the campaign took in approximately twenty-one thousand dollars per hour for four days, collecting over two million dollars in Internet donations.

In total, McCain raised $6.4 million in online donations, which amounted to about one-quarter of the campaign's overall receipts. More significant, however, was that the average donation was $112.[27] This amount is noteworthy because the presidential finance system rewards small donations. Candidates receive dollar-for-dollar matching funds from the federal government for donations of $250 or less during the presidential primaries. The small donations that McCain received from the Internet after his victory in New Hampshire made it possible for him to raise large amounts of money with astonishing speed. Likewise, in 2004, Howard Dean managed to raise approximately 40 percent of his total campaign funds through the Internet—about twenty million dollars. By comparison, Bush raised approximately fourteen million dollars online (5 percent of his total), and Kerry, eighty-nine million dollars (33 percent of his total).[28] What makes Dean's totals more impressive is that his campaign was effectively finished relatively early in the primary process, while the Bush and Kerry campaigns lasted for the duration.

Of course, no discussion of the use of the web in 2004 would be complete without a mention of blogs. Although most blogs are not under the control of the candidate, both presidential candidates in 2004 had their own official blogs. One has to assume that this constituted a tacit recognition of Howard Dean's successful marshaling of support via various blogs. While Dean's campaign demonstrated that blog support might not translate into enough votes to win, it remains the case that blogs connect supporters with each other, keeping them abreast of campaign developments. In addition to providing a forum to voice opinions, the hypertext format allows writers to link to other stories (pro or con) about the candidate. Howard Dean had several blogs that his campaign team supported, directly or indirectly, throughout 2003 and into 2004, including Dean Nation (the first Dean blog, at dean2004.blogspot.com), Change for America (www.changeforamerica.com, but as of this writing, offline), Howard Dean 2004 Call to Action Weblog (deancalltoaction.blogspot.com), and what eventually became his primary blog vehicle, Blog for America (blogforamerica.com).

These sites had a very significant effect on the Dean campaign throughout the preprimary campaign. Meetup.org allowed the campaign to gather momentum by connecting followers who met with each other in various cities and towns across the country. Dean finished first in an "online primary" that Moveon.org conducted, further raising his profile and generating momentum.[29] As noted, he raised an enormous amount of money by way of Internet donations. On June 30, 2003, for example, as the result of a massive effort on the blogs, the campaign raised eight hundred thousand dollars.[30] On one day in late December 2003, the campaign posted four hundred messages to Blog for America, prompting over four thousand responses or comments in the next twenty-four hours.[31] By the time of the Iowa caucuses, the campaign estimated some six hundred thousand online supporters.[32] And, while Dean did not win the Democratic Party nomination, both Kerry and Bush also had their share of blogs (see box 4.4, which presents text from one of the pro-Bush blogs).[33]

BOX 4.4

ABOUT "BLOGS FOR BUSH"

Founded by Matt Margolis, Blogs for Bush was launched in November of 2003 with the purpose [of] covering the 2004 Election, organizing a community of pro-Bush bloggers, and encouraging grassroots activity on behalf of President Bush. Blogs for Bush became one of the most popular blogs during the 2004 election, and was called 'a must read everyday' by nationally syndicated radio talk show host and bestselling author Hugh Hewitt.

Source: www.blogsforbush.com

E-MAIL

Another Internet contribution to modern electioneering has been the use of e-mail to mobilize potential supporters. The usual process is an e-mail that invites visitors to opt in or "subscribe" to a campaign newsletter. The visitor must enter his or her e-mail address and other information (e.g., full name, mailing address, telephone number, age, etc.). In 2004, Michael Turk, Bush's e-campaign director, reported that the campaign had an e-mail list of more than seven million subscribers.[34] This allowed campaigns to narrowcast their messages, personalizing them to specific individuals. The e-mail campaign is extremely efficient, both in terms of cost (negligible) and with respect to communicating with supporters. Candidates have incorporated e-mail into their campaign in a variety of different ways.

At the most basic level, an e-mail can keep supporters apprised of campaign news, including past and upcoming events, and candidate appearances as well as provide rapid response to opposition attacks or press reports, and so on. As aforementioned, Jesse Ventura used an extensive e-mail network to communicate with followers in his 1998 bid for the governorship of Minnesota. At one critical juncture, the campaign used e-mail to debunk rumors that suggested Ventura supported legalized prostitution.[35] In 2000, John McCain sent radio ads to supporters to preview before they aired.[36] At one point in early January 2000, an e-mail asked for volunteers to make ten phone calls to New Hampshire residents registered as independents or as Republicans. More than nine thousand did so. In early February 2000, the campaign sold approximately five hundred tickets at one hundred dollars apiece to an online question and answer session with the candidate himself.[37]

Four years later, John Kerry initially announced his choice of John Edwards as his running mate via an e-mail bulletin. Likewise, the Bush campaign sent e-mail to supporters that highlighted the issues important to the citizens of each state. The Bush campaign also included bulletins in their e-mail with a convenient link to forward them to a friend. According to one survey, some seventeen million people sent e-mail to friends and family throughout the 2004 campaign.[38] This lent a viral marketing component to the Bush campaign.[39] Forwarded e-mail could include political jokes and humorous political videos, as well as stories containing rumors and innuendo—starting "whisper campaigns." There is no telling, for example, how e-mail contributed to the attempt to discredit Teresa Heinz Kerry on various blogs.[40] One report estimates that thirty-two million Americans received or sent e-mail containing political jokes during the campaign.[41]

The Bush campaign, according to one report, also bested the Kerry campaign in terms of grabbing potential readers' attention by making clever use of subject lines. "Let the Voters Choose, Not the Lawyers" was the subject of one such electronic missive from the Bush campaign. This compares with a rather tame "Polling Update" from the Kerry campaign and a rather confusing (with potential for immediate deletion as spam) "Next Wednesday Morning" from the Edwards camp.[42] Finally, all candidates make use of e-mail to mobilize supporters as Election Day approaches, alerting them to campaign rallies in their area, reminding them to vote, and urging them to persuade others to do so as well.

CONCLUSION

So what are we to make of Internet campaigning at this early stage of its development? Certainly, it is difficult to predict the future with respect to anything related to technological advances. Nevertheless, modern Internet campaigning has several strengths and limitations that might foretell its future.

The Internet, both the web and e-mail, is an excellent way to connect and mobilize supporters. The Internet has become an invaluable campaign communications vehicle because of the relative ease and speed with which a campaign can deliver a message as well as the variety of formats available for the message. In addition, the Internet provides the ability to tailor messages to specific groups and does so at a cost that is a fraction of that associated with the writing, production, testing, and airing of television advertisements. This makes it possible, though not necessarily likely, that an underfunded outsider could wage a competitive campaign. Campaigns also make use of public (e.g., Google) and private (e.g., LexisNexis) networks to conduct thorough and speedy research on their opponents and themselves throughout the campaign.[43] Finally, some research suggests that messages on the Internet (web or e-mail) are multiplied when a small group of online influentials forward e-mails, links, and so on, to friends and family.[44]

However, the Internet's reach is not complete. Not all Americans have access to the Internet, and not all of those who have access use the Internet for political news and information. Moreover, those who do use the Internet for political information are likely to be browsing the sites of candidates they are already supporting. In short, the Internet is an excellent tool that modern campaign organizations can employ to rally the faithful, but it might be some time—if ever—before it replaces television as the main political campaign communication vehicle.

FOR MORE READING

Bimber, Bruce, and Richard Davis. *Campaigning Online: The Internet in U.S. Elections.* New York: Oxford University Press, 2003.

Cornfield, Michael. *Politics Moves Online: Campaigning and the Internet.* New York: Century Foundation Press, 2004.

Cornfield, Michael, and Jonah Seiger. "The Net and the Nomination." In *The Making of the Presidential Candidates 2004,* ed. William G. Mayer. Lanham, Md.: Rowman & Littlefield, 2004.

Howard, Philip N. *New Media Campaigns and the Managed Citizen.* Cambridge, UK: Cambridge University Press, 2006.

Williams, Andrew Paul, and John C. Tedesco, eds. *The Internet Campaign: Perspectives on the Web in Campaign 2004.* Lanham, Md.: Rowman & Littlefield, 2006.

5

Myth or Reality?

Presidential Campaigns
Have Become Nastier

In almost every election, political observers comment on the declining quality of political campaigns. One of the most frequently made charges is that negative campaigning has grown worse over the years. For example, the director of the nonpartisan Committee for the Study of the American Electorate called the 2004 election "the ugliest presidential election we've ever had."[1]

This reaction was due, at least in part, to a series of advertisements sponsored by the Swift Boat Veterans for Truth that attacked Democratic presidential nominee John Kerry. In one of the ads, the organization claimed that Kerry had "not been honest about what happened in Vietnam"; that he "lied about his first Purple Heart"; that he "lied to get his bronze star"; that he "lacks the capacity to lead"; that he is "no war hero"; and that he "betrayed the men and women he served with."[2] On the other side of the political aisle, filmmaker Michael Moore released an anti-Bush documentary film entitled *Fahrenheit 9/11* during the summer of 2004. The two-hour film makes the case that President Bush failed to address the threat of Islamic terrorism in the months leading up to the 9/11 attacks (one scene shows Bush casually playing golf as he answers a reporter's question about the threat of terrorism). The film then takes sharp aim at Bush's handling of the situation in the aftermath of the 9/11 attack. The documentary generated enormous publicity in the summer months preceding the November election and was one of the most memorable anti-Bush pieces of the 2004 campaign.

While few could argue that the Bush-Kerry contest was replete with egregious examples of political attacks, it is highly debatable that the 2004 election was the ugliest presidential election ever. Indeed, negative campaign tactics have always played a pervasive role in American presidential elections. Opponents of Thomas Jefferson suggested that his victory would lead to the rise of atheism and the burning of the Bible.[3] Andrew Jackson had to endure attacks by his political opponents that his deceased mother was a prostitute.[4] These and other examples illustrate that the mean-spirited, personal attacks of American campaigns are hardly new to the political landscape.

Of course, there is a subjective nature to evaluating just how negative a campaign is. Indeed, there are slightly different definitions in the literature about what exactly constitutes negativity in a campaign, although there is some agreement that it typically involves discrediting, criticizing, or publicizing the deficiencies of the opponent.[5] Some political scientists suggest that negative campaigning has had a deleterious effect on American democracy. Their research finds that negative advertisements heighten political cynicism, depress voter turnout, and reduce political efficacy.[6]

Others argue that negative advertisements provide important information to voters, help draw clearer distinctions between candidates, and improve voters' recall of information and memory of the ad.[7] Moreover, there is good justification for the notion that in a political campaign some mention of the opponent's background, experience, and public record should be part of the campaign discourse. Political ads that focus on these aspects are not negative but more properly thought of as comparative. These comparative ads bring or highlight some aspect of the opposition candidate's record or background that the voting public should know before they make their decision about who will best serve their interests if elected.[8]

Nevertheless, our intent in this chapter is *not* to quantify whether one campaign was more negative than another. Instead, the point of the chapter is more basic: We wish to demonstrate to the reader that the personal attacks of modern elections have long been a part of American politics. We focus on presidential elections. Although state and local elections certainly can be very negative at times, presidential races are the "Super Bowl" of campaigns, and perceptions of American elections are most heavily shaped by these contests. We review five presidential elections from the nineteenth century that each stand out as particularly negative. These historical examples cast some reasonable doubt on the repeated claims that "today's campaigns are the most negative ever."

THE ELECTION OF 1800

The election of 1800 pitted two of the nation's founding fathers against each other, President John Adams and Vice President Thomas Jefferson.

Both men had come to represent the views of two emerging political parties: the Federalists and the Democratic-Republicans. Federalists, who strongly opposed Jefferson, favored a strong central government, as well as domestic policies that supported the commercial and moneyed interests of the nation and a foreign policy that sided with Great Britain in its conflicts with France in the aftermath of the French Revolution. The Democratic-Republican Party, which formed its intellectual foundation from the ideas of Jefferson and James Madison, advocated a weaker federal government and stronger state governments, as well as domestic policies that favored small farmers and foreign policy that sided with France.[9]

While there were legitimate differences separating Adams and Jefferson on many issues, supporters of both candidates often focused their efforts on negative personal attacks. Adams's supporters spread stories that Jefferson had "cheated his British creditors, obtained property by fraud, robbed a widow of an estate worth ten thousand pounds, and behaved in a cowardly fashion as Governor of Virginia during the Revolution."[10] Federalists labeled Jefferson "mean-spirited" and claimed that he was the "son of a half-breed Indian squaw, sired by a Virginia mulatto father."[11]

These attacks, however, were only the beginning. Jefferson's opponents attacked his religious beliefs and moral values. One newspaper, the *Connecticut Courant*, opined that a victory for Jefferson in 1800 would result in the teaching and practice of "murder, robbery, rape, adultery, and incest" and added that the "air will be rent with cries of the distressed, the soil will be soaked with blood, and the nation black with crimes."[12] The president of Yale University, Timothy Dwight, believed that Jefferson's election would result in "the Bible [being] cast into a bonfire . . . our wives and daughters [becoming] the victims of legal prostitution."[13] Others attacked Jefferson as a dangerous rebel "who writes against the truths of God's word" and "without so much as a decent external respect for the faith and worship of Christians."[14]

Jefferson's supporters attacked Adams as a "fool, hypocrite, criminal, and tyrant."[15] They were sharply critical of Adams's support for the Alien and Sedition Acts (a federal law that made it illegal to speak or publish information critical of the government), which they saw as a betrayal of republican values and states' rights. Jeffersonians also planted several false stories about Adams, including one that suggested that were it not for a sword-wielding George Washington, Adams intended to arrange a marriage between one of his sons and one of the daughters of King George III in a plot to reunite the United States and Great Britain. Another rumor, spread by Jefferson's supporters, suggested that Adams had sent his running mate, General Charles Pinckney, to England on a trip to secure four mistresses, two for each of them. To these charges, Adams famously retorted, "If this be true, [then] General Pinckney has kept them all for himself and cheated me out of two."[16]

While negativity swirled in both directions, the political environment favored Jefferson in 1800. Adams would garner just 39 percent of the popular vote compared to 61 percent for Jefferson. In the electoral college vote, however, Jefferson received seventy-three of the necessary seventy electoral college votes to win the presidency, while Adams received sixty-five. However, because the electoral college at the time did not distinguish between votes for president and vice president, Jefferson's running mate, Aaron Burr, also received seventy-three electoral college votes, creating a tie and moving the election to the House of Representatives. There, Jefferson was finally elected president on the thirty-sixth ballot.[17]

The Twelfth Amendment eventually altered the chaotic process that ensued following the tie between Jefferson and Burr, giving the election of 1800 special historical significance. However, the election of 1800 was also significant in that many credit it as the first seriously contested campaign for the presidency. This first campaign certainly set a standard for negativity and viciousness that would generate notice, even by today's standards.[18]

THE ELECTION OF 1828

Many scholars consider the election of 1828 as one of dirtiest presidential contests in American history.[19] The 1828 election pitted incumbent President John Quincy Adams (the son of former President John Adams) of the Whig Party against challenger Andrew Jackson, a Democrat and former army general who led American troops to a decisive victory over the British in the Battle of New Orleans during the War of 1812. This election was a rematch of sorts of the 1824 election, which had ended in bitter controversy.

In the 1824 election, Jackson faced not only Adams but also William Harris Crawford of Georgia and Henry Clay of Kentucky. The four-man field divided the 261 total electoral college votes: Jackson received ninety-nine, Adams received eighty-four, Crawford received forty-one, and Clay received thirty-seven. Jackson also earned 41 percent of the popular vote—ten percentage points more than his closest competitor, Adams, who earned 31 percent of the popular vote. However, because no candidates received the required majority (131) of the electoral college votes, the election was thrust into the House of Representatives.[20]

In the House of Representatives, Clay was disqualified for finishing fourth (the Twelfth Amendment stipulates that the House may consider only the top three finishers). Clay, however, was the Speaker of the House, and wielded considerable influence in the chamber. He deeply disliked Jackson, referring to him as a "military chieftain" unfit to hold the office of the presidency.[21] Clay ultimately put his support behind John Quincy

Adams. With Clay's backing, Adams won the election on the first ballot, earning the votes of thirteen of the then twenty-four states (Jackson won seven states and Crawford four states). The result infuriated Jackson supporters who believed that their candidate deserved the election for winning the most popular and the most electoral college votes. To add to Jackson's outrage, Adams would name Clay his secretary of state, prompting critics to suggest that the two had struck a "corrupt bargain."[22] This history set the stage for a bitter rematch in 1828 between Jackson and Adams.

Jackson's supporters, often referred to as Jacksonians, attacked the Adams presidency for its excesses or what they described as the lifestyle of "King John the Second" to live in "kingly pomp and splendor."[23] This particular attack centered on Adams's purchase of a billiards table, which Jacksonians falsely claimed was purchased at taxpayer expense. Jacksonians also called into question Adams's religious sincerity, noting that he sometimes traveled on Sundays. These attacks came despite the fact that Adams was a Puritan and, by all reasonable accounts, a serious and devout Christian. The Jacksonians, however, went even further in their personal attacks, planting rumors that Adams and his wife had "premarital relations." Most outrageous was the Jacksonians' claim that Adams, while serving as the minister to Russia, handed over a young American girl to Czar Alexander I.[24]

The Adams campaign played equally dirty in attacking Jackson. Adams's supporters, known as the Friends of Adams, referred to Jackson as someone "destitute of historical, political, or statistical knowledge."[25] A pro-Adams political handbook added that Jackson was "wholly unqualified by education, habit and temper for the station of President."[26]

These criticisms, however, were tame compared to other accusations leveled against Jackson. Adams's supporters attacked Jackson with an endless barrage of scurrilous charges that included adultery, bigamy, gambling, drunkenness, theft, and even murder. The murder charge involved Jackson's approval to execute six militiamen for desertion during the Creek War in 1813. A pro-Adams editor described the event as "the Bloody Deeds of General Jackson" and portrayed the event as a cold-blooded murder in which Jackson sanctioned the killing of six innocent soldiers.[27] Not surprisingly, these charges outraged Jacksonians, who countered that Adams's supporters had distorted and even lied about the facts surrounding the event.

The attacks against Jackson even extended to his family. One newspaper story was particularly vicious, attacking Jackson's mother as a prostitute. According to the account, "General Jackson's mother was a COMMON PROSTITUTE, brought to this country by the British soldiers. She afterward married a MULATO MAN, with whom she had several children, of which GENERAL JACKSON IS ONE!!!"[28]

Jackson also had to endure attacks against his wife. Adams supporters spread misleading stories that Jackson's wife, Rachel, had committed adultery. The story underlying the charge, however, was much more complicated. Jackson's wife had been married previously and believed she had rightfully divorced her first husband, Captain Lewis Robards, when she began her relationship with Jackson. Unbeknownst to Rachel, Robards had delayed in finalizing the divorce. By the time Jackson and Rachel became aware of this, the two had already married. They would remarry after the divorce became final, but the entire event led to charges throughout Jackson's life, especially during the 1828 campaign, that his wife was an adulterer and a bigamist.[29]

In the end, Jackson defeated Adams in the 1828 election, winning 56 percent of the popular vote and 178 of the 261 electoral college votes. However, the victory came at deep personal cost to Jackson. His wife, Rachel, died a month after the election in December 1828. Jackson blamed Adams's supporters for their relentless attacks against his wife, referring to them as "murderers" and vowing never to forgive them. At her funeral, Jackson declared, "May God Almighty forgive her murderers, as I know she forgave them. I never can."[30]

The 1828 election certainly rises to the highest levels of negativity in American campaigns. Political scientist Kerwin Swint has labeled the 1828 election the most negative presidential campaign in history and the second most negative of all time (with only the George Wallace–Albert Brewer election for governor of Alabama in 1970 coming in higher).[31] As negative as modern campaigns can sometimes become, it seems difficult to argue that the 2004 election contained anything that surpassed the attacks of the 1828 election.

THE ELECTION OF 1864

The election of 1864 occurred during the Civil War and included only states that belonged to the union (i.e., southern states that belonged to the confederacy did not participate). The two principal candidates in the election were President Abraham Lincoln (Republican) and challenger General George McClellan (Democrat) of New Jersey. While Lincoln is revered today as one of the greatest presidents in American history, he was not nearly as popular in 1864. The Civil War that Lincoln led was ravaging the nation, with rising death tolls and mounting financial costs. Lincoln's opponents in the Democratic Party believed the difficulties of the war presented them with an opportunity to win the White House.

Many leaders in the Democratic Party saw the Civil War as a failure and called for an immediate cessation of hostilities. Numerous critics, even within the Republican Party, blamed Lincoln for the war's difficulties.

Lincoln's opponents labeled him ignorant, incompetent, and even corrupt. Others went further, referring to him as "Ignoramus Abe." Additional pejorative descriptions of Lincoln included ape, gorilla, Old Scoundrel, despot, liar, perjurer, thief, swindler, robber, buffoon, monster, fiend, and butcher.[32] *New York Herald* writer James Gordon Bennet, a critic of Lincoln's, said the "idea that such a man as he should be president of such a country is a very ridiculous joke."[33]

Another negative attack against Lincoln involved a story that he demanded one of his officers to sing to him a song after the Battle of Antietam. According to the story, Lincoln, McClellan (then the Union general under Lincoln), and officer Marshal Ward Hill Lamon rode together in an ambulance over the battlefield, passing the dead bodies of Union soldiers. During this rather solemn moment, Lincoln reportedly slapped Lamon on the knee and requested that he sing "that song about 'Picayune Butler.'" Despite objections from McClellan, Lincoln reportedly insisted, forcing Lamon to sing the song at this clearly inappropriate time. The story, however, proved to be false.[34]

Other anti-Lincoln groups relied on overtly racist appeals in their attempts to discredit Lincoln. One pamphlet, produced by a splinter group of northern Democrats (known as Copperheads) who opposed the Civil War, labeled Lincoln as "Abraham Africanus the First" for his opposition to slavery (see figure 5.1). Another pamphlet entitled "Miscegenation: The Theory of the Bending of the Races, Applied to the American White Man and Negro" claimed that Lincoln favored "race mixing" and actively encouraged and supported the "intermarriage" between whites and blacks. Many anti-Lincoln newspapers aggressively publicized the pamphlet.[35]

Lincoln supporters and the Republicans attacked McClellan personally as well. They labeled him a "coward," and criticized his "defeatism" and "lack of patriotism."[36] Some even suggested that the Democrats' opposition to the war constituted treason. Republicans ridiculed McClellan as "Little Mac," and attacked his military credentials as a general, noting that he had "nothing to offer but a tradition of defeat."[37] Republicans in Pennsylvania warned in one poster that a McClellan victory would lead to anarchy, despotism, and the end of civilization (see figure 5.2).

The election concluded with a clear victory for Lincoln, who received 212 electoral college votes (55 percent of the popular vote) to McClellan's 21 electoral college votes (45 percent of the popular vote). Lincoln's victory would have significant implications for American history, and his presidency would be long remembered for its high ideals. However, even "Honest Abe" could not avoid negative campaigning in the election of 1864.

Figure 5.1. Pamphlet Attacking Abraham Lincoln, 1864
Source: Answers.com, at www.answers.com/topic/united-states-presidential-election-1864.

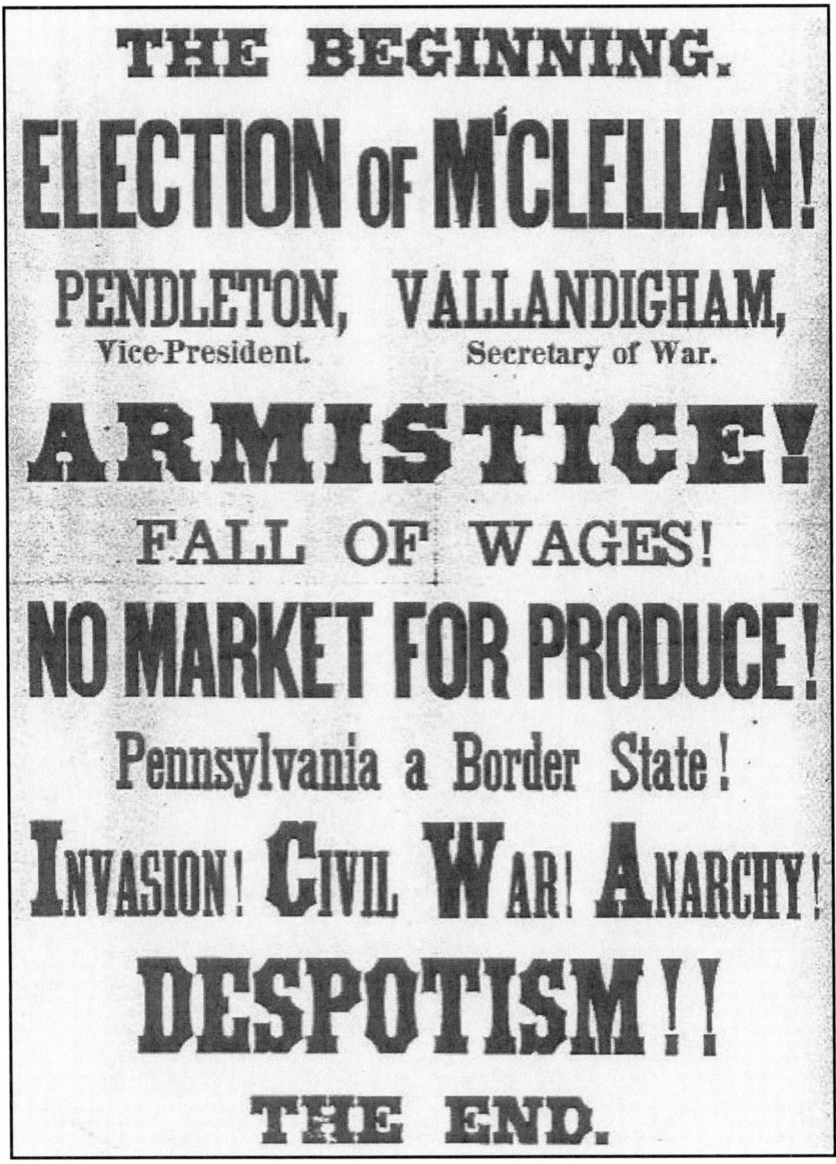

THE BEGINNING.

ELECTION OF M'CLELLAN!

PENDLETON, VALLANDIGHAM,
Vice-President.   Secretary of War.

ARMISTICE!

FALL OF WAGES!

NO MARKET FOR PRODUCE!

Pennsylvania a Border State!

INVASION! CIVIL WAR! ANARCHY!

DESPOTISM!!

THE END.

Figure 5.2.   Republican Party Election Poster, 1864
Source: Answers.com, at www.answers.com/topic/united-states-presidential-election-1864.

THE ELECTION OF 1872

The incumbent president heading into the election of 1872 was the former commander of the Union armies, Ulysses S. Grant. Grant, a Republican, won the presidency following his victory four years earlier over Democrat Horatio Seymour of New York (214 to 80 in the electoral college). Grant's first term in office, however, was marred with scandal, as the word "Grantism" became synonymous with corruption and nepotism.[38] Grant appointed personal friends and family members to political positions even when they had virtually no qualifications for the jobs. For example, he appointed Adolph Borie to be Secretary of the Navy, despite the fact that Borie's only experience was as a Philadelphia businessman.[39]

Corruption in the Grant administration led to a split in the Republican Party, as reformers opposed to Grant formed the Liberal Republicans. The major problem for the Liberal Republicans, however, was that they did not have a viable candidate to challenge Grant in 1872. The party ultimately settled on Horace Greeley, a well-known newspaperman without any political experience. Democrats, who feared the possibility of dividing the anti-Grant vote, decided not to run a candidate of their own, and instead endorsed Greeley—marking the first and only time in American history that a major party backed a third-party candidate for president rather than running a candidate from within the party.[40]

The Grant campaign mobilized all of its resources and attacked Greeley with a vengeance. Anti-Greeley cartoons were especially mean-spirited. One cartoon depicted Greeley as a bumbling fool, portraying him as a near-sighted clown with a pumpkin head. Another bitterly attacked Greeley for encouraging reconciliation between the North and South. In the cartoon, Greeley is shown handing over an African American man to a member of the Ku Klux Klan. Greeley even received abuse from his own supporters. The *Nation* viewed Greeley as a disappointing choice to be the Democrats' presidential nominee, while other periodicals and newspapers called the Greeley nomination a joke.[41]

Greeley supporters responded with their own sharp criticisms of Grant. A frequent line of attack was the issue of corruption in the Grant administration. One pro-Greeley pamphlet claimed the Grant administration was guilty of accepting bribes and even made charges that the Grant administration had encouraged other high crimes, such as robbery and murder.[42] A more mild attack mocked the president as "Useless" (rather than Ulysses) Grant.[43]

As the insults continued into the final days of the campaign, Greeley's wife, who had been suffering from health problems, died on October 30, 1872. Greeley, who was now grieving the death of his wife and had been savaged during the campaign by Grant and his supporters, fell ill shortly after the election. He passed away himself a month later on November 29, 1872.

Grant ultimately won reelection, earning 286 electoral college votes out of a possible 349 and 56 percent of the popular vote. Greeley received 43 percent of the popular vote, but due to his death after the election, he failed to receive any votes when the electoral college voted later in December. Thomas Hendricks, Grant's closest competitor in the electoral college, won just 42 votes. Despite Grant's comfortable victory, the election of 1872 was fiercely negative. As this example demonstrates, attack politics existed and thrived in nineteenth-century America.

THE ELECTION OF 1884

The presidential election of 1884 was an open-seat contest between New York governor Grover Cleveland, a Democrat, and U.S. senator James Blaine of Maine, a Republican. The race became open when the incumbent, Republican Chester Arthur (who became president after the assassination of James Garfield in 1881) decided not to run for president. Arthur had been privately suffering from Bright's disease (a kidney ailment), which had weakened his health and ultimately discouraged him from running for election.[44] With Arthur out of the race, Cleveland and Blaine became the candidates for president in what promised to be a very competitive election but ultimately became one of the most negative in American history.[45]

The election began with charges that Blaine had abused the power of his political office, specifically with respect to his "railroad connections." A story surfaced that Blaine pressured a railroad attorney, Warren Fisher, to sign a letter that Blaine had authored in which the senator exonerated himself of any misdealings with the railroad. Blaine, who communicated this request in a cover letter, wrote to Fisher that he would consider his signing of the letter to be an important favor. He then directed Fisher to destroy the letter. Democrats seized on controversies such as this one to question Blaine's honesty and integrity. One Democratic chant exclaimed, "Blaine! Blaine! James G. Blaine! The continental liar from the state of Maine!"[46]

Cleveland, who had earned a reputation as an honest public official, faced a more damaging personal scandal. On July 21, 1884, the *Buffalo Evening Telegraph* ran a story entitled "A Dark Chapter in a Public Man's History: The Pitiful Story of Maria Halpin and Governor Cleveland's Son." The story revealed that Cleveland as a young adult had fathered an illegitimate child with Maria Halpin, a widow from Buffalo. Cleveland provided financial support for both and did not deny the story, admitting that most of what appeared in the article was true. Cleveland's honesty, however, did not spare him from attacks. The *New York Sun's* Charles A.

Dana opined, "We do not believe that the American people will knowingly elect to the Presidency a coarse debauchee who would bring his harlots with him to Washington, and hire lodgings for them convenient to the White House."[47] Others attacked Cleveland as a "moral leper," a "gross and licentious man," and "worse in moral quality than a pickpocket." Republicans even taunted Cleveland supporters with the chant "Ma! Ma! Where's my pa?"[48]

Blaine, however, faced his own personal attacks. While Cleveland strongly discouraged his supporters from personally attacking his opponent, the *Indianapolis Sentinel* published a story that Blaine had premarital relations with his wife. According to the paper, "There is hardly an intelligent man in the country who has not heard that James C. Blaine betrayed the girl whom he married, and then only married her at the muzzle of a shotgun. . . . If after despoiling her, he was too craven to refuse her legal redress, giving legitimacy to her child, until a loaded shotgun stimulated his conscience—then there is a blot on his character more foul, if possible, than any of the countless stains on his political record."[49]

In the end, Cleveland won the election by a narrow margin, earning 219 electoral college votes to Blaine's 182. The popular vote was even closer, with Cleveland winning 48.5 percent of the vote to Blaine's 48.2 percent. While the election of 1884 is historically significant because Cleveland became the first Democrat to win the White House since 1856, the election was also one of the most personally mean-spirited campaigns in presidential history and certainly one that compares with any modern campaign.

CONCLUSION

As noted at the outset of this chapter, the 2004 presidential election had its fair share of negative attacks leveled against both John Kerry and George W. Bush. Certainly in living memory, the 2004 election was among the most negative, and in a somewhat troubling development, many of the attacks came from independent groups, which candidates and their campaigns could distance themselves from and avoid accountability. Yet, while the 2004 election contained numerous examples of nasty personal attacks from groups that supported Bush and those that supported Kerry, the 2004 election was probably not "the ugliest" presidential election in American history. As the five nineteenth-century presidential elections presented in this chapter make clear, vicious personal attacks and negative campaigning are virtually as old as the republic.

In addition to the negativity of these five campaigns, other examples exist. In 1876, one well-known speech favoring Rutherford B. Hayes strongly intimated that all Democrats were responsible for the assassination of Abraham Lincoln. The James Garfield campaign of 1880 portrayed the Democrat general Winfield Scott Hancock as favoring forceful and violent disenfranchisement of southern blacks.[50]

Indeed, there are even twentieth-century examples that compare in tone and negativity to the 2004 election. The 1964, 1972, and 1988 presidential elections all stand out as especially negative. In 1964, Democratic supporters of President Lyndon Johnson sponsored the infamous "Daisy commercial" in which a young girl plucks the petals of a daisy while the ad transitions into a nuclear countdown that ends in an atomic explosion. This ad's less than subtle suggestion that Republican challenger Barry Goldwater would lead the nation into nuclear war ranks among the most outrageous in presidential campaign history.[51]

Likewise, in 1972, Republican supporters of President Richard Nixon labeled the Democratic nominee, George McGovern, as the candidate of the three As: *acid* (for McGovern's position to decriminalize marijuana), *abortion* (for McGovern's pro-choice position on abortion), and *amnesty* (for McGovern's position to grant amnesty to those who resisted the Vietnam War draft at the conclusion of the war).[52] Four years earlier, Democrats attacked Nixon's running mate, Spiro Agnew, in what was probably one of the most well-known political advertisements in the television age. The commercial featured a shot of a television screen that displayed the words "Agnew for Vice President" and a soundtrack of a man laughing, at first softly, and then, increasingly louder. The advertisement ends with the following words on the screen: "This would be funny if it weren't so serious."[53]

The 1988 presidential election deserves special mention for the infamous "Willie Horton" advertisements in which supporters of Republican George H. W. Bush suggested that the Democratic candidate, Massachusetts governor Michael Dukakis, would turn a blind eye to violent crime. The ad featured the picture of a convicted murderer, Willie Horton, who raped a Maryland woman during a weekend furlough from a Massachusetts prison, as an announcer tells viewers, "Dukakis not only opposes the death penalty, he allowed first-degree murderers to have weekend passes from prison."[54] This charge, however, conveniently ignored the fact that the program had been adopted under the previous administration of Francis Sargent, a Republican. The advertisement also prompted charges of racism, as critics suggested that Bush supporters deliberately chose to feature an African American criminal to exploit "racist fears" about crime.[55]

There are certainly additional examples that one could note, but all would simply underlie the major point of this chapter, which is that negative campaigning has a long history in presidential elections. Future elections will undoubtedly bring about the familiar calls that the current election is the "most negative ever." Such lines certainly make for flashy headlines and provocative quotations; however, as the historical record rather plainly suggests, these claims come much closer to hyperbole than they do to reality.

FOR MORE READING

Boller, Paul F., Jr. *Presidential Campaigns: From George Washington to George W. Bush.* New York: Oxford University Press, 2004.

Jamieson, Kathleen Hall. *Dirty Politics: Deception, Distraction, and Democracy.* New York: Oxford University Press, 1992.

Mark, David. *Going Dirty: The Art of Negative Campaigning.* Lanham, Md.: Rowman & Littlefield, 2006.

Swint, Kerwin C. *Mudslingers: The Top 25 Negative Political Campaigns of All Time.* Westport, Conn.: Praeger, 2006.

6

Science or Voodoo?

Misconceptions about National Election Polls

I re-word Winston Churchill's famous remarks about democracy and say, "Polls are the worst way of measuring public opinion . . . or of predicting elections—except for all of the others."

—Humphrey Taylor, chairman of the Harris Poll[1]

Public opinion polls are ubiquitous. Rarely does a day pass without a major newspaper, such as *USA Today*, featuring the results of some poll. The frequency of polls only increases during an election season, and this is especially true during a presidential election. However, most people do not understand enough about polling to be able to interpret polls accurately. To make matters worse, the media occasionally misrepresent the results of polls. Pollsters themselves also miss the mark from time to time, providing forecasts and predictions that fail to materialize. This raises a few questions: Can national election polls be trusted? Are pollsters really able to gauge what Americans believe? One poll conducted in 2000 suggested that only 2 percent of Americans believe that national polls are "always right," while almost 60 percent believe they are right "only some of the time" and 7 percent "hardly ever."[2]

We offer a mixed answer to the question of whether people can trust polls throughout the election cycle. Our objective is less to dispel a particular myth but more to give the reader a better understanding of the enterprise of public polling during an election. This understanding is crucial to following news stories throughout the campaign. Our goal is to give readers a set of guidelines on how to actually use—read, analyze, and interpret—polling results during an election.[3] In the end, whether or not to trust a particular national opinion poll depends on a variety of factors.

THE BASICS OF PUBLIC POLLING

Election polls have a long history in the United States. Since 1824, newspapers have conducted and reported the results of so-called straws, or straw polls, during presidential elections.[4] Straw polls are informal polls taken to gauge public opinion (which way the wind is blowing the straw). During the nineteenth century, most newspapers were partisan publications. While newspapers purportedly used polls to give readers a sense of which candidate might be more likely to prevail, in actuality they were intended to advance the paper's partisan agenda by giving the public the impression that the paper's favored candidate was in the lead.

Indeed, the methodology of nineteenth-century polls was hardly scientific. To conduct a poll, a journalist might simply ask questions to passengers aboard a particular train or citizens attending a public gathering.[5] For example, in 1876, the following story ran in the *Chicago Tribune*: "An excursion train containing some 200 people from Dayton, [Ohio,] and neighboring towns, arrived last evening via the Pan Handle Road. . . . A vote was taken, resulting as follows: Hayes 65, Tilden 13, neutral 3, Cooper 2."[6]

Straw polls grew in popularity throughout the nineteenth century and by the early part of the twentieth century had become a regular feature in newspaper coverage of presidential elections. However, as popular as they were, they were not very useful in predicting the outcome of presidential elections. This was in part because people who did not sympathize with a given paper's partisan leanings would often refuse to return their questionnaires, leading to wildly biased estimates of the vote totals.

Among the many publications that conducted presidential polls was *Literary Digest*, which at the time was the most widely circulated general magazine in the nation. Starting in 1916, *Literary Digest* began to conduct polls predicting the presidential vote. While the magazine's predicted vote totals were often inaccurate, it correctly predicted the winner in five consecutive elections (1916–1932). However, in 1936, it predicted that the Republican candidate for president, Alf Landon, would receive 57 percent of the vote to Franklin Roosevelt's 43 percent. Of course, Roosevelt won, garnering 62.5 percent.[7]

The ushering in of the modern era of scientific polling began with the *Digest*'s failure in 1936. In addition to the fact that the magazine had incorrectly predicted Landon's victory, three enterprising individuals with backgrounds in market research correctly predicted the outcome. George Gallup, Elmo Roper, and Archibald Crossley were able to do so by employing more systematic methods of sampling.[8] To understand how Gallup, Roper, and Crossley correctly predicted the winner, and how the *Digest* did not, it is important to examine what pollsters do and how they do it.

A poll is a device used to measure what a group of people think about a particular subject or question. Because it is almost impossible to ask all of the people in a particular group (e.g., registered voters) what they think about a particular topic and because such an effort would be too time consuming or costly to be practical, a pollster asks a smaller group of people, or a sample. From this sample, pollsters then estimate what the larger group thinks.

To understand this process better, imagine trying to predict how a large lecture hall with five hundred students will vote in a presidential election. One approach would be to ask all five hundred students; however, by the time one handed out, collected, and counted all of the ballots, the class would be over. Is it reasonable to believe that one could *estimate* the *likely* vote outcome by polling only fifty people? Under certain circumstances, the answer is yes. Polling is based in part on the branch of mathematics known as probability theory, which attempts to quantify how likely it is that a certain event will occur.[9] The central limit theorem, for example, suggests that if one flips a coin one hundred times, it is likely that heads will land face-up about fifty times.

One important element, however, that needs to be considered is the number of times that one would need to flip the coin to have a rough idea of what the actual chance of heads landing face-up (about 50 percent) would be. Before one can estimate chance or probability, a certain number of actual observations are required. Probability theory allows pollsters to infer what Americans think based on answers given by only 1,500 people.[10]

Before applying the theories of probability to predicting vote outcomes, at least one condition needs to be specified. Based on previous research, we know that men and women, in general, vote differently. That is to say, women are more likely to vote Democratic, and men are more likely to vote Republican. Using the example of the class of five hundred, we would want to make sure that the poll sampled women and men in roughly similar proportions to their numbers in the whole class. If our class was evenly divided by gender (250 women, 250 men), we would want to poll approximately twenty-five women and twenty-five men. Furthermore, we know that people who frequently attend church vote differently than those who do not; that the more affluent cast their ballots differently than those who are less economically fortunate; and so on. Thus, to have any confidence that the results from our fifty-person sample would correctly predict the vote of all five hundred students, we would want to ensure that the fifty students polled were broadly *representative* of the entire class.

How is a representative sample identified by a pollster? There are four main strategies for doing this, and all rely on a random selection of individuals to take the poll. All, therefore, produce *probability* samples, a reference to the fact that randomness plays a central role in theories of probability.

The first strategy is *random sampling*. In a simple random sample, each person has an equal chance of selection. For example, if everyone in our hypothetical class of five hundred had a seat number, we could put slips of paper numbered one to five hundred in a basket, shuffle them around, and pick fifty. If conducted fairly (e.g., all sheets of paper are of equal size, folded in half to hide the number, sufficiently shuffled or mixed), the process would provide an equal chance for each student to be selected.

A second strategy, a variant of the first, is systematic sampling. Instead of selecting individuals randomly, *systematic sampling* involves moving through a list, which is assumed to be randomly distributed, and selecting names according to a preset strategy. For example, in systematic sampling, we could go through our alphabetical class roster and select every tenth name in order to create a fifty-person sample.

Another technique is *stratified sampling*. Here, the pollster selects the sampling frame, or the entire group, and divides it into strata, or groups. Within each stratum (group), the pollster selects a sample using simple random or systematic sampling. This helps to ensure that the sample sufficiently represents all relevant subgroups. For example, if our class has three hundred men and two hundred women, we would select a sample of thirty men and twenty women.

Multistage cluster sampling follows a similar principle, although geography rather than subgroup characteristics forms the basis. For example, a pollster could select a geographic unit (say, a state), and within that unit, select a smaller unit (a county), and within that unit, choose an even smaller one (a neighborhood) and then select potential respondents—at random— from the smallest unit. This process reduces costs for the polling firm by concentrating its efforts in several small areas. In our class example, we might think about selecting every fifth row of students, then randomly selecting respondents from each.

The important point with respect to sampling, regardless of the technique used, is that the respondents must be representative of the population that the pollster or researcher examines. Probability sampling rests on an assumption that if selected randomly, a sample will be representative of the population. Box 6.1 summarizes these four techniques.

This admittedly simplistic explanation of the polling process allows us to understand why the *Literary Digest* poll failed to predict Roosevelt's victory correctly in 1936. The magazine sent out over 10 million questionnaires, and of these, over 2.3 million people filled out the surveys and returned them. This was more than a sufficient number upon which to base a prediction of

BOX 6.1

TECHNIQUES FOR SELECTING A PROBABILITY SAMPLE

Random: Individuals are selected from the entire sampling frame by chance.

Systematic: Individuals are selected from the entire sampling frame according to a set strategy.

Stratified: The sampling frame is divided into subgroups, and within each, a certain number of individuals are selected either randomly or systematically.

Multistage Cluster: A number of geographic areas are identified, and within each, individuals are selected either randomly or systematically.

how the American public would vote. However, the magazine produced the list of people to mail the questionnaire from automobile registration and telephone number lists. In 1936, the people who owned automobiles or had telephones in their home were more likely to have been Republicans (thus, Landon voters) than Democrats (Roosevelt supporters). Additionally, subsequent research has shown that Landon voters were more likely to return their questionnaires. Coupled together, this produced a sample that was biased, or not representative of the general population.[11]

Assuming that researchers developed fairly worded questions and that they have administered the survey to a sufficiently large and representative sample, most polls can be trusted. However, not all polls are created equal. In particular, presidential campaign polls have some common pitfalls worth noting.

THE PROBLEM OF PSEUDO POLLS

There are many reputable polling firms as well as countless research institutions and university professors around the country that conduct scientifically grounded polls. In general, the results of these polls are trustworthy, if one uses a certain amount of discretion in interpreting the results. However, anyone can write and administer a poll. As noted earlier, a variety of different sources present us with various poll results every day. Which polls should we trust, or more to the point, which do we not trust?

"Pseudo polls" are one general category of polls to disregard, especially in understanding the dynamics of a presidential campaign. Websites (including blogs), local news organizations, talk radio, or college newspapers often administer these polls. The major problem with pseudo polls is that they typically rely on self-selected samples. Poll administrators simply invite people to participate in the poll and then tabulate the results. CNN's "QuickVote" is a good example of these types of polls. To be fair, CNN includes a disclaimer about the fact that the poll results were not representative of the general public, although it is unclear if the average viewer understands what this means.[12]

The problems with polls that rely on self-selected samples are twofold. First, not everyone has a chance to participate. For example, in the case of Internet polls, the sample includes only those who visit the poll's website. Moreover, most of these media cater to a specific type of person (i.e., most talk radio listeners tend to be conservative).[13] Another problem with this sampling technique is that people who have the motivation to take the time to respond to the poll usually have more extreme views than the general population. The end result is that the samples in pseudo polls are not representative of the population at large, nor are the views expressed in these polls representative of the views of the population at large.[14]

HOW TO DETERMINE LIKELY VOTERS?

A reliable poll of presidential preference should probably sample only those people who will actually vote. This is difficult to do. To understand the scope of this problem, consider that according to the Census Bureau, as of 2004, there were approximately 197 million citizens over the age of eighteen in the United States. Of these, roughly 142 million (72.1 percent) were registered voters in the presidential election, and only 125 million (63.8 percent of citizens over the age of eighteen) actually voted.[15] How then should a polling organization construct a sample of people who will vote or who will be likely to vote?

Unfortunately, there is no reliable or accepted way to determine whether an individual will exercise this most basic of political freedoms. Simply asking a person if they are likely to vote will not help identify likely voters. Most people, based on ideas about good citizenship, are reluctant to admit they might not vote. Thus, voter turnout is typically substantially lower than the percentage of people who say they are likely to vote. For example, the Pew Research Center conducted a survey prior to the 1996 election asking respondents about their intention to vote. Of those responding, 69 percent said they were "absolutely certain" they would vote, and another 18 percent replied they were "fairly certain." In actuality, voter turnout in 1996 was 49 percent.[16]

Most polling firms will use at least one, and typically several, screening questions in their attempt to narrow their sample down so it includes only likely voters. The first stage of this screening is almost always to ask whether the respondent is a registered voter. From those who respond in the affirmative, the polling firm will ask additional questions in an attempt to gauge how likely the registered voter is to vote. For example, the Gallup Organization has asked whether the respondent is likely to vote, how often they have voted in the past, whether they know where their polling place is, their level of interest in politics, their interest in a particular campaign, and their level of commitment to a particular candidate. Most of the reputable national polling organizations use some combination of questions similar to Gallup's to gauge whether an individual is likely to vote.[17]

In a presidential preference poll, especially one conducted close to the election, the sample should consist of only those who are registered and likely to vote. How well the polling firm constructs the sample in this regard can have a direct effect on the results. For example, a Harris Poll from October of 2004 suggested that President Bush was leading Senator John Kerry by two percentage points according to one measure of likely voters. A second method had Bush ahead by eight points (51 percent to 43 percent).[18]

Therefore, it seems prudent to take note of whether the poll bases its results on responses from registered or likely voters. Most major news organizations will include this information somewhere in the story. For example, a *Washington Post* story from early August 2004 reported that John Kerry had "the support of 50 percent of all *registered* voters." A story from late October 2004 suggested that Bush led Kerry "by 51% to 46% among *likely* voters" (emphasis added).[19]

WHAT ABOUT THE UNDECIDED VOTERS?

As complicated as it is to ensure that a poll sample includes only those voters most likely to vote, another issue is how to poll undecided voters. In most presidential campaigns, the number of "undecideds" is as high as 15 percent, and although this percentage drops as the campaign reaches its end, it can still be as high as 5 percent in the days prior to Election Day.

While it would be a simple matter for a news organization to report the percentage of undecideds in addition to the percentage that favor each candidate, most do not, because it makes for less interesting reading if the poll numbers present an uncertain picture. One strategy to deal with undecided voters is to have a follow-up question asking the respondent if he or she "leans" toward, or favors, either candidate.[20] While this reduces the number of undecideds, it paints an inaccurate portrait of voter preferences, given that many of these people subsequently change their minds.[21] This was one of the factors responsible for the Gallup Organization mistakenly calling the 1948 election for Thomas Dewey (morning newspapers proclaimed that Dewey won, when in fact Harry Truman was the victor).[22] Another way to reduce the number of undecideds is to present respondents with a secret ballot, but this requires face-to-face interviewing, a rather costly method.

A more common strategy is to allocate the undecideds to one candidate or the other, based on some formula. For example, one way to allocate them would be to assign them in proportion to the candidate's strength. If 46 percent of those have expressed a preference for Candidate A, then the pollster would allocate 46 percent of the undecided vote to Candidate A. This strategy, however, poses considerable risks, given that the closer Election Day looms, the more likely it is that momentum can shift, disproportionately favoring one candidate over the other. There are other formulas for allocating undecideds as well, including using the respondent's past voting record or partisan identification (if any) as a clue for future voting intentions, whether there is an incumbent in the race (undecideds are generally thought to be anti-incumbent), as well as other more complex solutions.

Additional ways to address this issue are to continue polling as close to Election Day as is feasible. This would eliminate many undecided voters. However, this strategy can result in less than perfect polls. One survey of the final preelection polls taken by major polling firms from 1980 to 2000 shows there is a fair degree of error in many of these polls when compared to the actual vote totals. Table 6.1, adopted from that study, lists the actual vote margin between the two candidates and the margin taken from the *least* accurate major poll, and the difference between these two figures, from each election cycle from 1980 to 2000.

To be fair, the survey also shows that with the exception of one year, at least one of the major polling firms projected the outcome either exactly or correctly to within one percentage point, and in only one case (the election of 2000) did any firm project the winner incorrectly. In 1980, all of the major firms underestimated Ronald Reagan's margin of victory over Jimmy Carter (NBC/AP came within three percentage points of the cor-

Table 6.1.   Actual and Projected Margins from Select Election Polls, 1980–2000

Year	Winner, Actual Vote Margin	Margin from Least Accurate Projection	Difference
1980	Reagan +10	Reagan +1 (CBS/New York Times)	9
1984	Reagan +18	Reagan +10 (Roper)/ +25 (USA Today)	8/7
1988	Bush +8	Bush +12 (Gallup)	4
1992	Clinton +8	Clinton +12 (Gallup/CNN/USA Today)	4
1996	Clinton +8	Clinton +18 (CBS/New York Times)	10
2000	Bush and Gore (even)	Bush +7 (Hotline)	7

Source: Adapted from Robert S. Erikson and Kent L. Tedin, *American Public Opinion: Its Origins, Content, and Impact*, 7th ed. (New York: Longman, 2005), 44.

rect margin). Seven organizations called the election for George W. Bush and two for Al Gore in 2000, while the actual vote was virtually even (Gore actually polled one-half of a percentage point more than did Bush). Table 6.1 illustrates the reality that many voters make their decision in the final days of the campaign, after the completion of the last polls. It also highlights the difficulties polling organizations have in dealing with these late-deciding voters.

THE PROBLEM OF TIMING: PHASES OF THE CAMPAIGN

Polls taken and released during certain periods of time during the campaign can be misleading, giving a false impression of a candidate's strength or weakness. Readers of these polls need to interpret them cautiously. This is especially true with respect to polls taken during the preprimary phase of the campaign, immediately after each party convention, and after debates.

Preprimary polls or those taken before the Iowa caucuses and New Hampshire primary have been a fairly good predictor of who will win the party nomination. Since 1980, all but one candidate who was leading in the Gallup poll immediately prior to the Iowa caucuses have won their party's nomination.[23] However, there is considerable fluctuation in these poll numbers before January of the election year. For example, in 2003, several candidates, including Joe Lieberman, Dick Gephardt, Wesley Clark, and the eventual presumed front-runner, Howard Dean, led in these preprimary polls.[24] John Kerry was the eventual winner of the Democratic nomination.

These "trial heat" polls do not measure actual preferences as much as they track name recognition or simple familiarity with the name of the individual.[25] In addition, these polls are sensitive to the news cycle. Before Wesley Clark's formal entrance into the race on September 17, 2003, most polls showed other Democratic candidates leading the field. However, in the month following his announcement to enter the race, Clark consistently ranked among the top tier of candidates. One can only assume this was at least partly the result of the media coverage generated by his announcement, because he won only one Democratic primary (the Oklahoma primary, held on February 3, 2004).[26] While polls taken immediately prior to the Iowa caucuses and the New Hampshire primary are a good indicator of who will be the eventual nominee, polls taken much earlier than November or December of the year prior to the election year are not very reliable.

In a similar way, polls taken immediately after each candidate's party convention (or a candidate debate) typically do not measure actual candidate strength. While there are exceptions (e.g., 1984, 1996), it is very common for each party candidate's numbers to go up 5 to 10 percent after the convention. Many political observers commonly refer to this as the "postconvention bump" or "bounce." Typically, challengers benefit more than incumbents from the postconvention bounce because they are less well known to the general public. However, convention bounces for either candidate can dissipate quickly, as was the case with Al Gore in 2000, but they can also be a prelude to a strong fall campaign, as happened for Bill Clinton in 1992.[27] In short, one should treat polls taken immediately after the conventions with caution.

Polls following presidential debates are similarly volatile. This is partly a function of the fact that firms must hastily conduct postdebate polls using smaller than normal samples (about six hundred people). In addition, postdebate polls are sensitive to media coverage of the debate.[28] Often different organizations report somewhat contradictory—or at least differing—results. For example, after the first presidential debate in 2004 (on September 30), one poll had Kerry winning the debate by a margin of forty-two percentage points (sixty-one to nineteen), another by thirty-two, (fifty-eight to twenty-six), and yet another by only sixteen (fifty-three to thirty-seven).[29] All clearly suggested that Kerry won but by varying margins. And all reported that Bush's slim lead going into the debate remained largely intact.[30] In other words, postdebate polls might suggest something about how voters viewed the candidates' performances in the debates, but they are a poor indicator of how well a particular candidate is doing in the campaign.[31]

Taken in isolation, few of these polls (preprimary, postconvention, postdebate) are good indicators of candidate strength. Moreover, as suggested above, there is often considerable variation in candidate strength as Election Day approaches. The closer to Election Day that one conducts a poll, the more likely it is to be accurate.

SAMPLES, DATA, AND REPORTING

As we have stressed throughout this chapter, most polls that the media report are well designed and administered. However, sometimes the media do not fully explain the results. For example, as aforementioned, some stories might not indicate whether their sample consisted of registered or likely voters. It is more common to misrepresent what a poll actually means, especially with respect to the margin separating the candidates. This leads to a discussion of the margin of error, also referred to as sampling error.

In discussing sampling, it is possible to infer what a population thinks by relying on the responses of a properly constructed sample. It is important to remember, however, that the theory driving this inference is one of probability, not certainty. So, if we flip a coin one hundred times, it is probable that heads will land face up about fifty times. However, common sense suggests that it might be as many as fifty-three times, or as few as forty-seven. Probability theory suggests that if one repeated the coin flip twenty times, heads would come up approximately 50 percent of the time in nineteen cases.[32] The difference between the expected outcome (heads fifty times, or 50 percent) and what repeated tests would actually yield is known as the margin of error.[33]

Most news organizations report the sampling error of a given poll by telling consumers that a poll is accurate to within a certain percentage. This number is given in plus or minus terms (+/−) and is variously referred to as the margin of error, sampling error, or the poll's error margin. For example, one story from 2004 reported that 42 percent of the people who watched the last presidential debate believed Kerry was the winner and that the poll "results have a 4.5 percent error margin."[34] Translated, this means that as few as 37.5 (42 minus 4.5) percent and as many as 46.5 (42 plus 4.5) percent thought Kerry performed better than Bush in the debate.

This is important to understand because headlines and news stories sometimes misrepresent what is actually happening in election polls with respect to sampling error.[35] Although the story qualified the claims, one Harris Poll report from October 2000 claimed that "Bush Leads Gore by Five Points," 48 to 43 percent. However, with the survey's margin of error (3 percent) factored in, Bush could have had as little as 45 percent, and Gore as much as 46 percent.[36] CBS News reported in 2000 that Gore won the last presidential debate by five percentage points over Bush (45 to 40 percent), but the margin of error for this poll was 4 percent—almost as much as the difference between the two.[37] Margin of error matters, especially if the two candidates are in a competitive election, which is usually the case in presidential elections.

Another point is that the media often report the poll numbers of various subgroups in preelection presidential polls as well. In these polls, a reliable sample size is sometimes a problem. A national poll based on responses from 1,000 individuals would have a 3 percent margin of error associated with it. If there was a split in the sample according to gender, there would be a subsample of approximately 490 men. The margin of error would be greater for this subsample. If there was a split in the sample for men according to their party identification, the sample would split further into three more categories: one each for Republicans, Democrats, and independents. The sample would continue to grow smaller with further divisions along race, income, or other socioeconomic characteristics. With each division, the sample becomes smaller and therefore associated with a greater margin of error. As such, group analysis of presidential polling data needs to be treated with caution, given that subgroups have higher margins of error associated with them.[38]

APPLYING NATIONAL POLLING RESULTS
TO A STATE-BY-STATE CONTEST

One particular problem with preelection presidential polls is centered on the fact that most of the preelection polls are national polls. If done well, the results mirror the outcome one would expect to find in a national vote for president. However, one problem arises in these polls: the United States does not have a national vote for president. Electoral college votes are allocated on a state-by-state basis, dependent (in all but two states) on the winner of the popular vote in that state. Only once in the past one hundred years has the loser of the popular vote been selected president, the election of 2000. Interestingly, most preelection polls during that campaign season had George W. Bush—the eventual loser of the popular vote and winner of the electoral college vote—ahead.[39]

For those who are only passively interested in following presidential campaigns, tracking national polls will probably suffice. However, if one is truly interested in the dynamics of the campaign, watching state polling results is the best answer. Fortunately, in the age of the World Wide Web, this has become fairly convenient. Several websites collate such information into easily accessible pages.[40] This approach is especially important in close races (as it was in 2000 and 2004) when it is known in advance that the outcome might hinge on the results from a few key "battleground" states (states with a fairly large number of electoral college votes that could realistically swing to either candidate). Watching state polls allows one a more nuanced—and accurate—view of how each candidate is doing and, more importantly, where each candidate is doing well or poorly.

CONCLUSION

Is polling an art, a science, or some form of modern voodoo? As we hope our discussion has made clear, polling is a science but hardly an exact science. Table 6.1 is a good example of this point. One objective of this chapter was to provide the tools to become better consumers of preelection presidential polls. Box 6.2 summarizes the various points made throughout the chapter in short question form. While it is not necessary to study every poll intensively, moving mentally through this checklist is a helpful way to understand what the polls are really telling us.

BOX 6.2

INTERPRETING PREELECTION POLLS: A CHECKLIST

- Who conducted the poll?

- Is the poll based on a representative sample of the population?

- Is the poll based on responses from registered or likely voters?

- How has the poll dealt with undecided voters?

- Is the poll focused on too narrow a phase of the campaign, and if so, does the accompanying story account for that?

- Is the sample or subsample large enough to base inferences on?

- Does the accompanying story or headline properly account for the poll's margin of error?

- In a close presidential race, does the story accompanying the poll account for the fact that certain state races will be more important in determining the electoral college winner?

FOR MORE READING

Asher, Herbert. *Polling and the Public: What Every Citizen Should Know.* 6th ed. Washington, D.C.: CQ Press, 2004.

Erikson, Robert S., and Kent L. Tedin. *American Public Opinion: Its Origins, Content, and Impact.* 7th ed. New York: Longman, 2005.

Traugott, Michael W., and Lavrakas, Paul J. *The Voter's Guide to Election Polls.* 3rd ed. Lanham, Md.: Rowman & Littlefield, 2004.

7

"It's the Ratings, Stupid"

Misconceptions about Media Bias

M any Americans believe there is bias—either liberal or conservative—
in the mass media's coverage of politics. According to a recent poll,
a majority (53 percent) of people believe that "news organizations are
politically biased, while just 29 percent say they are careful to remove bias
from their reports."[1] In another poll, 67 percent agreed with the following
statement: "In dealing with political and social issues, news organizations
tend to favor one side."[2] Another report found that "78 percent of adults
agree with the assessment that there is bias in the news media,"[3] and yet
another showed that almost two-thirds (64 percent) disagreed with the
idea that "the news media try to report the news without bias."[4] Most
Americans (51 percent) describe news organizations as "liberal," while a
smaller segment of the public perceives the press as "conservative" (26
percent) with an even smaller group that believes the press is neither liberal nor conservative (14 percent).[5] Still, in one poll, 46 percent of respondents viewed their newspaper as more liberal than they are, while 36
percent perceived their newspaper to be more conservative than they are.[6]
In short, healthy percentages of Americans see ideological bias—whether
liberal or conservative—in the press.

But, is campaign news really biased? Does news coverage of campaigns
favor one candidate or the other? How objective has reporting been in
recent elections? In this chapter, we explore these questions. First, we
review the basics of the legal environment in which the press operates.
Second, we discuss some of the major issues surrounding media bias and
consider what the public should realistically expect from the press in its
coverage of campaigns and elections. We also review the emergence of

objective journalism as a professional norm in the United States. For the first one hundred years or so of the republic, it was well understood and accepted that the news carried with it a partisan slant.

Finally, we examine the various ways in which news coverage of a presidential campaign might reflect the bias of news organizations. This discussion first focuses on what researchers have found with respect to charges of partisan bias in the media. Then, we discuss the idea that most of the bias (or nonobjectivity) that some claim exists in the coverage of campaigns and elections in the media are a direct result of commercial pressures on news organizations. As many studies report, if there is media bias, it is primarily a commercial bias, or orientation, that they display.

FREEDOM OF THE PRESS AND ITS IMPLICATIONS FOR NEWS

The U.S. Constitution does not prohibit the press from presenting the news in a biased fashion. Quite the contrary, the First Amendment of the Constitution clearly states that "Congress shall make no law . . . abridging the freedom of speech, or of the press." While many people associate this constitutional provision with the ability to say or write whatever they wish (with the exceptions of libel and slander), our focus here is on the implications for the organization of the media. In particular, if the law specifies that Congress cannot abridge these freedoms, then it is also saying that government cannot control the media. This not only applies to government regulations concerning censorship but also to media ownership. As the old adage goes, "He who pays the piper calls the tune."

Private ownership characterizes the media environment in the United States; government-owned or government-sponsored media outlets are minimal. Partial exceptions exist, but these are restricted mainly to foreign broadcast services (e.g., the Voice of America), which cannot air in the United States. So-called public broadcasting (National Public Radio and the Public Broadcasting System) are actually joint ventures that rely heavily on many partners, including federal, state, and local governments, universities, and private sponsors and foundations.[7] In most other constitutional democracies, there is both private and government ownership of media outlets, especially broadcast (radio and television) media.[8]

Publicly owned media outlets are, to some extent, freed from the pressures of making money. This is because the government partially funds them. Conversely, private media outlets (unless philanthropically oriented) are continually under pressure to make money. In the case of newspapers and magazines, this translates directly into selling copy. For television and radio, this means selling airtime for advertisements. The greater number of viewers or listeners a television or radio station or network has, the more it can charge for its advertising time. In the end, television and radio stations attempt to attract viewers, much in the same way that newspapers and magazines try to sell copy. All media outlets are thus under the same pressure to make money by orienting their product toward what consumers (viewers, listeners, readers) want. Commercial considerations, which are inevitable products of the First Amendment, are never far from the minds of those responsible for news production in the United States.

A BRIEF HISTORY OF JOURNALISM IN THE UNITED STATES

In colonial times, no norm or expectation of journalistic objectivity existed. Printers, who were small businessmen, originally produced newspapers. These individuals attempted to maintain editorial neutrality primarily because they were interested in avoiding controversy and selling papers. The news that they printed in their pages was mainly foreign news from London because it created less potential for controversy. This began to change, however, as conflict with England intensified during the Revolutionary War period. After winning independence and following a period of government under the Articles of Confederation, debate over the Constitution had begun in the various states. During this time, Federalist sympathizers controlled most newspapers. Antitreason and sedition laws in several states as well as the Sedition Act of 1789, a federal statute, helped suppress antigovernment opinion. Indeed, the government charged many defiant editors under the Sedition Act. It was not until 1800 that the act expired, although this did not change the views of most editors and printers concerning press objectivity or neutrality, which was clearly not the accepted norm of the time.[9]

Throughout the nineteenth century, most newspapers had an identifiable partisan bias. For example, the Albany *Argus* was the newspaper of the nation's first political machine, the Albany Regency (the Democratic Party machine).[10] While the *Argus* prided itself in the accuracy of its reporting, coverage of campaigns remained selective at best. This was true of many other newspapers during the Golden Age of political parties—a time when politics meant *party* politics, and the party machine was the most influential political institution, at least at the local level.[11]

The demise of the partisan press began with improvements in printing technology. Two major advancements were the rotary and, later, the steam press, which made it possible to mass produce newspapers at a low price. New urban centers provided potential markets for these "penny papers," and as a business, many thrived, attracting major advertising dollars. By the late 1800s, owners and editors began to understand that partisan presentation of news effectively cut them off from half of their potential market.

Conservatives, for example, would not buy a liberal-leaning newspaper, and vice versa. The notion of presenting the news impartially was therefore not a high-minded ideal but rather a response to commercial considerations.

As the century progressed, newspapers began to feature more local news stories in a further attempt to increase sales.[12] This helped usher in the era of yellow journalism. Somewhat similar to the contemporary era of news production, "stories of crime, sex, and violence captured the headlines and sold papers. . . . Joseph Pulitzer's *New York World* and William Hearst's *New York Journal* set the standards for this era of highly competitive 'yellow journalism.'"[13] Driven by sales, this focus on local stories meant that newspapers began to employ more reporters. For example, one report suggests that by 1895 the *New York World* employed twelve hundred people, scores of whom were reporters.

It was perhaps natural that as the number of reporters increased, so did "journalism as an occupational culture." Reporters began frequenting the same clubs, restaurants, and taverns. The Missouri School of Journalism, the world's first, opened in 1908. The Columbia University School of Journalism, where classes started in 1913, was endowed by Joseph Pulitzer for the purpose of raising "journalism to the rank of a learned profession." Within a few decades other schools had begun programs as well. These schools began to inculcate in their students a "self-conscious ethic of objectivity."[14] By the 1920s, these journalists and others began to articulate this ethic as a professional norm. The American Society of Newspaper Editors, formed in 1922, adopted the "Canons of Journalism," one of which was impartiality. Other newly formed professional associations (e.g., the Newspaper Guild, formed in 1933) followed.[15]

The norm of objectivity thus emerged in part because of the commercial nature of news production. As newspaper production technology improved, supply increased and prices dropped, while at the same time demand grew. Part of the increased demand included a desire on the part of readers for more local news rather than stories about foreign affairs previously printed in London or elsewhere. The desire for local news created a need for more reporters, who, as they increased in numbers, began to see themselves as professionals with their own code of ethics. This code of ethics included the notion that journalists report their stories fully and accurately, devoid of value judgments. Further driving a move toward impartiality was the emergence of, and reliance by newspapers on, the national wire services. Following the same commercial logic that drove local papers away from partisanship, the Associated Press and United Press wire services understood that neutrality in reporting was necessary for them to sell stories.[16] In short, the development of news as an industry and as big business helped drive the emergence and acceptance of objectivity as a journalistic norm.

BIAS

Before proceeding any further in our discussion of bias in the news, it might be useful to define the terms we are using. Bias, as it relates to news, refers to the idea that the selection and presentation of a particular story explicitly or implicitly reflects the views of some person or persons involved in the news production process. That is, the introduction of bias into the news results in a presentation that does not adequately or completely reflect reality. Another point that should be clarified is that when we talk about news bias, we are not talking about essays that appear in the editorial and opinion pages of the newspapers. They are, by definition, biased.

When we refer to bias in campaign news, we are typically referring to unequal coverage or treatment of one or the other candidate or party. It can take many forms. For example, greater news coverage of one or the other candidate, casting a story about one candidate in favorable terms, and focusing on the negative aspects of a candidate's character are but a few ways in which news about the campaign might be biased. The notion that election news should be impartial is based on the idea that voting should be an informed choice, and the only way for citizens to make an informed choice is to have facts, not value judgments or opinions, at their disposal. Therefore the standard that news organizations adhere to and that citizens use to evaluate them is one of objectivity. As one scholar notes, "The objectivity norm guides journalists to separate facts from values and to report only facts."[17]

Is objectivity in the media an attainable goal? In many matters, for example, law, it is most certainly a standard worth striving to achieve. Politics, however, concerns itself with values, which makes it difficult at best to be objective. Polls show that while most people who see bias in the news believe it to be a liberal bias, there is some relationship between a person's party identification and the type of bias they see in the news. In other words, Democrats see a conservative bias, while Republicans see a liberal bias.[18]

If campaign news *is* biased, where would we look to find evidence? How exactly might the selection and presentation of the news reflect a particular bias? We should first specify that for the sake of space we will look only at national media organizations. Fortunately, there is an abundance of academic research informing us on this subject. One place to look would be the political leanings of those responsible for news production (e.g., editors, producers, reporters, and so on). Studies conducted in the past two decades show that newspaper reporters are more liberal than the average citizen. Similar studies (surveys of reporters) also show that reporters tend to vote Democratic.[19] Other research has demonstrated that the owners of media organizations tend to be more conservative and vote Republican.[20]

Do these tendencies manifest themselves into an ideological or partisan slant in the news?

Some observers make the case that conservative bias exists in the modern media environment and have reported that Republican presidential candidates, on average, win more newspaper endorsements than Democrats.[21] Other studies have examined the content of political coverage and determined that mainstream coverage favors Democratic elites over their Republican counterparts.[22] The top-rated cable news networks, Fox News and CNN, have been two of the most frequent targets for charges of ideological bias. Among several claims, liberals routinely note that the owner of Fox News, Rupert Murdoch, is a well-known conservative advocate and that Roger Ailes, a former Republican operative, is the president of Fox News. On the other side of the political aisle, conservatives, such as former House Majority Leader Tom DeLay, have dubbed CNN the "communist news network" for what they perceive to be its left-wing bias in news coverage.[23]

Yet despite these charges, most scholars have concluded that there is no convincing evidence of media bias in either direction. One recent and comprehensive study found no ideological or partisan bias in newspapers and a slight but statistically insignificant Republican bias in news magazines and Democratic bias on television.[24] In fact, some suggest that because reporters tend to be more liberal they overcompensate to some extent in their treatment of political candidates, slightly favoring Republicans.[25] Overall, however, the weight of the evidence suggests that Republican and Democratic candidates receive roughly equal treatment in the press. The fact that so many Americans see otherwise suggests that selective reception might explain the widespread belief in media bias.

If there is little if any partisan bias in the news, then are there any other patterns that can be detected that might suggest that campaign coverage is less than adequate or complete? In the next section we turn to that question. The evidence suggests that commercial considerations are significantly more important than ideology or partisanship in shaping campaign coverage.

COMMERCIAL BIAS IN CAMPAIGN COVERAGE

In an environment where there is a constitutional guarantee of a free press, media organizations must rely on profit for survival. This puts pressure on news organizations to keep costs down and sales up. This pressure is manifested in campaign coverage, which displays a distinct commercial bias.[26] A need or desire to cut costs while continuing to attract market share shapes campaign news.

Ultimately, the news is the product of a series of decisions made by owners, editors, producers, reporters, and journalists. While the masthead of the *New York Times* claims the paper presents "all the news that's fit to print," in actuality there are any number of newsworthy events that occur in a given day that go *un*reported or *under*reported. The individuals working in news organizations decide what stories are worthy of attention and how to present them. Commercial factors also balance these considerations. Editors, for example, are more likely to choose stories that will generate the average news consumer's attention. This explains why there is so much celebrity news or why scandal and sex are often prominent features of news coverage.

Most campaign coverage falls into the category of what political scientist and media scholar Thomas Patterson labels "horse race" coverage.[27] This refers to the fact that most stories focus on or frame themselves around the competitive or strategic aspect of the campaign—who is leading, who fell behind, and why. This type of coverage dominates news about the campaign from the preprimary season through Election Day.[28] According to one authoritative source, substantive (issue-oriented) stories accounted for only 18 percent of the coverage on the three major television networks (ABC, CBS, and NBC) in 2004. This was down from 22 percent in 2000 and compares with an overall average of 26 percent from 1988 to 2004.[29] The reason this type of coverage dominates campaign news is rather straightforward: it makes for a more exciting story, and all other things being equal, more exciting stories sell better.

In the next section, we explore commercial considerations, or bias, in the production, selection, and presentation of campaign coverage. Horse race coverage, as we will explain, drives campaign coverage. Thus, despite the overwhelming attention paid to ideological and partisan bias in the media, commercial bias is ultimately what shapes news coverage.

The Press as Kingmaker or Winnower

The decisions that news organizations make about the deployment of their resources and the stories that they run often have a profound impact on who will eventually win the party nomination. In part, this is because most people do not know much—if anything—about many of the aspirants for their party's nomination. This is especially true in years when there are many candidates vying for the nomination. In the year preceding the election, media organizations make decisions about which candidates they will and will not cover. These decisions translate directly into the amount of coverage a given candidate receives in print or on television. Here, the rule of thumb is that a better-known candidate is more likely to be the subject of a story than a lesser-known opponent.

This is partly due to simple economics: In a crowded field of aspirants, media organizations must make decisions about how to deploy scant resources. News organizations simply cannot assign a reporter to cover every candidate and every campaign event. In 2004, the cable television network MSNBC assigned an "embedded" journalist to travel with and cover each of the nine Democratic hopefuls, but this was an exception to the rule.[30] Democratic long-shot candidate Dennis Kucinich, for example, publicly criticized ABC News for withdrawing its reporters from his campaign.[31]

Generally, news organizations decide which candidates will likely be viable candidates. They focus primarily on candidates who are leading in early, preprimary polls (those taken the year prior to the Iowa caucuses). This, of course, means that candidates who are not doing well in public opinion polls receive less attention in the news, thus making it more difficult for them to raise their public profile, attract campaign contributions, and ultimately, do well. To overstate the case somewhat, the hidden decisions made by news organizations about *whom* to cover, in effect, become self-fulfilling prophecies.[32]

For example, in 2003, Howard Dean, Wesley Clark, John Kerry, and Joseph Lieberman were the focus of most of the television news stories about the Democrat hopefuls. They were also, not coincidently, leading in the preprimary polls throughout the year.[33] After January 1, the pattern of coverage shifted to account for John Edwards's increased popularity and Joseph Lieberman's decreased popularity (as well as the fact that he did not compete in Iowa).[34] Similarly, in 1999, Al Gore and George W. Bush had more than double the television news coverage than their main rivals for the nomination—Bill Bradley and John McCain, respectively—combined. Although coverage was much more evenhanded as the Iowa caucuses and New Hampshire primary approached, it became even more lopsided afterward, with more than quadruple the number of stories about Gore and Bush than about their opponents.[35]

Winnowing also occurs in the substance of the coverage. For example, one analysis of articles by several leading political pundits in early 2004 suggests that Democrat candidates Carol Moseley Braun, Dennis Kucinich, and Al Sharpton were all but dismissed in analyses by these writers.[36] Few were as blunt as Ted Koppel, the host of ABC's *Nightline*, who hosted a Democratic debate in Durham, New Hampshire, on December 9, 2003. In preparation before the debate, Koppel asked staffers,

How did Dennis Kucinich and Al Sharpton and Carol Moseley Braun get into this thing [the debate]? Nobody seems to know. Some candidates who are perceived as serious are gasping for air, and what little oxygen there is on the stage will be taken up by one-third of the people who do not have a snowball's chance in hell of winning the nomination.

During the debate, Koppel asked provocative questions of each of these three candidates and at one point asked directly whether they would eventually "drop out" or continue their "vanity" candidacies.[37] Koppel's apparent resentment of the minor candidates and their dismissal by others is related to the fact that news organizations have limited resources with which to cover the campaign. Moreover, likely losers do not make for good stories.

The amount and substance of news coverage toward presumed frontrunners has the effect of forcing lesser-known candidates to withdraw from the race earlier than they otherwise might. While it is highly unlikely that Dennis Kucinich, Al Sharpton, or Carol Moseley Braun would have been able to secure the Democratic nomination in 2004, each was a recognized candidate whose inclusion in the race added something to the democratic process. Whether intentional or not, bias in the form of noncoverage or less than favorable coverage—based in commercial considerations—contributed, at least slightly, to their early withdrawal and thus detracted from the campaign.

The Expectations Game

In addition to helping winnow the field of primary candidates early by way of devoting less coverage to those who are doing poorly in the polls, the press handicaps the primaries. The expectations game actually starts long before the primaries begin, escalating during the fall of the year prior to the Iowa caucuses. Pundits regularly report on who is leading in the polls, who is raising how much money, who is endorsing which candidate, and more. Based on this, they typically anoint a front-runner who is therefore expected to win either the Iowa caucuses, the New Hampshire primary, or both. If the presumed front-runner loses either, the resulting story line is typically framed in terms of the uphill battle faced by the candidate in upcoming contests. Interestingly, however, if the candidate does worse than expected—even if he wins—the story is framed in terms of a loss or setback.

In 1992, for example, George H. W. Bush, who was expected to win in New Hampshire, was declared the loser after placing first, *only* sixteen percentage points ahead of Pat Buchanan. This was the result of Bush falling short of expectations and Buchanan exceeding them. In 2000 John McCain's victory in the New Hampshire primary over favored George W. Bush propelled him to front-page news, while Al Gore defeated his Democratic rival Bill Bradley in what one source called an "uncomfortably tight race."[38] While the victories of both men were indeed newsworthy, few observers believed that given their financial and organizational resources they could actually secure the nomination.

In addition, because the primary season begins early, the media often pay a disproportionate amount of positive attention to the candidate trailing in the race—the underdog. During the latter part of 2003, for example, when Howard Dean was the front-runner for the Democratic nomination, he was the recipient of much negative press. Shortly after his loss in Iowa, however, coverage became more favorable.[39] John McCain was the media favorite throughout the 2000 Republican primary season, in part because he was trailing Bush. The reason for this focus on the underdog is simply that it makes for a more exciting and compelling story.

Focus on the Negative

Similar to its ability to anoint a winner, the press can also help drive candidates from the field with a focus on mistakes, scandals, and gaffes. This is especially true during the primary season. In 1988, Democratic candidate Senator Joseph Biden was charged with plagiarizing parts of his speeches. He withdrew from the primary race after a flurry of negative media attention. That same year the Democrat Gary Hart dropped out of the race after a widely publicized sex scandal. Bill Clinton was the notable exception, overcoming numerous charges of marital infidelity in 1992 to secure the Democratic nomination.

Negative campaign coverage is also important because it can shape the issue agenda. In 1988, for example, George Bush delivered a campaign speech in which he mistakenly referred to September 7 as the anniversary of the attack on Pearl Harbor (the actual date is December 7). His audience caught the mistake, and based on their reaction, he quickly corrected himself. While the audience seemed to pay no further attention to the incident, all three television networks featured a story about it that evening. Their coverage was less than flattering. Dan Rather of CBS News, for example, told viewers that "Bush's talk to audiences in Louisville was overshadowed by a strange happening."[40] In addition to simple gaffes, the media often focus on more salacious stories. An inordinate amount of coverage centered on charges that Bill Clinton had been unfaithful to his wife, had experimented with marijuana, was a draft dodger, and had burned an American flag while a student in England.[41] This negative focus on simple mistakes, scandals, and so forth, is part of a pattern in American journalism referred to by Larry Sabato as "attack journalism." Sabato uses the metaphor of "feeding frenzy" to describe how the press is drawn to, highlights, and repeats any negative news from the campaign trail.[42]

Often the focus on the negative is not scandal related but simply mistakes made on the campaign trail. In 2000, for example, days of coverage were devoted to an alleged subliminal message ("rats") found in a George Bush campaign ad or the fact that Bush, thinking his microphone was off, referred to long-time reporter Adam Clymer as a "major league ——hole." In 2004, media organizations ran numerous stories about John Kerry's testimony to the Senate after his service in Vietnam, whether President Bush had lied about his National Guard service, the fact that Kerry mentioned Vice President Dick Cheney's gay daughter, Lynn, during the final presidential debate, and more.

According to one study, in 1968 there was only one instance where a television network newscast took notice of a "minor incident unrelated to the content of the campaign."[43] The reason for the change is best summarized by the "orchestra pit" theory of politics coined by former Republican media consultant and now president of Fox News Channel Roger Ailes. As Ailes explained, "If you have two guys on stage and one says, 'I have a solution to the Middle East problem,' and the other guy falls into the orchestra pit, who do you think is going to be on the evening news?"[44]

Pack Journalism

Exacerbating the commercial patterns of campaign coverage noted above is a phenomenon known by many as "pack journalism." A term originally coined by Timothy Crouse in his 1973 account of the Nixon campaign,[45] it refers to the fact that much of what appears in the news media is remarkably homogeneous. Crouse argued this was because reporters who spend a great deal of time together (on the campaign trail) end up with similar ideas, but the homogeneity of news coverage has other sources as well. For example, the competitive pressure of knowing that another network or newspaper is running a particular story exerts pressure on producers and editors to do the same.[46]

The pressure to meet deadlines also contributes to uniformity in the news, as reporters have less time to explore a story. Smaller media organizations tend to take their cues from more prestigious outlets (*New York Times, Washington Post*) and, in many cases, subscribe to the same wire service stories (Associated Press, Reuters). The end result is uniformity in campaign coverage. If the aforementioned commercial biases were not operative, this might not be problematic. However, pack journalism only multiplies these biases as each story repeats itself.

Other Commercial Biases

There are several other patterns evident in the news coverage of presidential primaries that reflect a commercial bias in the media. One is a focus on attractive personalities. In particular, there is a tendency for the media to give attractive personalities more positive press, especially during the primary season. This particular bias was apparent in 2004. The highly telegenic and upbeat John Edwards received the best press of any major candidate since 1988. A full 96 percent of the coverage of Edwards by the three major television networks (ABC, CBS, and NBC) from January 1 through March 1, 2004, was positive.[47]

Another pattern, evident during both the primary and general election season, is an anti-incumbency bias. This is because sitting presidents (or vice president, in the case of George H. W. Bush in 1988 or Al Gore in 2000) are not fresh "news." The challenger, on the other hand, adds something new to the race, thus making it more attractive to news consumers. While Bill Clinton received more favorable coverage than challenger Bob Dole in 1996, virtually all incumbents since Jimmy Carter in 1980 have been the recipients of negative press during their reelection campaign. This also holds true for the incumbent vice presidents George H. W. Bush in 1988 and Al Gore after the first presidential debate in 2000. In 2004, coverage of the incumbent George W. Bush on the three broadcast networks from September through November was only 37 percent positive, as compared with John Kerry's 59 percent. In addition, Bush was the target of almost twice as many jokes on late night television as was Kerry.[48]

CONCLUSION

Criticizing the media has become something of a national pastime. However, in a media environment dominated by private ownership, news organizations must attract viewers or readers. This makes commercial bias inevitable. Of course, this is a welcome trade-off to government ownership of the media, which is anathema to the First Amendment and to a free and independent press.

Because of the need to attract viewers, attack journalism has become the norm. The sharp and sometimes unfair criticisms of political candidates frequently bring about charges of ideological bias in the media. Yet despite a good deal of research on the subject, there is no clear consensus to support those charges. Instead, the pressure for profit rather than some broad left-wing or right-wing conspiracy is what predominantly shapes media coverage of American elections and campaigns.

FOR MORE READING

Bennett, Stephen Earl, Staci L. Rhine, Richard S. Flickinger, and Linda L. M. Bennett. "Video Malaise Revisited: Public Trust in the Media and Government." *Harvard International Journal of Press/Politics* 4(4) (1999): 8–23.

Bennett, W. Lance. *News: The Politics of Illusion.* 7th ed. New York: Longman, 2007.

Fallows, James. *Breaking the News.* New York: Vintage, 1996.

Graber, Doris. *Mass Media and American Politics.* 7th ed. Washington, D.C.: CQ Press, 2006.

Jamieson, Kathleen Hall, and Paul T. Waldman. *The Press Effect: Politicians, Journalists, and the Stories That Shape the Political World*. New York: Oxford University Press, 2002.

Patterson, Thomas E. *Out of Order: An Incisive and Boldly Original Critique of the News Media's Domination of America's Political Process*. New York: Vintage Books, 1994.

8

A "Dime's Worth
of Difference"?

Political Parties and the Myth of
Tweedledum and Tweedledee

In 1968, former Alabama governor George Wallace ran for president as a candidate of the American Independent Party, famously declaring that "there's not a dime's worth of difference" between the Democratic and Republican Parties.[1] A recent book uses Wallace's statement in its title,[2] and presidential candidate Ralph Nader repeated this claim during his 2000 and 2004 campaigns.[3] Nader—among others—is known for referring to the two major parties as "Tweedledum and Tweedledee," a reference to the twins in Lewis Carroll's *Through the Looking-Glass and What Alice Found There.*[4]

Many Americans agree with this assessment of political parties. For example, in one survey from August of 2000, 39 percent of respondents agreed with the statement, "There is little difference between the candidates and policies of the Republican Party and the candidates and policies of the Democratic Party."[5] In 2004, 43 percent of nonvoters claimed they saw no difference between the two parties.[6]

The notion that both parties are similar is an enduring myth held by the public. To dispel this myth, we compare each prominent issue position contained in the Republican and Democratic Party platforms, demonstrating that each has significantly different ideas about the role of government in society. Next, we examine how this myth came about and why it is that many people believe it to be true. Finally, we conclude by discussing how the moderate rhetoric of the campaign trail is often quite different from how the parties actually govern.

THE DIFFERENCES: IN THEIR OWN WORDS

The two major American political parties are, in fact, quite different from each other in terms of the positions they take on any variety of issues. However, the differences between the Republicans and the Democrats are not as great as the differences between major parties in some other democracies. Most democracies have multiparty systems, and parties in these systems represent the full range of the ideological spectrum. For example, in most European democracies there is a significant socialist or social democratic party on the left. Great Britain has the Labour Party; France has its Socialist Party; and in Germany, it is the Social Democratic Party.[7] These same countries also have conservative or Christian democratic parties that oppose them from the right side of the ideological spectrum. Examples include Great Britain's Conservative Party; France's Gaullist party, Rally for the Republic; and Germany's Christian Democratic Union and their smaller sister party, the Christian Socialist Union. In addition to these main parties of the left and right, most European democracies (as well as other established democracies) have minor parties that win a significant share of the vote in national and local elections (for a listing of some of these parties, see table 8.1).[8] A recent show of minor party strength occurred in France where ultranationalist candidate Jean-Marie Le Pen of the National Front Party finished a surprising second in the presidential election of 2002.

In terms of their placement on a spectrum that includes the major political ideologies of the world, American political parties occupy a similar space. To be more specific, both American political parties come from the same classic liberal tradition. Both take, as a matter of faith, classic liberal ideas about individual freedoms. These ideas find acceptance in the economic realm of a market economy and in the political realm of democratic governance. In this sense, there is not a "dime's worth of difference" between the Republican and Democratic parties.

However, it is within this ideological slice of classic liberalism that American politics takes place. Indeed, there is a wide gulf separating the

Table 8.1.   Minor Parties in European Democracies

Party Type	Examples
Classic Liberal	Free Democratic Party (Germany), Liberal Democrats (Great Britain)
Green	German Green Party, Green Party (France)
Regional	Scottish National Party (Great Britain), Northern League (Italy)
Ultranationalist	National Front (France), Austrian Freedom Party
Radical Socialist or Communist	Party of Democratic Socialism (Germany), French Communist Party

two parties when it comes to their prescriptions for American society. As noted earlier, party activists and campaign donors in each of the two parties hold intense and sharply different opinions on various policy issues. Members of Congress have grown more polarized over time as well, suggesting that elites in the two parties find few issues on which to agree (see chapter 2).

This gulf is also evident by the party platforms adopted at the national conventions every four years. A party platform is an official document that outlines, either very specifically or in expansive terms, the position the party takes on a variety of issues. The first party platform, written in 1832, occurred when the first Democratic National Convention met to renominate Andrew Jackson. However, while Jackson's renomination was a certainty, the party wrote what they termed an "address," which was the first party platform.[9] The drafting of the platform is sometimes contentious and actually begins before the national convention.

Drawing on statements taken from the 2000 and 2004 platforms, table 8.2 compares the positions of the two parties on a variety of selected issues. Table 8.3 presents several other specific issue positions taken by each party. Together, these tables illustrate that there is more than a "dime's worth of difference" between the two parties.

Much of the difference between the two parties in the past two decades is in the positions each party takes on social and cultural issues, such as abortion and civil rights.[10] The Republican Party has consistently staked the more conservative or traditional positions on these so-called cultural issues. For example, Republicans generally oppose abortion in cases in which the mother's life is not at stake, gay marriage, gays in the military, and embryonic stem-cell research, and favor school prayer. Most Democrats, conversely, favor a women's right to choose an abortion (even if it means that the state would have to pay for it), civil unions, gays in the military, and embryonic stem-cell research, and oppose school prayer.

Many Republicans oppose affirmative action, while a large percentage of Democrats favor programs to redress past discrimination. Democrats usually support hate crime legislation, while Republicans typically oppose this (although with some notable exceptions, such as when President George H. W. Bush signed the Hate Crimes Statistic Act in 1990). Additionally, many Democrats are more willing to pass legislation regulating certain aspects of gun ownership (e.g., waiting periods for the purchase of handguns). Most Republicans perceive these laws as an infringement on their Second Amendment rights and oppose them.

On issues related to education, Democrats generally advocate putting more money into the public school system, whereas a large number of Republicans believe that the problem of failing schools should be addressed by some measure of privatization (namely, school vouchers). Democrats are

Table 8.2.   Comparing the 2000 and 2004 Party Platforms: Selected Issues, Part I

Issue	Democrats	Republicans
Abortion	Choice is a fundamental, constitutional right (2000)	Ban abortion with Human Life Amendment to the Constitution (2004)
Gay Marriage	Regulate marriage at state level; no federal gay marriage ban (2004)	Constitutional amendment banning same-sex marriage (2004)
Affirmative Action	Support affirmative action to redress discrimination (2004)	Affirmative Access, without preferences or set-asides (2004)
Crime	Fight crime with prevention, community police (2000)	Best way to deter crime is to enforce existing laws (2004)
Education	U.S. needs public school account-ability, not vouchers (2000)	Promote school choice and homeschooling (2004)
Energy and Oil	We cannot drill our way to energy independence (2004)	Provide tax incentives for energy production (2000)
Environment	Honor hunting and fishing heritage via more conservation lands (2004)	Open more public land to hunting (2004)
Gun Control	Reauthorize assault weapons ban, close gun show loophole (2004)	No gun licensing (2004)
Stem Cells	Pursue embryonic stem-cell research (2004)	Ethical research, yes; embryonic stem-cell research, no (2004)
Immigration	Path for undocumented aliens to earn citizenship (2004)	Amnesty encourages illegal immigration (2004)
Social Security	Oppose privatization and oppose raising retirement age (2004)	Workers should have choice to invest their payroll taxes (2000)

Source: www.ontheissues.org.

Table 8.3.   Comparing the 2000 and 2004 Party Platforms: Selected Issues, Part II

Democrats On:
- *Abortion*: Support the right to choose, even if the mother cannot pay (2004)
- *Profiling*: Racial and religious profiling is wrong (2004)
- *Hate Crimes*: Pass hate crime legislation, including protection for gays (2000)
- *Corporations*: End corporate welfare as we know it (2004)
- *Welfare and Poverty*: Raise Earned Income Tax Credit, and minimum wage to $7 (2004)

Republicans On:
- *Gays in the Military*: Homosexuality is incompatible with military service (2004)
- *Civil Rights*: Let Boy Scouts exercise free speech and ban gays (2000)
- *Education*: Support voluntary student-initiated prayer in school (2004)
- *Environment*: No Kyoto Treaty, and no mandatory carbon emissions controls (2004)
- *Health Care*: No assisted suicide (2004)

Source: www.ontheissues.org.

more likely to be in favor of legislation and regulation to protect the environment, Republicans less so. (The Bush administration's withdrawal from the Kyoto Protocol on greenhouse gas emissions, and Al Gore's scathing criticism of this decision in his documentary *An Inconvenient Truth,* are examples of this difference.) Democrats are generally in favor of greater government involvement in the realm of health care in order to reduce the number of uninsured and underinsured. Republicans typically oppose government involvement in managing the nation's health care system.

In the economic realm, Republicans tend to favor policies that emphasize personal initiative and responsibility, while Democrats are more inclined to see a role for the federal government. For example, Republicans are generally in favor of tax cuts (broadly defined) while many Democrats prefer using tax revenues to reduce the federal deficit or to increase federal spending on programs addressing social needs. Democrats often call for increases in the minimum wage to assist the working poor. Many Republicans believe that this is harmful to business and ultimately to workers if the wage increase forces business to cut its costs with layoffs. Finally, Republicans have historically been the party that takes a more hawkish stand on foreign policy disputes and favors greater military spending when compared to those in the Democratic Party.

In short, there are noticeable differences between the issue positions of the two parties. Moreover, the two parties each have a reasonably good record of pursuing the programs they claim to favor.[11] These differences are often evident in the issue positions that candidates take on the campaign trail.

THE MEDIAN VOTER THEORY
AND CANDIDATES' RESPONSE

The notion that there are few discernable differences between the two major parties is based on the fact that candidates sometimes moderate their policy positions when campaigning for office. This occurs as a result of the electoral environment in the United States, and in particular (1) the fact that all national elections in the United States are single-member district contests decided by plurality winner rules; (2) a stable two-party system; and (3) the fact that American public opinion on most political issues is moderate. Together, they create an environment conducive to moderation in campaigns.

Single-Member Districts

In most elections in the United States, including all elections to federal office, there is only one election winner per district. For example, in U.S.

House elections, only one representative wins a seat in the Congress for each of the 435 districts. Similarly, each state elects two senators but only one senator at a time (elections to the Senate are staggered so that no state elects both its senators in the same election year). Finally, in every state except Maine and Nebraska, the winner of the popular vote receives all of the electoral college votes awarded to that state.[12] This system is known as a single-member district system.

In many local elections, other methods might apply. For example, at-large elections often determine city councils. Under this system, voters select candidates for all of the seats on the council, and the seats are then awarded to the highest vote recipients. Some city and town councils and even a few state legislatures have so-called multimember districts in which voters elect at least two candidates to represent the district. Philadelphia, Cincinnati, and Seattle are a few cities that use an at-large system to select their city councils, while the state of Maryland uses the multimember district system to select members to the state legislature.[13]

Plurality Winner Rules

Plurality rules determine the winners in single-member districts. Referred to by some political scientists as "winner takes all" or "first past the post," the winner is the candidate who receives the most votes, even if no candidate receives a majority of the votes. With the exception of Louisiana, plurality winner rules apply to U.S. House and Senate elections.

In parliamentary systems, however, it is common to select multiple representatives from a single election district (e.g., the entire country or a region) according to a principle of proportionality. Under this system, known as proportional representation, citizens vote for a party. Each party then receives seats in parliament based on the proportion of votes it earns in the election. Hypothetically, in a national legislature with one hundred seats, the party that receives 30 percent of the vote would win thirty seats. The formulas governing proportional representation rules are typically much more complex;[14] however, the proportional principle still applies.

Two-Party System

Another aspect of the U.S. electoral environment is that there has been a stable two-party system for most of the nation's history, and the same two parties have dominated national politics since 1860. Several theories have been advanced to explain the stability of the two-party system in the United States. Political scientist V. O. Key suggests that there is a lasting duality of interests in American society that, while shifting (East-West, North-South, urban-rural), naturally coalesces to a two-party system.[15]

Another theory is the social consensus theory, which suggests that because America did not have a feudal past, there has been historic agreement on the basic values that provide the foundation for the republic (democratic government, a market economy). Therefore, two parties have always been needed to forge compromise.[16] These theories are centered primarily on the idea that parties are an outgrowth of social forces.

The most common explanation for the emergence and stability of the two-party system is Duverger's Law. In an influential book, French political scientist Maurice Duverger suggested that countries with single-member district electoral systems where a plurality determines the winner will tend to have two-party systems.[17] However, there are some exceptions. For example, while the British use a single-member district plurality system, there is a significant third party (the Liberal Democrats) and several significant regional parties (the Scottish National Party, the Welsh Plaid Cymru).

Despite these exceptions, third parties typically struggle to remain viable in single-member, simple plurality systems. To illustrate the difficulties that third parties confront, consider the following hypothetical example in which there are three political parties. Two of the parties are clearly stronger than the third: Party A commands 44 percent of the vote; Party B, 40 percent; and Party C, 16 percent. In a straight three-party race, Party A would win but only by a plurality (44 percent). Given the relatively close margin of victory, Party A would try to align with Party C to bolster its strength. However, Party B would also attempt the same alignment to build a majority. Parties A and B are unlikely to align with each other according to the minimal winning coalition rule posited by William Riker, which suggests that parties or groups have no incentive to get a larger majority than is necessary.[18]

There would be a variety of incentives for Party C to allow itself to be absorbed by one of the larger two parties. First, Party C would face a rather obvious choice: align with a major party and share power or remain independent but consigned to last place with no power. Given that most political parties ultimately desire power, few third parties opt for the latter option. Second, the larger parties could offer other incentives such as a position for Party C leaders in the future administration or the adoption of an important issue position important to Party C. These conditions create an environment that is optimal for the parties to consolidate so that only two parties remain.

After repeated elections, the weakest party will eventually die, as voters, candidates, and supporters understand that it is both politically expedient and strategically wise to align with another party. Duverger's Law suggests that under single-member, simple plurality electoral rules, third parties are practically squeezed out of these systems. Duverger identifies what he calls the "mechanical effect" (third parties are typically underrepresented in government under systems with plurality rules). For example, based on the results in the earlier example, Party C would receive zero seats in the Congress or Parliament under plurality rules, despite winning 16 percent of the vote. This would encourage Party C and its supporters to defect to one of the major parties in an effort to win at least some representation and gain a voice in the halls of government. Duverger also identifies what he calls the "psychological factor." According to this explanation, voters simply do not want to waste or "throw away" their votes on a likely loser. These two forces ultimately explain why single-member plurality rule erodes the ability of third parties to compete and survive.

A Comparatively Moderate Electorate

A final element that explains the development of the two-party system in the United States is that the American electorate is generally moderate, at least in comparison to citizens in many other nations.[19] While there are relatively few people who claim to be extremely liberal or extremely conservative on most issues,[20] a considerable academic debate has emerged over the past decade concerning the existence or severity of a culture war in the United States. Some issues, such as abortion or gay marriage, are divisive (see chapter 2).

Nevertheless, if we accept that aggregate opinion is moderate on most other issues, it would be depicted as bell-shaped curve, or normal distribution (see figure 8.1). In figure 8.1, the horizontal axis represents the hypothetical positions that can be taken on any given issue, ranging from extremely liberal (Democratic) on the left to extremely conservative (Republican) on the right. The vertical axis represents the number of people who take these positions. For example, at the extreme right end of the x-axis, these individuals would be classified as extremely conservative Republicans. A majority clustered in the middle area of the spectrum indicates that most people are relatively moderate. The shaded area of the figure represents the number of voters who are one standard deviation off the mean, or the midpoint, and are the individuals who are closest to the middle. This shaded area represents 68.3 percent of the distribution (the total area of the figure).

Candidates from two parties competing for votes among a moderate electorate in which there will be only one winner will attempt to moderate their campaign message—move to the middle—in order to capture the greatest number of votes. This is known as the median voter theorem. Originally the work of economists, the theorem was first articulated in an article by Duncan Black and subsequently expanded upon in Anthony Downs's influential *An Economic Theory of Democracy*.[21]

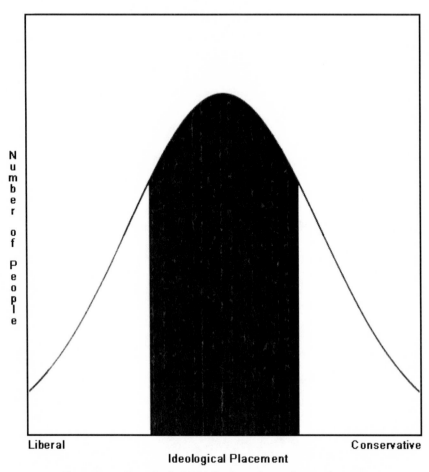

Liberal   Conservative
Ideological Placement

Figure 8.1.   Hypothetical Distribution of a Moderate Electorate

Downs's theorem suggests that in an electoral environment consisting of single-member districts, plurality winner rules, a two-party system, and a moderate electorate, individuals will vote for the party or candidate that is closest to them on the ideological spectrum. Because voters cluster in the middle of the spectrum (in statistical terms, normally distributed), parties and candidates have an incentive to avoid taking and articulating extreme issue positions during the campaign, instead moderating their messages or moving to the center. As candidates from both parties moderate their messages or issue positions, their resulting messages will appear to be, or might actually be, quite similar.

Of course, "the middle of the spectrum" takes on a different meaning in the primary election than it does in the general election. Because primary voters tend to be more ideologically extreme than the general election electorate, the primary median voter is considerably less moderate.[22] Thus, candidates must first adopt positions that satisfy their party's base. This often complicates a candidate's ability to move to the middle of the spectrum in the general election. In addition, as noted in chapter 2, political donors and party activists, who are critical to a candidate's ability to wage a competitive campaign, are also more ideologically extreme, further complicating a candidate's ability to move to the middle of the spectrum in the general election.

ON THE CAMPAIGN TRAIL: BLURRING THE LINES

The electoral environment in the United States explains why candidates have an incentive to blur the differences between the two political parties in their pursuit of moderate voters. Beyond this, the platform is the party's official policy document. However, it is ultimately a candidate-centered document. Recall that the first platform was actually written as a "platform" to support Andrew Jackson's reelection effort. While there are many influences on the party platform, presidential candidates have always been central to the process of drafting the document.[23]

During the past few decades, however, the "party platform has become [even] more of a presidential campaign document" than was previously the case.[24] Because direct primaries and caucuses effectively decide the party, the presidential nominee is known several months before the convention begins. Moreover, an increasing number of states have moved their primary or caucus election to an earlier date in the calendar. This "front-loading" of contests means that the party's presidential nomination battle can be decided as early as March of the election year (as it was for John Kerry in 2004)—some six months before the official convention takes place.

This schedule provides the nominee with more of an opportunity to become involved in shaping the party platform. Indeed, the language of the party platforms reflects that they are candidate-centered documents. For example, Michael Dukakis's campaign team heavily influenced the 1988 Democratic Party platform. Similarly, George H. W. Bush's organization selected the team that drafted the 1992 Republican Party platform. During his 1996 reelection effort, Bill Clinton, along with the Democratic Leadership Council, dominated the process of drafting the Democratic Party platform. His opponent, Bob Dole, effectively had veto power over the language adopted in the Republican Party platform dealing with the party's most contentious issue, abortion.[25] In 2000, the Democratic Party platform contained 99 references to Al Gore. George W. Bush was mentioned in the 2000 Republican Party platform 44 times. Similarly, in 2004, John Kerry's name appeared in the Democratic Party platform 22 times, and the Republican Party platform contained a whopping 250 references to George W. Bush. This candidate-centered document allows candidates, especially presidential candidates, virtually to ignore the party platform on the campaign trail. An example of this occurred in 1996, when Republican presidential hopeful Bob Dole freely admitted that he had not even read the document.[26]

Because candidates are responsible for the conduct of their own campaigns, they can easily ignore the party platform. Candidates, for example, build their own campaign organizations in order to win the party nomination, as competition for the nomination is intraparty, and they cannot rely on personnel or other resources that the party has available for the campaign. People loyal to the candidate become staff, and campaign professionals are hired to work for the candidate. Also, candidates actively go outside the party to seek endorsements and support from interest groups and prominent individuals. Candidates are largely responsible for raising the funds necessary to conduct their campaigns, and current campaign finance laws aid candidates rather than parties. This allows the candidate to have the final say in how campaign funds are spent. Among other things, this means that they can and do craft campaign messages that are often at odds with the policy positions contained in the party platform.[27]

If candidates, especially presidential candidates, stray too far from the party platform, the party has little if any power to sanction the candidate. The party cannot control important endorsements from outside groups or political notables, can only marginally affect a candidate's financial base, and most importantly, cannot deny a candidate the party nomination—the ultimate prize. This electoral environment provides candidates with some flexibility to moderate their positions. When this occurs, critics such as Ralph Nader often seize on this as confirmation that the two major parties are not fundamentally different. However, while the campaign trail can often blur the lines between the parties' presidential candidates during the general election (as noted earlier, the process operates quite differently in the primary), the most current research overwhelmingly demonstrates that the moderate rhetoric of presidential candidates is a poor indicator of how members of the two parties actually govern, especially in the U.S. Congress. Increasingly, the empirical evidence makes clear that Democrats and Republicans find very little upon which to agree when casting their roll-call votes on legislation in Congress.

POLARIZATION IN GOVERNING

Partisan differences among members of the U.S. Congress have always been present, although contrary to the myth of Tweedledum and Tweedledee, polarization has increased in recent years. At the turn of the twentieth century, Democrats and Republicans held rather distinct ideological positions, with Republicans voting in a consistently conservative direction and Democrats voting in a more liberal direction. However, Democrats and Republicans began to vote in a moderate direction during midcentury. Indeed, throughout the early 1970s, there was "considerable overlap" among Democrats and Republicans.[28] By the 1980s, and especially the 1990s, that pattern reversed, with both parties moving increasingly apart.

The dominant explanation for this development is the partisan realignment of the South. Southern conservatives joined the Republican Party, while African Americans affiliated with the Democratic Party. This significantly altered the ideological base of the two parties (see chapter 2 for more information and an explanation for this development).[29] Also, as noted earlier, the bases of the two parties are comprised of more ideologically extreme members. Political activists, individual donors, and interest groups all exert pressure on elected officials to stand firm on certain core party principles, making moderation more difficult.[30]

A third and popular explanation credits the redistricting process for polarization in Congress. Every ten years, each state determines its congressional district boundaries through what is usually a highly political process. In many instances, "bipartisan" redistricting schemes are adopted in which both parties cooperate with one another to protect their respective incumbents. As a result, elected officials often represent districts with heavy concentrations of voters from their own political parties, creating little incentive to reach across party lines and develop a more pragmatic approach to governing.[31]

Not surprisingly, ideologically moderate members of Congress have declined in number over the past several decades, leaving behind what is now best described as a "polarized, unidimensional Congress."[32] According to political scientist Keith Poole, "Moderates have virtually disappeared during the thirty years between the 93rd and 108th Congresses and the parties have pulled apart."[33] The result is growing polarization in Congress and perhaps clearer and more pronounced differences between the parties than at any time in recent memory. Indeed, researchers have concluded that polarization during the 109th Congress reached a post-Reconstruction high in the U.S. Senate and ranked third highest in the U.S. House over a 120-year period (see figure 8.2).[34] In sum, the evidence coming from roll-call data in Congress make clear that the Democratic and Republican parties do not look alike, as some have suggested.[35]

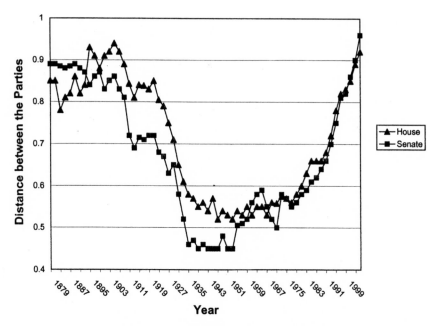

Figure 8.2.   Party Polarization, 1879–2006
Source: Nolan McCarty, Keith T. Poole, and Howard Rosenthal, *Polarized America: The Dance of Ideology and Unequal Riches* (Cambridge, Mass.: MIT Press, 2006), chap. 1. See also the authors' website, at polarizedamerica.com/#politicalpolarization.

CONCLUSION

The rhetoric on the presidential campaign trail can make it appear as if candidates from both parties are taking the same positions on the issues. A recent example occurred in the second presidential debate of 2000, between Al Gore and George W. Bush, as the candidates agreed with each other on 37 percent of the issues, leaving Bush to describe the debate as "a great lovefest."[36] In fact, the word "agree" was used thirty-one times throughout the debate (see box 8.1).

While this example is extreme, the statements of individuals should not be confused with the positions of the parties they claim to represent. Candidates are not parties. There *is* a party line—or to be more precise, two party lines—even if candidates do not always follow that party line. Each party's platform—an official document—reflects fundamental differences in the positions of both parties.

It is also important to remember that these differences are not simply words in some irrelevant party platform that are ignored by elected officials. In the halls of Congress, party differences are clear as the roll-call

BOX 8.1

THE "GREAT LOVEFEST" OF 2000: AL GORE AND GEORGE W. BUSH

Gore: We ought to recognize the value to our children and grandchildren of taking steps that preserve the environment in a way that's good for them.

Bush: Yeah, I agree.

Bush: If we're a humble nation [other countries will] respect us.

Gore: I agree with that.

Moderator: There was no U.S. intervention [in Rwanda]. . . . Was that a mistake not to intervene?

Bush: I think the [Clinton] administration did the right thing.

Gore: I think [hate crimes are] intended to stigmatize and dehumanize a whole group of people.

Moderator: You have a different view of that?

Bush: No, I don't really.

Bush: A marriage should be between a man and a woman.

Lehrer: Vice President Gore?

Gore: I agree with that.

Moderator: Is there any difference?

Gore: I haven't heard a big difference in the last few exchanges.

Bush: Well, I think it's hard to tell.

Moderator: How do you see the connection between controlling gun sales and the incidence of death by accident or intentional use of guns?

Gore: I believe that—well, first of all, let me say that the governor and I agree on some things where this subject is concerned.

Gore: I agree with Governor Bush that we should have new accountability. Testing of students.

Bush: You know, I support the [Clinton] administration in Colombia.

Bush: It seems like we're having a great lovefest tonight.

Source: "Debate Transcript: The Second Gore-Bush Presidential Debate," Commission on Presidential Debates, October 11, 2000, at www.debates.org/pages/trans2000b.html.

data increasingly demonstrate. Members of the two major parties do govern differently—even if the rhetoric of their presidential candidates can sometimes make the parties seem very similar.

FOR MORE READING

Hershey, Marjorie Random. *Party Politics in America*. 12th ed. New York: Longman, 2007.

McCarty, Nolan, Keith T. Poole, and Howard Rosenthal. *Polarized America: The Dance of Ideology and Unequal Riches*. Cambridge: MIT Press, 2006.

Reichley, A. James. *The Life of the Parties: A History of American Political Parties*. Lanham, Md.: Rowman & Littlefield, 1992.

White, John Kenneth, and Daniel M. Shea. *New Party Politics: From Jefferson and Hamilton to the Information Age*. Boston: Bedford/St. Martin's, 2000.

Zeigler, L. Harmon. *Political Parties in Industrial Democracies*. Itasca, Ill.: F. E. Peacock, 1993.

III

UNDERSTANDING ELECTION OUTCOMES

9

Selling the President
The "Image Is Everything" Myth

C an presidential candidates be marketed, packaged, and sold? With sufficient funding, can a team of professional campaign managers take
any reasonably attractive, well-spoken individual, craft an image for him
or her, and win the Oval Office? While it is often only implied and under-
stated, one myth about presidential elections is that the success of modern
presidential candidates depends primarily on their ability to "sell" themselves. This notion formally originated with Joe McGinniss's *Selling of the
President* in 1969, which described how Richard Nixon was remade by campaign and advertising professionals in order to capture the White House in
1968.[1] McGinniss, who joined the campaign as an observer, presents a
fairly cynical picture of what politicians will do in order to win elective
office. The theme of the book is that the public face of the candidate is all
that really matters, whether genuine or not. One of the implications of the
selling the president metaphor (or marketing myth) is that slick campaigns
and candidates can easily fool the American electorate.

Journalists, political observers, and many scholars have adopted this
metaphor. One of the classics in presidential campaign literature remains
Theodore White's *Making of the President* series, the first of which appeared
in 1961. As the title of this work implies, campaign management is the critical ingredient to a winning campaign.[2] One well-known account of the
1980 presidential election, *Blue Smoke and Mirrors*, suggested that the presidential campaign of Ronald Reagan hoodwinked the public.[3] A recent
text focused on the financial aspect of the marketing myth, adopting the
provocative title *The Buying of the President 2004.*[4] A 1997 Gallup poll also
reported that 59 percent of Americans believe that elections are "generally

for sale to the candidate who can raise the most money." Another well-known study of presidential campaign advertising discusses *Packaging the Presidency*.[5] Other recent scholarship focuses on various aspects of presidential image making, political marketing, and how television advertising wars present presidential candidates.[6] Other accounts have focused on the role of ad agencies and image specialists in presidential campaigns and the handling of the candidate on the campaign trail.[7]

Presidential candidates themselves might believe in the marketing myth as well. One of the reasons that McGinniss's book made such an impact was that in his previous presidential campaign (in 1960) Nixon had refused a proposal by a major advertising firm to manage his campaign using the latest marketing and media techniques.[8] Nixon also reportedly refused to wear makeup to improve his skin color in his first debate with John F. Kennedy in 1960. Many accounts suggest that this hurt Nixon. According to one summary,

> In substance, the candidates were much more evenly matched. Indeed, those who heard the first debate on the radio pronounced Nixon the winner. But the 70 million who watched television saw a candidate still sickly and obviously discomforted by Kennedy's smooth delivery and charisma. Those television viewers focused on what they saw, not what they heard. Studies of the audience indicated that, among television viewers, Kennedy was perceived the winner of the first debate by a very large margin.[9]

The poor reaction to Nixon's television debate performance led many to conclude to that image and physical appearance were most critical in the media age. Indeed, after viewing the 1972 Robert Redford film, *The Candidate*, Dan Quayle concluded that not only was he more attractive than the popular actor, but with the assistance of the right campaign professionals, he could one day make a serious run for the White House.[10] Senator Henry Jackson of Washington provides perhaps the best example of how this prevailing wisdom began to affect politicians. Jackson had plastic surgery, lost twenty pounds, purchased a new wardrobe, and even hired speech instructors to improve his public speaking skills.[11] Likewise, Al Gore, in the months leading up to his 2000 candidacy for the presidency, consulted former actor and image consultant Michael Sheehan on body language, intonation, and wardrobe.[12]

The selling of the presidency metaphor suggests that the presidency is a commodity to be packaged and sold to an unwitting public. Explicit in McGinniss's account of the 1968 campaign is that the marketing of presidential candidates is something new to the television mass-marketing age. The truth is slightly more nuanced. Successful presidential campaigns focus to some degree on image, and this has been true throughout the history of the nation. It is true that presidential image making has become more scientific and sophisticated with the advent of new technologies. Related to this development is the emergence of a class of campaign professionals, men and women whose job it is to manage all aspects of political campaigns. This management revolves around the crafting, presentation, and preservation of candidate image.

However, like all metaphors, the selling of the president captures only part of the reality of a presidential campaign. Even in the television age, campaign organization matters. Behind the scenes of television advertising, there are interest groups, unions, citizen groups, campaign organizations, political party organizations, and individual citizens that attempt to persuade others, through person-to-person contact, to vote for their candidate.

This chapter will explore the marketing myth by deconstructing the selling of the president metaphor. First, we present a review of image making in presidential campaigns prior to the television age, illustrating that presidential campaigns have always been elite-driven, managed affairs that place a great emphasis on image. Next, we examine the emergence, growth, and specialization of a class of individuals engaged in the business of campaign management. We then focus on foot soldiers, or the organization of presidential campaigns, and what they do. A successful presidential campaign relies on equal parts image and campaign organization.

PRESIDENTIAL IMAGE MAKING
IN THE PRE-TELEVISION ERA

While campaign management has evolved into a highly specialized and lucrative profession, it was not simplistic or even primitive in the pre-television era. Politics is a high-stakes game, with presidential campaigns at the top. A focus on crafting a presidential image is certainly not new to the television age.[13]

There are three aspects to presidential image making in the pre-television era. The first is the image makers themselves. Who is responsible for crafting and presenting the candidate's image to the voting public? Who are the campaign managers? Second, how do these managers present the candidate's image? This question involves a discussion of the modes and content of campaign communication as well as the basics of presidential electioneering practices in the pre-television era. Finally, what were some images presented of the candidates? A brief discussion of each of these elements illustrates that presidential image making mattered in the pre-television era.

With regard to personnel, presidential image making in the nineteenth century was largely the domain of professional politicians and party leaders. Typically this meant a good number of government officials, elected or otherwise. Campaign organizations were formed immediately after the national party convention and usually included a representative from each state. This ensured that the campaign within each state ran efficiently. Because the technology of political communication was limited to the written and spoken word, campaign managers during this period were not specialists. These professionals were responsible for the crafting of the candidate's image, while the presentation—the implementation—was left to newspapers writers (editors and journalists), cartoonists, pamphleteers, and other authors, as well as orators (speech makers).

In general, presidential candidates did not hit the campaign trail. Most politicians in the nation's early history considered campaigning to be unseemly, or unpresidential.[14] In addition, campaigning for office generally indicated that a candidate was trailing his opponent.[15] Furthermore, campaign managers and parties feared the candidate might make statements that would damage the candidate's image or election effort. Keeping the campaign out of the public spotlight—and off the campaign trail—was especially important for poor public speakers. In a letter written during the campaign of 1872, Ulysses S. Grant wrote,

> My judgment is that it will be better that I should not attend any convention or political meeting during the campaign. It has been done, so far as I remember, but by two presidential candidates heretofore, and both of them were public speakers, and both were beaten. I am no speaker, and don't want to be beaten.[16]

A good example of keeping a candidate off the campaign trail was the "front porch campaign" of Republican James Garfield in 1880. Most of his involvement in the campaign was in the form of receiving thousands of visitors on the front porch of his farm in Mentor, Ohio. This strategy was adopted in spite of the fact that many people considered Garfield to be one of the better public speakers of his time.[17] Because political campaigns emulate what works in previous campaigns, Benjamin Harrison (in 1888) and William McKinley (in 1896) modeled their campaigns after Garfield's.

Even in the early days of presidential elections, campaign managers worked hard to protect the image of their candidates. These campaign managers were individuals who led the efforts to build party support for the candidate before and during the national convention to secure the nomination. This was mainly a back room effort. Also, they directed the overall direction of the campaign during the general election season and managed the details of the ground campaign. John J. Beckley managed the 1796 campaign of Thomas Jefferson,[18] Martin Van Buren the 1828 campaign of Andrew Jackson,[19] and Illinois judge David Davis managed the 1860 campaign of Abraham Lincoln.[20] Mark Hanna directed the campaign of William McKinley in 1896, bringing new-style advertising techniques to presidential campaigning.[21] Ohio political boss Harry M. Daugherty arranged Warren Harding's nomination and served as his campaign manager in 1920.[22] James A. Farley and Louis Howe managed Franklin Roosevelt's 1932 campaign.[23]

Before the era of electronic media, image making was done either orally or in print. Speeches made by party leaders, notables, and orators served to garnish the presidential candidate's image. Printed materials included pamphlets that both created and propagated the image the candidate was trying to portray, short treatises by or letters from the candidate on particular issues, and the candidate's biography. Another popular form of campaign literature was the campaign textbook, which consisted of various editorials, cartoons, and issue tracts that the party used to promote the candidate's image and a common campaign theme. Campaign slogans contributed to the candidate's image making. Newspapers also helped by printing favorable articles, editorials, and political cartoons. In addition, banners, buttons, hats, flags, clothing, and other campaign materials were printed with the candidate's or party's name, campaign slogan, or theme.[24]

Finally, the campaign would commission songs, shouts, chants, and poems to build and spread the image of the candidate. For example, in 1840,William Henry Harrison's supporters sang—all to popular tunes—various short songs entitled "The Soldier of Tippecanoe," "The Farmer of North Bend," "The Log Cabin Song," "Old Tip and the Log Cabin Boys," and more.[25] In 1864, crowds of Lincoln supporters might have been heard singing the following:

> Old Abe Lincoln came out of the wilderness,
> Out of the wilderness, out of the wilderness,
> Old Abe Lincoln came out of the wilderness,
> Down in Illinois.[26]

Box 9.1 is a select list of the titles of other campaign songs that were associated with presidential campaigns through the years.

The evolution of presidential image making tied in closely to developments in communications technology. Presidential campaigns have always taken advantage of the latest technological advances. William Jennings Bryant was the first political candidate to record a speech (in 1900) and also the first to appear in a campaign movie short (in 1908). Both parties used radio in the presidential campaign of 1924, and by the 1940s, radio advertising accounted for up to one-third of the budget of presidential campaigns. Alf Landon was the first to produce a candidate biography film in 1936.[27]

Presidential image making is no simple affair. Crafting a presidential image is the art of building on certain characteristics of the candidate in order to portray him or her as a capable, positive, strong leader. Typically, presidential candidates also attempt to convey the idea that they are trustworthy and understand the problems of the average citizen.[28] This was true even in the pre-television era when image making was less sophisticated. Box 9.2 illustrates selected images and their origins from the pre-television era.

BOX 9.1

SELECTED TITLES: PRESIDENTIAL CAMPAIGN SONGS

"Follow Washington" (George Washington)

"Adams and Liberty" (John Adams)

"For Jefferson and Liberty" (Thomas Jefferson)

"Huzzah for Madison, Huzzah" (James Madison)

"Monroe Is the Man" (James Monroe)

"Jackson and Kentucky" (Andrew Jackson)

"Rockabye, Baby" (Martin Van Buren)

"The Harrison Yankee Doodle" (William Henry Harrison)

"Rumadum Dum" (Zachary Taylor)

"Lincoln and Liberty" (Abraham Lincoln)

"Just before Election, Andy" (Andrew Johnson)

"If the Johnnies Get into Power Again" (James A. Garfield)

"He's All Right" (Benjamin Harrison)

"Roosevelt the Cry" (Theodore Roosevelt)

"Get on a Raft with Taft" (William H. Taft)

"Wilson, That's All" (Woodrow Wilson)

"Harding, You're the Man for Us" (Warren Harding)

"Keep Cool and Keep Coolidge" (Calvin Coolidge)

"If He's Good Enough for Lindy" (Herbert Hoover)

"I'm Just Wild About Harry" (Harry S Truman)

"I Like Ike" (Dwight D. Eisenhower)

Source: Song titles from *Presidential Campaign Songs, 1789–1996*, sung by Oscar Brand, *Smithsonian Folkways Recordings*, May 18, 1999, SFW45051.

BOX 9.2

PRESIDENTIAL IMAGES FROM
THE PRE–TELEVISION ERA

Andrew Jackson (1828): "Stonewall Jackson," and "Hero of New Orleans," in reference to his victory over the British in 1815. Also known as "Old Hickory," a reference to his robust nature and common roots.

William Henry Harrison (1840): "Old Buckeye," a reference to his common Ohio roots as well as a take-off on "Old Hickory." Better well known was the campaign slogan, "Tippecanoe and Tyler Too." This was a reference to the Battle of Tippecanoe in 1811, in which Harrison defeated the Shawnee chief Tecumseh, as well as his running mate, John Tyler.

Abraham Lincoln (1860): The image of Lincoln as a "Rail Splitter" highlighted his roots as a hard working, common man. The term "Honest Old Abe" refers to his integrity, another common characteristic in presidential image making.

Ulysses S. Grant (1868): Grant parlayed his success as the victorious Union general into an image of someone equally capable of leading the nation.

James Garfield (1880): "Boatman Jim" was portrayed as a commonsense man of the people, highlighted also by the front porch campaign in his hometown of Mentor, Ohio.

Theodore Roosevelt (1904): The "Rough Rider" image drew attention to his energetic, adventurous, and vigorous spirit, implying that he would bring these qualities to the White House.

Woodrow Wilson (1916): The campaign slogan "He kept us out of the war" (and others) drew attention to the fact that, until that point, Wilson had been steadfast in keeping the United States out of the European war.

Dwight D. Eisenhower (1952, 1956): "Ike" was painted as a nonpartisan choice who, by virtue of his military record of leading the allies to victory in Europe in World War II, would be the best choice to lead the country.

Source: Paul F. Boller Jr., *Presidential Campaigns: From George Washington to George W. Bush* (New York: Oxford University Press, 2004).

The art and science of packaging presidential candidates was well developed by the early part of the twentieth century. By creatively using the available communications technologies of the day, presidential campaigns paid a great deal of attention to crafting an image for their candidate. The packaging the president metaphor came about with the invention and widespread penetration of electronic media and the development of more advanced marketing techniques. However, the emergence of a new class of campaign specialists is especially important in this regard.

IMAGE SPECIALISTS: THE NEW "ELECTION MEN"

In 1973, David Rosenbloom published a book entitled, *The Election Men*, describing a new breed of professional campaign management specialists.[29] As previously noted, campaign managers are not new to presidential campaigning. However, the emergence and development of a profession in which increasingly specialized individuals, independent of party, sell their services to candidates at all levels is new. As Robert Agranoff observed in 1976, "The party professional has given way to a different type of professional—the advertising and public relations man, the management specialist, the media specialist, the pollster—who performs services for the candidates based on skills he has acquired in nonpolitical fields."[30]

The birth of political consultancy as a business is credited to two Californians, Clem Whitaker, a political reporter, and Leone Baxter, a public relations worker for the local Redding, California, chamber of commerce. In 1933, both worked on a local initiative campaign and the following year formed Campaigns, Inc., a political consultant business. Their firm applied mass-marketing techniques to politics. Republican presidential candidate in 1936, Alf Landon, employed an ad agency to help conduct his campaign. Over the next two decades, other presidential candidates did so as well, using various agencies to produce television advertisements. During this time, public opinion polling became an established industry, and professionals explored its applications to campaign strategy. Early pioneers of the industry include Joe Napolitan, Clif White, Matt Reese, Bill Roberts, Stu Spencer, Joe Cerrell, Bill Hamilton, Bob Squier, and Walter deVries, all of whom began working in the field during the 1950s.

John Kennedy's 1960 campaign proved to be a turning point for professional campaign management in that he assembled one of the largest teams of consultants, strategists, pollsters, and media advisors.[31] By 1969, the American Association of Political Consultants (AAPC) formed, originally numbering only twenty-five members. Since then, membership in the association has exploded, with several thousand active members and many nonmembers in the business as well. It is now almost impossible to successfully run for federal office without employing the services of these campaign professionals.

Not only has the business grown, but it has become increasingly specialized. *Campaigns and Elections*, the trade magazine for the AAPC, depicts nearly every type of campaign activity in articles, features, and advertisements. This includes "fund raising, polling, electoral mobilization, accounting and compliance, research, the production and distribution of audio-visual advertising, direct mail and literature, internet services," and more.[32] A good deal of the specialization in the industry has come as the result of developments in technology. Computer-assisted dialing, the Internet, database technology, and satellite teleconferencing are just a few technologies that have emerged, as well as demand specialists who are capable of using them.[33]

Crafting and producing a presidential image—much of which is done via television—is integral to the specialization of campaign management. These specialists include pollsters who pretest and posttest images on voters and potential voters and inform others in the campaign on what seems to work. Also included are all the individuals involved in the production of television ads (meaning writers, producers, etc.). After ad production, the campaign distributes ads to broadcast and cable television networks and stations, which involve ad buyers as well as voter and media market researchers and pollsters to target the right image to the right audience.

In fact, presidential campaigns spend a majority of their money on media-related products or services. From April 1995 through July 1996, the Clinton campaign paid $8.7 million to two advertising firms (Squier Knapp Ochs and November 5 Group Broadcast).[34] While all television advertising is not necessarily image-based advertising, it is essential to maintain the correct image in any ad. An analysis from the 2004 presidential campaign suggests that

> the two largest consultants . . . were the media consultants for the Bush and Kerry presidential campaigns. The media group that created the president's television commercials, Maverick Media, was paid a combined $177 million by the Bush campaign and the Republican National Committee. Riverfront Media, the group led by consultant Bob Shrum, worked on John Kerry's media campaign and was paid $150 million by his campaign and the Democratic National Committee.[35]

Presidential candidate image making is now a specialized big business. This is mainly a product of the television age and is likely the reason that the idea of the packaged presidency emerged and has become a popularly accepted myth. However, image making is not exclusively a product of the modern era, nor is it the *only* ingredient for a successful campaign. In the next section, we look at the "ground war" in presidential campaigns. In the television age, the ground war (as opposed to the "Air War"[36]) is as crucial to winning the White House as it was in the previous era.

THE GROUND WARS: THEN AND NOW

A less noticed, but central, element of any campaign is the effort to mobilize voters and potential voters. In particular, campaigns expend a great deal of energy registering new voters and motivating citizens to vote. It does a candidate little good to persuade people that he or she are the right person for the job if these supporters have not taken the time to register to vote or stay home on Election Day. In the pre-television era, this grassroots mobilization was done in person.

Martin Van Buren developed one of the first models for efficient, grassroots mobilization for the New York Democratic Party ("The Democracy," as it was referred to) in preparation for the 1828 presidential campaign of Andrew Jackson. He divided responsibility for the state campaign among other party leaders at the local level, who in turn recruited other volunteers. Other states organized in a similar manner. Local volunteers, called "Hurra Boys," planted hickory trees or handed out hickory sticks at campaign rallies in honor of Jackson, whose nickname was "Old Hickory." In this model, mobilization of volunteers was both efficient and systematic or what one campaign historian has referred to as "army style" organization.[37] These volunteers often organized into clubs, described by James Bryce as follows:

> [They] usually bear the candidates' names [and are] formed on every imaginable basis, that of locality, of race, of trade or professions, of university affiliation. There are Irish clubs, Italian clubs, German clubs, Scandinavian clubs, Polish clubs . . . young men's clubs, lawyer's clubs, dry-goods clubs, insurance men's clubs, shoe and leather clubs . . . [and] clubs of the graduates of various colleges.[38]

These clubs performed many functions. In some cases they marched the streets, often accompanied by a marching band, charged with whipping up support for the candidate.[39] According to one account, there was a "Democratic parade (which drew roughly 6,000 spectators) consisting of 1,600 mounted men and roughly the same number on foot in Anderson, South Carolina. . . . Another puts better than 25,000 businessmen, organized by profession, marching parade-style in New York City for James Blaine in late October of 1884."[40]

The ground game was elaborately and systematically organized. During the 1880 campaign of James Garfield, the canvassing effort in New York City included a list of three hundred thousand voters, organized by precinct.[41] The ground campaign was so important to parties that they did not rely on volunteers alone. Paid workers, sometimes numbering in the thousands, distributed campaign materials and canvassed voters in the attempt to build support.[42] Parties hosted picnics, clambakes, and barbeques, attempting to generate enthusiasm for the candidate. In 1880, Standard Oil mobilized two thousand of its employees in the state of Indiana for the Garfield campaign and counted on the active support of better than twenty-five thousand of the candidate's fellow church members.[43]

As Election Day nears, campaigns direct their efforts to ensuring that people turn out to vote. Get-out-the-vote (GOTV) efforts in this era were extremely aggressive. Party leaders went to any lengths to produce the number of votes needed for victory. For example, if the infamous Tammany Hall machine in New York City needed extra votes to put their candidate over the top, they would import extra voters from New Jersey or Pennsylvania.[44] Parties were also not averse to buying votes. Stephen Dorsey, one of the campaign managers of the 1880 Garfield campaign, reportedly bought thirty thousand votes in Indiana for two dollars apiece.[45]

As with other aspects of political campaigns, voter mobilization efforts are more systematic and sophisticated today. Party organizations mainly fund these efforts and conduct them at the state and local levels. Each party's efforts reflect differences between their respective base supporters. For example, many self-identified Democrats are generally less likely to vote and come from the lower end of the socioeconomic scale. Thus, the Democratic Party expends a good deal of effort to help this segment of the population register and vote. On Election Day, the party might arrange for transportation to the polls and provide or arrange for child care for those who need it.

Mobilization efforts are important as well. Research demonstrates that voters are more likely to vote if they are contacted by political parties, candidate organizations, or other interested groups.[46] And, voter turnout can be the critical difference in an election outcome. In 1968, for example, the Democratic Party did not heal its wounds after its bitter and divisive national convention until late October. This resulted in fewer Democrats registering and, thus, fewer votes for the party's presidential nominee Hubert Humphrey. The Democrats in 1976, with the help of organized labor (which plays a central role in Democratic GOTV efforts),[47] registered more voters than Republicans. Jimmy Carter's 1976 win was also attributed to the party's successful drive to register African Americans. Republicans, who rely on volunteers, housewives, small business owners, and retirees,[48] mounted a sophisticated and largely successful effort to increase turnout in 1984, contributing to Ronald Reagan's victory.[49]

In 2000, both parties engaged in intensive turnout efforts in battleground states. The Democratic Party had an estimated forty thousand volunteers making personal contacts with voters, in addition to sending an estimated fifty million pieces of mail. Several key interest groups aided this effort. For example, the National Association for the Advancement of Colored People (NAACP) actively raised voter awareness among African Americans in Florida, whose turnout in 2000 was almost double what it was in 1996. Their campaign included recorded telephone messages from President Clinton and African American leaders urging people to vote as well as reminders from the ministers of black churches of the importance of voting. Republicans were active as well. In the last week of the campaign they made approximately eighty-five million telephone calls and sent over 110 million pieces of mail. During the final two weeks, they distributed roughly sixteen million pieces of campaign literature to people's doors, 1.2 million yard signs, and over one million bumper stickers. The National Rifle Association, pro-life, and other groups helped in this effort.[50]

Despite these efforts, the Republican attempt to turn out the vote in 2000 fell short—at least according to Bush's main political strategist, Karl Rove. According to Rove, some four million conservative voters stayed home in 2000. Given the closeness of the 2000 election, he built a GOTV operation designed to ensure that more Republicans than Democrats turned out in 2004. This effort focused on election districts "where Republican candidates underperformed against the Democratic profile of the district."[51] The plan included the purchase of commercial databases to pinpoint voters based on, among other things, their shopping habits and magazine subscriptions. Gun owners, for example, were targets, as were subscribers to magazines like *Christianity Today*.[52]

Republicans tested this operation in the 2002 Congressional elections and increased their turnout over 1998 by five million voters, while turnout increased by only two million for the Democrats.[53] In the run up to the 2004 election, Rove was focused on increasing registration numbers, and he intensified the effort accordingly.[54] To mobilize young adults, the Republican Party unveiled Reggie the Registration Rig, a fifty-six-foot, eighteen-wheeled mobile voter registration center, dispatching it to various youth-oriented events such as MTV's "Total Request Live."[55] The commercial databases the Bush campaign purchased targeted its appeals to members of thirty-two different subgroups, who were also cultivated with tickets to Bush appearances.[56]

As the election neared, efforts intensified in nine or ten battleground states. The Bush strategy was threefold. First, the campaign focused on people who had recently moved. This helped register approximately 3.4 million of these voters. Second, it focused on a group of roughly 7 million identified Republicans who do not always vote. Finally, the campaign targeted another 10 million unaffiliated voters.[57] In all, one report suggests that the Bush campaign allocated $125 million for voter mobilization, more than three times the amount spent in 2000. Other groups (e.g., Progress for America Voter Fund[58]) assisted in the effort, and the campaign used churches as well. For example, the Bush campaign asked the coalitions coordinator in Pennsylvania (a battleground state) to identify 1,600 friendly congregations that might help in the campaign effort.[59]

The Bush campaign made aggressive and innovative use of new technologies in the 2004 ground war effort. In particular, the campaign used the Internet to build networks of individuals who would canvass their neighborhoods and contact friends in other states as well.[60] On the Bush website, people could type in their zip codes and receive links to local talk radio as well as boilerplate letters to the editor. It also enabled people to create virtual precincts where typing in their addresses would return a list of five people in their immediate area, with directions to their homes and directions to their polling places. This model was based on the effort in the Iowa caucuses in 2000, and the 2002 congressional elections in South Dakota, where a volunteer could become a team leader by bringing ten other people into the campaign. Daily messages and communications from national team leaders encouraged these local leaders and kept them informed.[61] This "one-on-one politics" effort was a throwback of sorts to an earlier era—but with a modern twist. One person would volunteer to recruit a few people, each of whom in turn recruited several more, resulting in a network of volunteers connected by e-mail to the national campaign organization. This resulted in approximately 1.4 million volunteers in key battleground states.[62]

Taken together, the Bush campaign reported that they made between fourteen and eighteen million attempts to contact voters in battleground states in the last four days of the campaign.[63] Of course, the Democrats were active as well. The Kerry campaign reportedly spent sixty million dollars in voter mobilization efforts, more than twice the amount spent by the Democrats in 2000. In addition, organized labor led by the American Federation of Labor and Congress of Industrial Organizations (AFL-CIO) spent forty-five million dollars in sixteen battleground states.

America Coming Together raised $125 million and employed 2,500 people to register and stay in contact with new voters. They claim to have made approximately sixteen million telephone calls in the last three weeks of the campaign, sent twenty-three million pieces of mail, and delivered eleven million flyers. In one survey, 38 percent of respondents reported being contacted by one of the two campaigns in 2004, representing the third consecutive election cycle that this percentage has increased (it was approximately 20 percent in 1960).[64]

CONCLUSION

Packaging, marketing, selling, or otherwise crafting and propagating presidential candidate images are not new to the television era. It is an old practice in presidential campaigns. What has changed with the rise of television are the tools with which a new breed of highly specialized election people, or campaign managers, can craft and sell these images to the public. This has most assuredly made image making in the television era more sophisticated, but it is a far cry from implying or intimating—by way of metaphor or otherwise—that the practice is new.

In addition, while image building has its importance, it should not detract from the fact that political campaigns are largely fought on the ground. In short, all of the slick advertisements designed to persuade voters are pointless if no one votes. This is not to suggest that image is irrelevant. Certainly in a close election, such as Bush-Gore in 2000, every vote counts, and even the smallest details could potentially mean the difference between victory or defeat for a candidate, as the literature on campaign effects suggests.[65] Nevertheless, it is important to remember that behind every campaign are volunteers, workers, and other individuals who carry their messages to others and remind people of the importance of their vote. In recent election cycles, turnout has been a prime determinant of victory. The Bush campaign made innovative and aggressive use of information technology to mobilize supporters. This resulted in a national network of committed supporters who encouraged, cajoled, and otherwise persuaded others to register and vote for their candidate. This particular sales job was personal—one on one—and, in the end, effective.

FOR MORE READING

Baumgartner, Jody. *Modern Presidential Electioneering: An Organizational and Comparative Approach*. Westport, Conn.: Praeger, 2000.

Dinkin, Robert J. *Campaigning in America: A History of Election Practices*. New York: Greenwood, 1989.

Melder, Keith. *Hail to the Candidate: Presidential Campaigns from Banners to Broadcasts*. Washington, D.C.: Smithsonian Institution Press, 1992.

Polsby, Nelson W., and Aaron Wildavsky. *Presidential Elections: Strategies and Structures of American Politics*. 11th ed. Lanham, Md.: Rowman & Littlefield, 2004.

Wayne, Stephen J. *The Road to the White House, 2004: The Politics of Presidential Elections*. Belmont, Calif.: Wadsworth, 2004.

10

The Misconception
of Competitive
Congressional Elections

If a group of planners sat down and tried to design a pair of assemblies
with the goal of serving members' reelection needs year in and year out,
they would be hard pressed to improve on what exists.

—David R. Mayhew[1]

Democratic theorists agree that in a democracy citizens elect most of
their leaders in free, fair, and regular elections.[2] The notion that these
elections should be competitive is almost self-evident. There would be little reason to hold an election if the outcome was a foregone conclusion.
While competitive elections have important implications for democratic
theory, most Americans are unaware that most congressional elections in
the United States are uncompetitive. According to a recent poll, nearly
three out of every five Americans anticipate a "close" contest in their district for the U.S. House, and of the respondents who could even venture a
guess, more than 71 percent answered that they expect a close election.[3]

Of course, a significantly smaller percentage of congressional races are
actually competitive. This chapter discusses the lack of electoral competitiveness in many congressional districts. We begin by demonstrating
that congressional elections have become less competitive in recent years,
especially elections to the House of Representatives. In particular, we illustrate that incumbents rarely, if ever, lose in their bid for reelection. As
Ronald Reagan once quipped, there was more turnover in the former
Soviet Union's presidium than in the U.S. Congress.[4] Incumbents' margins
of victory have also increased over time due in part to the variety of advantages they have in their bid for reelection, including various institutional

prerequisites and greater access to interest groups and political action committees (PACs), which help finance their campaigns. In addition, they are advantaged by a "scare-off" effect, which depresses the entrance of quality and adequately funded challengers, and recent trends in redistricting, which advantage incumbents of both parties.

In the final part we are shifting gears somewhat, discussing how incumbents can lose. We focus on the fact that the scare-off effect does not always work, on how presidential politics affects congressional elections, and on the occasional effect of "national tides." We conclude that while American elections satisfy most of the conditions for a democracy, the lack of competitiveness in congressional elections poses some problems for a healthy democratic system.

BACKGROUND

For many years Congress was not considered a career. Until the 1900s, it was quite common for a member of Congress, especially in the House, to serve only one or two terms (senators were not directly elected until after the ratification of the Seventeenth Amendment in 1913). There were a relatively high number of incumbents who did not seek reelection each election cycle. There are typically three general explanations given for this.

First, in earlier times, the notion of a "career" in Congress was not desirable to most ambitious professionals. Mediocre salaries, hot and humid summers in Washington, D.C., long stretches of time away from home, and the rather limited responsibilities of the federal government all combined to make the job of a U.S. Congressman less attractive than today. Second, most accounts suggest that even those who wished to stay in Washington for multiple successive terms were hard pressed to do so. Most congressional elections were highly contested, close contests. Third, many members did not want to run, or were prevented from running, for more than one or two terms. In many states, especially nonsouthern states, party organizations had informal term limits that prevented members from seeking the nomination more than one or two times (during this time, political parties controlled the nomination process).[5] However, as the century progressed, the percentage of House incumbents running for reelection increased, and the percentage of those retiring—voluntarily or otherwise—decreased (see table 10.1).

The results indicate that, over time, considerably more House incumbents ran for reelection and a much smaller percentage opted to retire. Another way to look at this would be to track the number of first-term members (freshman) or the mean number of terms served by members over time.[6] As seen in table 10.2, the percentage of freshman in the House

Table 10.1. House Incumbents Running for Reelection and Retirement Rates, 1850–1910

Decade	Number Running for Reelection	Percentage Retiring
1850s	60	27.1
1870s	64	22.8
1880s	66	20.0
1890s	73	17.3
1900s	80	11.2

Source: Samuel Kernell, "Toward Understanding 19th Century Congressional Careers: Ambition, Competition, and Rotation," *American Journal of Political Science* 21 (1977): 684, table 2; and John B. Gilmour and Paul Rothstein, "A Dynamic Model of Loss, Retirement, and Tenure in the U.S. House of Representatives," *Journal of Politics* 58 (1996): 57, table 1. Data for the 1860s is not included because Southern states did not hold elections to Congress during the Civil War years.

dropped more than thirty percentage points (from 51.3 to 20.4), and the mean number of terms that members served more than doubled (from 1.88 to 4.34) in the century after 1850. Together, tables 10.1 and 10.2 suggest a pattern of steadily increasing tenure in the House from the mid-1800s forward. The pattern of increased numbers of incumbents running for and winning elections accelerated in the post–World War II era (see table 10.3). Since 1946, an average of 91 percent of House incumbents have sought reelection per election cycle, and the percentage of those seeking reelection has dipped below 87 percent only once. This occurred in 1992, in the aftermath of a major check-writing scandal, when only 84.6 percent of House incumbents sought reelection. Of those seeking reelection, a few were defeated in either the primary or general elections. This was an exception. During this period, 5.2 percent of incumbents did not win their

Table 10.2. Percentage of First-Term Members and Mean Tenure, House of Representatives, 1851–1949

Decade	Percentage First-Term Members	Mean Number of Terms
1850s	51.3	1.88
1870s	49.1	2.09
1880s	39.0	2.47
1890s	39.7	2.54
1900s	23.8	3.43
1910s	26.2	3.55
1920s	19.6	3.99
1930s	25.6	3.92
1940s	20.4	4.34

Source: Nelson W. Polsby, "The Institutionalization of the U.S. House of Representatives," *American Political Science Review* 62 (1968): 146, tables 1 and 2.

Chapter 10

Table 10.3. Reelection Rates for House Incumbents, 1946–2006

Year	Number of Incumbents Seeking Reelection (%)		Sought Reelection, Defeated in Primary (%)		Won Primary, Defeated in General Election (%)		Total Percentage Reelected
1946	398	(91.5)	18	(4.5)	52	(13.7)	82
1948	400	(92.0)	15	(3.8)	68	(17.7)	79
1950	400	(92.0)	6	(1.5)	32	(8.1)	91
1952	389	(89.4)	9	(2.3)	26	(6.8)	91
1954	407	(93.6)	6	(1.5)	22	(5.5)	93
1956	411	(94.5)	6	(1.5)	16	(4.0)	95
1958	396	(91.0)	3	(0.8)	37	(9.4)	90
1960	405	(93.1)	5	(1.2)	25	(6.3)	93
1962	402	(92.4)	12	(3.0)	22	(5.6)	92
1964	397	(91.3)	8	(2.0)	45	(11.6)	87
1966	411	(94.5)	8	(1.9)	41	(10.2)	88
1968	409	(94.0)	4	(1.0)	9	(2.2)	97
1970	401	(92.2)	10	(2.5)	12	(3.1)	95
1972	390	(89.7)	12	(3.1)	13	(3.4)	94
1974	391	(89.9)	8	(2.0)	40	(10.4)	88
1976	384	(88.3)	3	(0.8)	13	(3.4)	96
1978	382	(87.8)	5	(1.3)	19	(5.0)	94
1980	398	(91.5)	6	(1.5)	31	(7.9)	91
1982	393	(90.3)	10	(2.5)	29	(7.6)	90
1984	409	(94.0)	3	(0.7)	16	(3.9)	95
1986	393	(90.3)	2	(0.5)	6	(1.5)	98
1988	408	(93.8)	1	(0.2)	6	(1.5)	98
1990	406	(93.3)	1	(0.2)	15	(3.7)	96
1992	368	(84.6)	19	(5.2)	24	(6.9)	88
1994	387	(89.0)	4	(1.0)	34	(8.9)	90
1996	384	(88.3)	2	(0.5)	21	(5.5)	94
1998	402	(92.4)	1	(0.2)	6	(1.5)	98
2000	403	(92.6)	3	(0.7)	6	(1.5)	98
2002	398	(91.5)	8	(2.0)	8	(2.1)	96
2004	402	(92.4)	3	(0.7)	7	(1.8)	98

Source: Gary C. Jacobson, *The Politics of Congressional Elections*, 6th ed. (New York: Longman, 2004), 24, table 3.1; 2004 data from Michael Barone and Richard E. Cohen, *The Almanac of American Politics: 2006* (Washington, D.C.: National Journal Group, 2006). Data from 1982, 1992, 2002, and 2004 include races pitting one incumbent against another.

party's primary, and the average number defeated in the general election was just 1.7 percent.

Most incumbents who survive their primaries win in the general election. In only six elections since World War II has the percentage of incumbents winning reelection fallen below 90 percent, and in the past four decades, the number has not fallen below 88 percent. Ninety-nine percent

Table 10.4.   House Incumbents with No Major-Party Opposition in General Election, 1982–2002

Year	Number Running Unopposed (%)
1982	49 (12.5)
1984	63 (15.4)
1986	71 (18.1)
1988	81 (19.9)
1990	76 (18.7)
1992	25 (6.8)
1994	54 (14.0)
1996	20 (5.2)
1998	94 (23.4)
2000	63 (15.6)
2002	78 (19.6)

Source: Paul S. Herrnson, *Congressional Elections: Campaigning at Home and in Washington*, 4th ed. (Washington, D.C.: CQ Press, 2003), 30, table 1.3.

of incumbents won their races in 1998 and 2000, and only six were not reelected. Even in 1974, a bad year for Republicans tainted with the scandal of Watergate, a full 77 percent of the Republicans seeking reelection were returned to office.[7] From 1982 through 2002, an average of 15.4 percent of incumbents faced no major-party opposition in the general election (see table 10.4). In 1998, almost one in four incumbents (23.4 percent) had no major-party opposition. Races like these are clearly uncompetitive.

While the House returns a very high percentage of incumbents, the Senate is slightly more competitive. In the post–World War II era, 82.7 percent of Senate incumbents sought reelection (see table 10.5). Approximately one in twenty (4.9 percent) lost their primary bids, and of those who gained their party nomination and stood in the general election, less than one in five (17.8 percent) lost. Taken together, 78.4 percent of incumbent senators seeking reelection were successful. While there is more variation in reelection rates than in House races, the general trend of elections becoming less competitive is similar. For example, in the eleven election cycles from 1982 to 2002, only 3 of 306 Senate incumbents faced opposition in their party primaries.

Congressional incumbents are not only winning, but they are doing so by larger margins. In 1974, political scientist David Mayhew noted that fewer elections in the postwar era could be classified as competitive. Mayhew dubbed this trend "the case of the vanishing marginals," a reference to the fact that close races in the House were becoming rare (Senate races tend to be more competitive, for reasons we will discuss shortly).[8]

As figure 10.1 shows, this trend has become more pronounced over time, especially in the House. In figure 10.1, the dotted line represents the

Table 10.5. Reelection Rates for Senate Incumbents, 1946–2002

Year	Number of Races	Sought Reelection (%)	Sought Reelection, Defeated in Primary (%)	Won Primary, Defeated in General Election (%)	Total Reelected (%)
1946	37	30 (81.1)	6 (20.0)	7 (29.2)	57
1948	33	25 (75.8)	2 (8.0)	8 (34.8)	60
1950	36	32 (88.9)	5 (15.6)	5 (18.5)	69
1952	35	31 (88.6)	2 (6.5)	9 (31.0)	65
1954	38	32 (84.2)	2 (6.3)	6 (20.0)	75
1956	35	29 (82.9)	0 —	4 (13.8)	86
1958	36	28 (77.8)	0 —	10 (35.7)	64
1960	35	29 (82.9)	0 —	1 (3.4)	97
1962	39	35 (89.7)	1 (2.9)	5 (14.7)	83
1964	35	33 (94.3)	1 (3.0)	4 (12.5)	85
1966	35	32 (91.4)	3 (9.4)	1 (3.4)	88
1968	34	28 (82.4)	4 (14.3)	4 (16.7)	71
1970	35	31 (88.6)	1 (3.2)	6 (20.0)	77
1972	34	27 (79.4)	2 (7.4)	5 (20.0)	74
1974	34	27 (79.4)	2 (7.4)	2 (8.0)	85
1976	33	25 (75.8)	0 —	9 (36.0)	64
1978	35	25 (71.4)	3 (12.0)	7 (31.8)	60
1980	34	29 (85.3)	4 (13.8)	9 (36.0)	55
1982	33	30 (90.9)	0 —	2 (6.7)	93
1984	33	29 (87.9)	0 —	3 (10.3)	90
1986	34	28 (82.4)	0 —	7 (25.0)	75
1988	33	27 (81.8)	0 —	4 (14.8)	85
1990	35	32 (91.4)	0 —	1 (3.1)	97
1992	36	28 (77.8)	1 (3.6)	4 (14.8)	82
1994	35	26 (74.3)	0 —	2 (7.7)	92
1996	34	21 (61.8)	1 (4.8)	1 (5.0)	90
1998	34	29 (85.3)	0 —	3 (10.3)	90
2000	34	29 (85.3)	0 —	6 (20.7)	79
2002	34	27 (79.4)	1 (3.7)	3 (11.5)	85

Source: Gary C. Jacobson, *The Politics of Congressional Elections*, 6th ed. (New York: Longman, 2004), 24, table 3.1.

percentage of races in which the winner received more than 60 percent of the vote. As the results indicate, the winning candidate received more than 60 percent of the vote (defined traditionally as an uncompetitive election) in an astonishing 80 percent of all U.S. House elections in 2002—a high for the post-Watergate era. In addition, 18 percent of all U.S. House elections were uncontested in 2002—equaling the high mark set in 1988 during the post-Watergate era.[9]

Congressional elections, especially for the House of Representatives, have become increasingly noncompetitive in the period following World

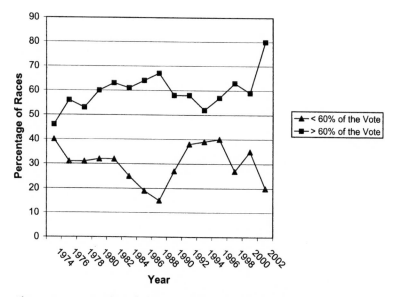

Figure 10.1.   Margins of Victory, House of Representatives, 1974–2002
Source: Roger H. Davidson and Walter J. Oleszek, *Congress and Its Members*, 9th ed. (Washington, D.C.: CQ Press, 2003), 136, table 5.3.

War II. Not only are more incumbents running, but they are winning as well and doing so by greater margins (although it should be noted that seats often become competitive again when incumbents retire or run for another office). Some scholars have attempted to quantify the value of incumbency in an election. Various measures suggest that incumbency in the House was worth between 2.1 to 3.3 percent of the vote from 1946 to 1966 and jumped to between 7 and 8.6 percent from 1968 to 2000. In the Senate, from 1914 to 1960, incumbency was worth a bit more than 2 percent of the vote and jumped to 7 percent from 1962 to 1992.[10]

Why are congressional elections so noncompetitive? There are several contributing factors, most of which revolve around the various advantages incumbents enjoy by virtue of being the current officeholder. This is the subject of the next section.

ELECTORAL ADVANTAGES AND
THE POWER OF INCUMBENCY

Our discussion of the advantages of incumbency is divided into several sections. The first section deals with various institutional factors, or perks, of the office. This class of incumbency advantages includes a large staff working for members of Congress as well as office space, computers, and so on. In addition, members of Congress employ various ways to communicate with their constituents at the taxpayer's expense. Incumbents also aggressively solve various bureaucratic problems for members of their district in hopes that these favors will be returned on Election Day. Finally, there are various norms guiding legislative activity itself that favor incumbents, allowing them to build and present their record in a favorable light.

In addition to these institutional advantages, there are other aspects of incumbency that give incumbents an advantage over their challengers. One is the overwhelming edge in raising campaign funds, which can sometimes scare off quality challengers.[11] Congressional redistricting efforts have also helped incumbents in recent years. Finally, the criteria that people use to make their voting decisions favor incumbents as well. Together, these factors provide the current officeholder with an enormous edge in his or her bid for reelection.

Office and Staff

Institutional advantages are those associated with doing the job of a congressperson. Congressional office comes with various perks, some of which aid in the reelection efforts of members, and some are often referred to (e.g., in American government textbooks) as "in kind" advantages. One advantage is the fact that each member of Congress has a staff that also serves as the nucleus of a permanent campaign organization, and the number of these staffers has increased dramatically in the past century.

The number of employees in the House of Representatives increased approximately sevenfold since 1930. In 1950, the House employed slightly fewer than two thousand staffers. By 1990, that number exceeded 7,500. Individually, the average member has fourteen employees (staffers) but is allowed eighteen full-time and four part-time employees.[12] Total staff growth of the Senate has been slightly less. In 1955, there were approximately one thousand staffers on the Senate and, by 1990, four thousand. However, individually they average thirty-four staffers per senator, from as few as thirteen to as many as seventy-one. There are no limits to the number of staffers a senator may employ.[13] Furthermore, the home district uses congressional staffers for casework, more so if it looks to be a tight race. The percentage of total staff working for House members in their districts nearly doubled from 1972 to 1992 (22 to 42 percent), and for senators the percentage almost tripled during the same period (from 12 to 32 percent).[14]

Members of Congress are also given allowances for "travel, communications, office rental, stationery, computer services, and mail."[15] House members average about 2.3 offices in their districts, while senators average four offices per district (state).[16] All of this comes at the expense of the taxpayer. While these staffers technically cannot be used for the campaign, there is a fine line between campaigning and constituency service. The press secretary is especially important in this regard, helping to generate favorable news about the congressperson at the local level.[17]

Direct Communications

Members of Congress take full advantage of what is known as the "franking" privilege. This is the right of members of Congress to send letters to their constituents informing them about what is happening in Washington, at government expense. The precedent for this dates back to 1660 in the British House of Commons and was granted by the Continental Congress to members in 1775. Subsequently, the first U.S. Congress passed a law granting its members the privilege in 1789.[18] The health of a representative democracy depends in part on an informed citizenry, and central to this is knowing what our representative is doing in Washington.

One widely circulated account suggests that new members are urged to "use the frank,"[19] and by all accounts, they do so. Members of Congress send mass newsletters and more narrowly tailored messages to different segments of their electorate. Often recipients are invited in these messages to send their thoughts to their member of Congress. Estimates suggest that from the mid-1960s to 1990, the volume of mail has at least tripled and perhaps quadrupled. Importantly, the amount of franked mail is higher during election years.[20] In 1990, Congress enacted new regulations limiting the amount of franked mail to one piece per address per state for a senator and three pieces per address per House district. Other regulations, such as prohibiting personal photographs of or references to the member and integrating franking costs into the members' office expenses were added. However, at minimum, these communications keep the incumbent's name fresh in voter's minds and provide an enormous advantage, especially for members of the House.

Bureaucratic Ombudsmanship

It is not unusual for an ordinary citizen to need assistance from time to time navigating or circumventing the bureaucracy that makes up modern government. Citizens might contact their member of Congress for any number of reasons, which could include, for example, requests or questions about an expired passport only days before a planned trip or a tax problem with the Internal Revenue Service. Here, the member would be acting in a capacity analogous to that of an ombudsman (or ombudsperson), a government-appointed individual who looks after the rights and needs of citizens in disputes with government. Originally a Scandinavian concept, ombudsmen are found in virtually all modern bureaucracies. Members of Congress take this type of work—referred to as case work—very seriously.

Each member of Congress receives thousands of such requests each year. While it is impossible for members to handle each request personally, much of the staff work handled in district offices is devoted to resolving citizens' problems and answering requests. This is an extremely effective way to win the loyalty and votes of citizens and others. A favor done for a constituent makes it more likely that he or she will repay the kindness come election time—and perhaps even tell others. This type of interpersonal, word-of-mouth, advertising is invaluable.[21]

Favorable Local Media

Incumbents have certain advantages with various media that make it easier to boost name recognition among their constituents as well as communicate and cultivate a favorable view among supporters and potential supporters. First, all members of Congress have their own websites, which allow interested parties to learn about what they are doing in Washington.[22] The government pays for these websites, and members use them to publicize their achievements, downplay their shortcomings, and invite visitors to send comments and feedback.

Second, both parties in each house of Congress, as well as the chambers themselves, have state-of-the-art audiovisual studios. Members can produce short statements to the press, interviews, and other types of programming. Along with satellite link technology, this allows incumbents to feed the local media, which is always looking for story material, especially on 90- or 120-minute evening newscasts.[23] Some members are regular guests on various local programs; others have their own local programs (e.g., a call-in show). Almost all produce press releases on a fairly regular basis that local news organizations air unedited, presenting them as news.

The link with local media outlets is important because studies show that local news organizations are rarely as confrontational as the national press. When members are featured in a thirty-second spot answering a few questions, the questions are rarely difficult and the answers rarely challenged. This is in part because the news organizations in question (typically the electronic media) are in need of material as well as the fact that local reporters are often less well prepared for the interview or versed in national politics in general. The result is generally favorable coverage in local media, which is especially helpful for members of the House, who run on local issues.[24]

Legislative Norms

In a representative democracy, an assumption exists that there is a link between what people want and what elected officials work to accomplish. Members of Congress understand this and understand that this is what people expect. Therefore, it is not surprising that their legislative activity is geared toward working—or at least appearing to work—for the people in their district. With so many decentralized committees and subcommittees in Congress, new members have almost no trouble seeking out and receiving an assignment on a committee that deals with policy concerns important to their district. For example, if the legislator is from Washington state, he or she might seek assignment on the Merchant Marine and Fisheries Committee; if from the Midwest, on agriculture. Because the details of most policy is worked out in committees, this allows the legislator to go back to the district and claim to be doing something for the district.[25]

Another legislative norm is that a member is not required or expected to vote with his or her party if that vote will do damage electorally. Weak party discipline allows members to protect themselves if the party's position contradicts what constituents expect. Finally, most members cooperate with other members when it comes to distributive legislation. If there is "pork" (government projects that benefit a specific locale) to be spread around, everyone gets a piece to take home to the district. Additionally, a member will support another member's bill with a full expectation of reciprocity. This reciprocity is referred to as "logrolling," and allows members at the end to claim credit for passing legislation that is popular back home.

Financial Advantages

Congressional elections cost a great deal of money. The expectation in 2006 was that "candidates, national political parties and outside issue advocacy groups [would] spend roughly $2.6 billion" in the 472 congressional elections.[26] Unlike other incumbent advantages, financial aspects of congressional campaigns are easy to quantify, and a good deal has been written on this subject.[27] Since the 1970s, the United States has had the most transparent campaign finance system in the world.[28] This provides a detailed understanding of the financial advantage incumbents have over their challengers.

Most incumbents start their next campaigns with money left over from the previous campaign. This is referred to as their "war chest." In 2002, the average returning House member had three hundred thousand dollars left in a campaign coffer after the election.[29] But even with this advantage, incumbents continue to raise enormous sums of money. They

BOX 10.1

WHAT IS A PAC?

A political action committee (PAC) is a legal entity formed by an organized group (a corporation, union, interest group, citizen action group, etc.) whose purpose is to raise money for, and make contributions to, the campaigns of candidates for federal office.

It is important to understand PACs because they are the only legal way that an organized group—of any kind—can contribute money to a campaign for federal office.

do this because reelection is never a certainty,[30] and raising large amounts of cash can scare off challengers.

Furthermore, incumbents raise money more easily than do most challengers. This is especially true when soliciting funds from Washington-based political action committees (see box 10.1), who are six times more likely to give to an incumbent.[31] One reason for this is that PACs know that incumbents are more likely to win, and they want to ensure future access by backing the winning candidate. Incumbents also have financial backing from congressional party campaign committees. There is a committee for each party in each house and for national and state party organizations. Also, individual donors who give large sums of money are more likely to give to incumbents. Challengers therefore find it difficult to raise the necessary resources to be competitive, given that a majority of the money goes to the incumbent.

During the past two decades, the financial advantages of incumbents have grown tremendously. In 1990, for example, House incumbents had a four to one financial advantage over challengers, while in the Senate the ratio was two to one in 1990. By 2004, that ratio had grown to almost six to one in the House and almost nine to one in the Senate (see table 10.6).

Lack of Quality Challengers

Another reason why incumbents enjoy high reelection rates is the lack of quality challengers. A quality challenger is an individual that possesses a combination of characteristics that can convince voters that he or she is qualified to be their representative. These qualities include, but are not

Table 10.6.   Incumbent Financial Advantage in Congressional Elections, 2004

Type of Candidate	Number of Candidates	Total Raised ($)	Average Raised ($)	Ratio
House				
Incumbent	407	456,990,049	1,122,826	5.81:1
Challenger	583	112,682,816	193,281	
Senate				
Incumbent	26	223,964,927	8,614,036	8.95:1
Challenger	83	79,852,042	962,073	

Source: "The Big Picture, 2004 Cycle: Incumbent Advantage," Center for Responsive Politics, at www.opensecrets.org/bigpicture/incumbs.asp?cycle=2004.

limited to, having previously held public office (either elective or otherwise), being a celebrity (show business, sports, etc.), or being a prominent local business, religious, or community leader. Generally, there is some name recognition in the community (or district, state) and enough ties to support fund-raising efforts to raise the money necessary to challenge a congressional incumbent.[32] The top challenger also possesses some political experience.

This explains why most challengers in congressional elections are amateurs, or lesser quality candidates. Most lack some, or all, of the various characteristics, background, and experience mentioned. Experienced politicians or prominent leaders have enough political savvy to know that the chances of beating an incumbent are slim. Generally, only open-seat races attract quality candidates. Amateurs are more likely to challenge an entrenched incumbent. Fund-raising efforts by incumbents further deter quality candidates. Raising early money, as well as being active in the district, goes a long way toward deterring potential challengers. This is the so-called scare-off effect,[33] and while it is clear that anything *can* happen in a campaign, most challengers are amateurs who pose little threat to incumbents.[34]

Congressional Redistricting

House district boundaries in almost every state are redrawn every ten years following the census. This ensures that districts contain approximately equal numbers of people. Few voters know about or pay much attention to this process.[35] Redistricting is a very contentious exercise as it almost always gives an advantage to a certain party or group.

An example of this would be a state with twelve equal and distinct geographic divisions (think of them as neighborhoods), with each division containing equal numbers of straight partisan voters. All voters in each division vote the party line every time. From this state, four congressional

BOX 10.2

EXAMPLE: PARTISAN EFFECTS
OF DISTRICTING (D = DEMOCRAT,
R = REPUBLICAN)

Partisan Distribution				Districting Plan #1				Districting Plan #2			
R	R	R	R	R	R	R	R	R	R	R	R
R	R	D	D	R	R	D	D	R	R	D	D
D	D	D	D	D	D	D	D	D	D	D	D

Source: Michael D. Robbins, "Gerrymander and the Need for Redistricting Reform," October 25, 2006, at www.fraudfactor.com/ffgerrymander.html.

districts, each containing roughly equal numbers of voters and containing three of these geographic divisions, is drawn. Box 10.2 illustrates this as well as which divisions belong to which party (D = Democrat, R = Republican) in the left-most column, under "Partisan Distribution." With the first districting plan, Democrats and Republicans will each win in two districts. However, if the district lines are slightly different, as seen in the second districting plan, Democrats win in only one district, while Republicans win in three.[36]

Drawing district lines to maximize the electoral advantage of a political group, party, or faction is "gerrymandering." The term, first used in 1812, characterized the salamander-like redistricting plan drawn up by Massachusetts governor Elbridge Gerry. Partisan gerrymandering, or redistricting that favors a specific party, enjoys a long history in the United States. While not an exact science, since the 1990s gerrymandering has evolved into a practice of incumbent-based, or "sweetheart," gerrymandering. This is a true bipartisan effort where district lines drawn ensure that there is a high concentration of each party's supporters in "their" respective districts.[37] Thus, the status quo (incumbents of each party) is protected. While some recent research suggests that the effect is minimal, many suggest that incumbent-based districts lead to a decline in the number of competitive elections, at least in the House, as more districts are "packed" on a partisan basis.[38]

Voting Behavior

To round out our discussion, we should also say something about voting behavior, or how people vote. A few aspects of voting in congressional elections are important with respect to incumbent advantages. First, the electorate knows incumbents better than challengers. Second, with more campaign funding, incumbents can advertise more, beyond the free advertising they receive from franking, local media, and so on.

In House elections from 1980 to 2002, on average, respondents were almost twice as likely to recognize the incumbent's name as opposed to the challenger's name (92 to 53 percent) and better than twice as likely to be able to recall—unprompted—the incumbent's rather than the challenger's name (46 to 17 percent). For Senate candidates, the percentages are more even, but incumbent names are recognized and recalled more than those of their challengers (97 to 77 percent recognition, 58 to 35 percent recall). While people do not always cast their votes for the better-known candidate, the converse of this is probably a fair assumption: people are less likely to vote for an unknown candidate.[39] This is especially true in midterm elections where the turnout of the voting age population has decreased from approximately 47 to 37 percent from 1960 to 2002.[40] Generally, lower turnout is an advantage to incumbents.

Another factor favoring incumbents is the party loyalty of voters. Ticket splitting, or casting one's vote for the presidential candidate of one party while voting for the congressional candidate of the other party, increased consistently throughout the middle part of the past century. This trend seems to have reversed itself. In 1972, 192 districts split their votes in this way. In 2000, only 86 did so, and in 2004, the number fell to 59, the lowest number since World War II.[41] In short, voters, who are packed into increasingly partisan-leaning districts are voting to support their party. But since recent redistricting efforts have generally protected incumbents, "their party" is more likely to be the party of the incumbent.

Finally, it should be noted that members of Congress pay special attention throughout their careers, and especially during the campaign, to the way in which they present themselves. Here, the landmark study of Richard Fenno is useful.[42] Fenno followed and observed a number of House members, concluding that they self-consciously adopted a style or persona that was compatible with the culture of their district. He labeled this their "home style." For example, a House member from rural Georgia would be hard pressed to win an election if he traveled the district in a three-piece Brooks Brothers suit. In a district like this, a candidate would likely present himself as a common member of the local community, hoping to establish a connection with the majority of voters. This example is a bit exaggerated, but according to Fenno's work, not by much. And it seems to pay off. In short, incumbents have any variety of advantages in their bid to be returned to Washington. The next section briefly reviews some of the situations that might contribute to an incumbent defeat and offers some concluding thoughts.

CONCLUSION: CAN INCUMBENTS LOSE?

Challengers clearly face uphill battles. However, there are some factors that make it more likely that a challenger can be competitive. First, the scare-off effect does not always work.[43] Incumbents sometimes show signs of weakness or are weakened by circumstance. This can be the result of any number of factors including unfavorable redistricting, a small war chest, press criticism, or scandal. All of these can make incumbents look vulnerable, attracting quality challengers to the fray. Or, more simply, any of these factors can actually make an incumbent more vulnerable, giving challengers a better chance to win.

Second, presidential politics sometimes affects congressional elections. The two most obvious ways in which this occurs are either the "coattail" effects of a popular presidential candidate or the historic tendency for a president's party to lose seats in midterm elections. In the first case, an extremely popular presidential candidate can increase the popularity— and thus the chances for victory—of the congressional candidates in his party. This happened, for example, in 1980, when Ronald Reagan's popularity helped the Republicans win control of the Senate for the first time since 1954. Alternatively, it is also the case that, historically, the president's party usually loses seats in the midterm elections (see table 10.7).

Some midterm elections bring greater losses than others, but in most, a fairly significant number of the president's party loses. Some of these losses are inevitably suffered by incumbents. In 2006, Republicans lost their majorities in both the U.S. House and Senate, in part because of their association with President George W. Bush whose popularity gradually and steadily dropped following his reelection in 2004.

The final factor is the occasional effect of what scholars refer to as "national tides" on congressional elections. Local elections generally favor incumbents. Congressional elections are primarily local affairs, more so in the House than in the Senate. However, sometimes congressional elections are influenced by national political factors, favoring one party over the other. This was the case, for example, in 1974, when an anti-Watergate sentiment swept the country, and the Democrats made large gains. In 1980, anti-Carter sentiment and a national recession helped produce a significant number of victories for Republicans. Anti-incumbent

Table 10.7. Midterm Losses for Presidential Party

Year	President (Party)	House	Senate
1946	Franklin Roosevelt and Harry Truman (Dem.)	45	12
1950	Harry Truman (Dem.)	29	6
1954	Dwight Eisenhower (Rep.)	18	1
1958	Dwight Eisenhower (Rep.)	48	13
1962	John Kennedy (Dem.)	4	(3)
1966	Lyndon Johnson (Dem.)	47	4
1970	Richard Nixon (Rep.)	12	(2)
1974	Richard Nixon and Gerald Ford (Rep.)	48	5
1978	Jimmy Carter (Dem.)	15	3
1982	Ronald Reagan (Rep.)	26	(1)
1986	Ronald Reagan (Rep.)	5	8
1990	George H. W. Bush (Rep.)	8	1
1994	Bill Clinton (Dem.)	52	8

Note: Numbers in parentheses were gains for the presidential party.
Source: Gary C. Jacobson, *The Politics of Congressional Elections*, 6th ed. (New York: Longman, 2004), 104, table 4.2.

and anticongressional feelings in 1992 (surrounding various congressional scandals and the Clarence Thomas hearings) helped 110 newcomers win election to Congress. Republicans won both houses of Congress for the first time in more than four decades in 1994, partly as the result of an anti-Congress and anti-Clinton mood prevailing in the country. In 1998, anti-impeachment sentiment helped the Democrats reverse historical trends and gain seats, and in 2002, national security concerns helped Republicans do the same. In all of these cases, a prevailing mood in the country overcame local concerns to help oust a significant number of incumbents.

In short, incumbents rarely lose, although challengers can sometimes capitalize on national conditions that might be in their favor (as in 1994). The word "campaign" was originally used to refer to military operations and adopted for political use later. To use this metaphor, challengers face an overwhelming disadvantage given that their opponents have been gearing up for months, are already on the field, and have an arsenal in place.

Certainly, we are not the first observers to note that congressional elections have become less competitive over the course of the last century.[44] However, many Americans do not realize or appreciate how uncompetitive congressional elections have become. While the high rate of incumbent victories might, to some degree, equate to voter satisfaction, it more likely reflects the numerous advantages that incumbents have. This has undoubtedly increased the number of uncompetitive congressional contests, which, as noted earlier, has consequences for the type of democracy that exists in the United States.

FOR MORE READING

Fenno, Richard F., Jr. *Home Style: House Members in Their Districts*. New York: Longman, 2003.

Herrnson, Paul S. *Congressional Elections: Campaigning at Home and in Washington*.
4th ed. Washington, D.C.: CQ Press, 2003.

Jacobson, Gary C. *The Politics of Congressional Elections*. 6th ed. New York: Longman, 2004.

Mayhew, David R. *Congress: The Electoral Connection*. New Haven, Conn.: Yale
University, 1974.

11

Presidential Campaigns and "Kingmaker" States

The Myth of a National Contest

In the previous chapter we discussed how many Americans are unaware that congressional elections are becoming increasingly less competitive. This chapter has a similar orientation. In it, we discuss another misconception about American elections, but in this chapter, we turn to presidential elections. The idea that every four years a handful of men and a few women take their messages to citizens across the nation in order win the White House is, we believe, at least implicitly shared by most citizens.

And in many respects this is true. Presidential candidates and their parties fund, build, and mobilize campaign organizations in literally hundreds of locations throughout the country. Candidates and their surrogates (wives, children, parents, and more) take the campaign messages to countless towns, villages, and hamlets. They, their parties, and other groups craft messages designed to persuade voters and air these messages on national media throughout the campaign. National media organizations spend enormous amounts of money gathering news about the campaign and reporting it to a national audience. Indeed, presidential campaigns seem to be as national an event as the celebration of Independence Day. In other respects, however, they fall short of being truly national contests. As we will illustrate in this chapter, presidential campaigns in both the primary and general election season focus their efforts in only a select few states and to only a select few voters.

This chapter is divided into two main sections. The first will deal with the presidential primary season. After a brief history of presidential nomination systems and the emergence of direct primaries and caucuses, our focus will turn to the evolution of the modern nomination system. Under this system, relatively few citizens vote in presidential primaries or participate in caucuses. Likewise, the general election reaches only a limited audience. Because of the electoral college system, presidential campaigns spend proportionately greater resources on a minority of voters in only a few battleground states.

THE HISTORY OF PRESIDENTIAL PRIMARIES AND CAUCUSES

There have been three different systems for selecting presidential nominees throughout our history. The first, known as the legislative caucus, functioned by having legislators from each party select their presidential candidate. The second, the convention system, allowed party leaders and party regulars to select the nominee. The third and current method, the primary system, permits voters to select their party's presidential nominee.[1] In the section that follows, we discuss each system briefly, focusing on the idea that the trend has been toward increased citizen participation.

During the colonial period and immediately following ratification of the Constitution, partisans within the state legislature selected party candidates for local and state offices. Shortly after the ratification of the Constitution, many state legislative caucuses began selecting party candidates for national offices as well. Although they were not identifiable as parties, two informal caucuses emerged in Congress in 1796. The first, a pro-administration faction, supported the presidential candidacy of John Adams, while the second, an antiadministration faction, backed Thomas Jefferson. In 1800, the same informal caucuses supported each of these candidates again.

In the first four presidential elections, electors in the electoral college cast two votes for president. The candidate who received the majority of votes became president, while the runner-up became vice president. In 1796, this process resulted in a president (John Adams) and vice president (Thomas Jefferson) from two different factions. The election of 1800 was eventually decided by the House of Representatives, because Jefferson finished in a tie with his running mate Aaron Burr in the electoral college vote (see chapter 5 for more information about the election). Jefferson prevailed, but because the previous two elections had demonstrated two different flaws in the electoral college system, Congress passed and the states ratified the Twelfth Amendment in 1804. The amendment stipulated that electors cast one vote each for president and for vice president. One of the results of the passage of the Twelfth Amendment was that congressional caucuses (parties) began to nominate tickets comprising both a presidential and a vice-presidential candidate. This system, known as "King Caucus," was used to nominate presidential candidates until 1824.

In 1824, the splintering of the dominant Democratic-Republican Party led to a contested nomination between William Crawford, Andrew Jackson, John Q. Adams, and Henry Clay, foreshadowing the death of King Caucus. By the election of 1828 there was no discernible nomination system. This, as well as growing pressure for increased popular participation in the nomination process, led to the first national nominating convention. In 1831, leaders of the Anti-Masonic Party—from all levels of government—met in a convention in Baltimore to choose their presidential candidate. The two dominant parties of their time, the Democratic and Whig parties, adopted the same process shortly thereafter, and the convention system of presidential nominations was born.

The objective of using a national convention to nominate a presidential candidate was to widen the circle of participation. Under the convention system, state party leaders, party activists, and party regulars gathered every four years in the summer of the presidential election year in a national meeting lasting several days. The primary purpose was the selection of the party's presidential candidate. Party leaders used this system well into the twentieth century. However, because a few party leaders seemed to control conventions, the system had its detractors.

One alternative that seemed to hold out the promise of greater participation was the party primary, where voters themselves select (either directly or indirectly) their party's candidates for public office. The first primary was held by the Democratic Party of Crawford County, Pennsylvania, in 1842. In an attempt to mollify detractors within the party, party leaders experimented by giving citizens the chance to vote directly for their choice of party candidate. The Crawford County System, as it became known, spread to many other counties throughout the state within a few years. In a relatively short period of time, parties in different locales in other states, including California, Virginia, Ohio, and New York, had experimented with direct primaries. Primaries were still optional at this stage and were not being used to select presidential candidates.

Another alternative emerged in 1846, when Iowa (which had just become a state) used presidential nominating caucuses to select delegates to the national party convention. A presidential nominating caucus is actually a series of caucuses held to select delegates to the national convention. The first round narrows the field and selects the candidates to participate in the next round and is held at the local level, at schools, public buildings, and in some cases in private homes, all over the state. As the process repeats itself, the caucus finally selects delegates to represent the state at the national convention. In Iowa, for example, the first caucuses happen at the precinct level, the second at the county level, and the third at the congressional district level. The final caucus is a state-level caucus.

Because the evolution of state-level presidential nominating caucuses is less important to our story of nominating systems than primaries, our focus will be on primaries.

In 1901, Florida passed legislation that gave the state Democratic Party the option of selecting delegates to the national convention in a primary election. Wisconsin mandated that both parties do so in 1905. A year later, a Pennsylvania law allowed convention delegates to place their presidential preference on a primary ballot. Some amounted to little more than a presidential preference vote; in others, convention delegates pledged to vote for particular candidates; and some fulfilled both functions.

A split in the Republican Party in early 1912 over the nomination battle between former president Theodore Roosevelt and then president William Howard Taft provided the impetus for states to adopt a primary system. Roosevelt supporters, recognizing that they could not win the nomination by relying on party regulars at the convention, persuaded five more states to hold primaries, bringing the total number of states holding primaries to twelve. The hope was that party leaders might be swayed by a demonstration of Roosevelt's popularity. Although Roosevelt lost the Republican nomination through the convention system, primaries proved to be quite popular. By 1916, the number of states holding primaries peaked at twenty.

For the next sixty years, candidates used primaries to demonstrate their popularity and their ability to be elected. For example, in 1944, dark-horse Republican candidate Wendell Willkie used this strategy to help secure the nomination, as did Dwight Eisenhower in 1952. John F. Kennedy also employed this strategy in 1960. Kennedy's decision to enter the primary in heavily Protestant West Virginia was a strategic move designed to demonstrate that he—a Catholic—could win a Protestant state.[2] Kennedy's strong showing there helped convince party leaders to make him the party nominee, even though early indications were that party leaders had been leaning toward giving the nomination to Lyndon Johnson.

The pivotal year in the move from the convention to the primary system was 1968. By the time the Democratic convention convened in Chicago that summer, the country had witnessed the assassinations of Martin Luther King Jr. and Senator Robert Kennedy of New York as well as growing protest against the Vietnam War. Both Kennedy, before his assassination, and Senator Eugene McCarthy from Minnesota had entered and won several primaries before the convention. However, Vice President Hubert Humphrey, who had not entered a single primary, was favored by party regulars and secured the party nomination at the convention. Protests erupted in the convention hall and in the streets as Chicago police responded with violence in an attempt to control the situation.

To reunite the party for the general election, party leaders, activists, and supporters agreed to reform the nominating procedures. The McGovern-Fraser Commission, one of the two commissions appointed to examine the process, proposed increasing the number of state-level primaries. Recommendations by the commission led to six more states adopting primaries for the 1972 election season, bringing the total number of states holding primaries that year to twenty-one, including most of the more populous states. This makes 1972 the first year of the primary system for nominating presidential candidates. It was the first year that the majority of convention delegates (roughly two-thirds) who pledged to support a particular candidate were selected by primaries. This change in the process effectively shifted power out of the hands of party leaders and to the party electorate. However, in making this change, many have argued that the current primary system empowers more than voters. Interest groups and the mass media also play a very influential role in the process.[3]

Under the current system, it is all but impossible to capture the nomination for president unless one competes in and wins presidential primaries and caucuses in many states. This is because the objective of a party primary is to win the pledged support of delegates attending the national convention. Since 1972, the percentage of pledged delegates selected from presidential primaries and caucuses in various states has increased in almost every election year.

The exact number of primaries and caucuses varies from one election year to the next. These variations are the result of the fact that states are responsible for conducting elections, and the national party organizations give state parties a fair amount of latitude with respect to how they select their state delegations. In 2004, there were thirty-five primaries and fifteen caucuses (this number does not include caucuses held in U.S. territories). From these events, the Republican Party selected 2,509 delegates. Of the 4,317 delegates to the Democratic convention, 82 percent (3,502) were selected in primaries of caucuses.[4] The remaining delegates are the so-called superdelegates, typically elected officials or other party leaders who come to the convention officially uncommitted to any particular candidate.

There are three types of primaries and caucuses, distinguished according to which voters are allowed to participate.[5] In a closed primary or caucus, only those registered with the party may vote. For example, only registered Republicans are allowed to vote in a closed Republican primary. An open primary or caucus is open to any registered voter, and that voter may vote for either party's candidates. Semi-closed primaries allow party members and independents to participate in the party primaries. Under these rules, only registered Republicans and independents may vote in a Republican primary, while only registered Democrats and independents may vote in a Democratic primary.[6]

PRIMARIES AND REPRESENTATION

The primary system of selecting presidential nominees is less representative than it appears. While more citizens are involved in the selection of their party's presidential nominee than was the case under the legislative caucus or convention system, relatively few are actually involved in the choice. There are three main aspects of the primary system that make it less than fully representative: the disproportionate importance of the Iowa caucuses and the New Hampshire primary, increased front-loading of the primaries, and the small number of citizens who actually vote in the process.

The Winnowing Effect of the Iowa Caucuses and the New Hampshire Primary

Since 1972, the Iowa caucuses have been the first delegate selection event of the year, a place secured for the state in the rules of the Democratic National Committee. New Hampshire held their first primary in 1916 and has been the first primary in the delegate selection season since 1920. In fact, state law mandates that they hold their primary before any other state, and Democratic Party rules allow them to do so. Together, the delegate selection events of these two states are the first test for those aspiring to the presidency, and doing well in both states is critical to the pursuit of the party nomination. Therefore, candidates pay an extraordinary amount of attention to these two events.

Jimmy Carter spent seven days campaigning in Iowa in 1975 and early 1976. In 1987, major-party candidates spent an average of fifty days in Iowa and thirty-seven days in New Hampshire.[7] Fourteen major presidential aspirants (from both parties) devoted approximately 35 percent of their campaign time to these two states from mid-March 1999 through July of 1999.[8] Shortly after the 1998 congressional elections, Al Gore placed approximately two hundred telephone calls to supporters and potential supporters in New Hampshire in preparation for his bid for the presidency in 2000. From 2001 to 2002, ten Democratic candidates spent a combined total of sixty-five days campaigning in the state and three hundred days in 2003.[9] John Kerry spent seventy-three days campaigning in Iowa from January 2003 to January 19, 2004. Howard Dean spent approximately three million dollars in television advertising in Iowa in 2003 and early 2004, and some estimates suggest that, in total, Democratic candidates spent almost one hundred dollars for television advertising per voter in that state during that same time period.[10]

The media also pay an inordinate amount of attention to these two delegate selection events. For example, one analysis of the 1980 campaign by

United Press International and *CBS News* suggested that 14 percent of the coverage was devoted to the Iowa caucuses. The *New York Times* ran approximately seventy stories in 1987 and almost fifty in 1988 about the Iowa caucuses. Similarly, another study found that in 1984 network news and the *New York Times* devoted more coverage to the New Hampshire primary than to any of the twenty-four primaries in southern, border, and Rocky Mountain west states. An analysis of the coverage by ABC, CBS, NBC, and CNN from January 1995 through June 1996 found that of all the stories devoted to the primary season, the 1996 Republican New Hampshire primary was the subject of one-fourth of the coverage.[11]

The delegate selection events in Iowa and New Hampshire serve to winnow the field of presidential candidates. From 1972 to 2004, the winner of fourteen contested nominations won in New Hampshire nine times and placed second five times. However, during that same time period, George McGovern (1972), Michael Dukakis (1988), and George H. W. Bush (1988) placed third in the Iowa caucuses and went on to win the nomination; Bill Clinton won the Democratic nomination in 1992 after finishing behind senators Tom Harkin and Paul Tsongas in Iowa. All of the other nominees during that time period finished first or second.[12]

Doing poorly in either or both of these contests can effectively end a campaign. No candidate placing third or lower in New Hampshire ever went on to win the nomination. In 2004, Dick Gephardt withdrew immediately after the Iowa caucuses after finishing fourth with 11.2 percent of the vote. Joseph Lieberman, who did not enter the Iowa caucuses, finished fourth in New Hampshire with 8.6 percent of the vote, and did not win a single one of the five primaries held one week later. He withdrew immediately afterward. In 1996, Steve Forbes placed fourth in both Iowa and New Hampshire and withdrew after receiving only 20 percent of the vote in his home state of Delaware on February 10.[13] Al Gore's 1988 bid for the Democratic nomination was also cut short after poor finishes in both Iowa and New Hampshire.

Given their relative weight in the overall electoral process, it is somewhat puzzling that these two states have such power over who the eventual nominee will be. For example, Iowa and New Hampshire combined have a total of eleven electoral votes (Iowa, seven; New Hampshire, four). New Hampshire primary voters were responsible for choosing less than 1 percent of delegates to the Democratic Party convention in 2004.[14] The relative number of votes that determine the winners in these events is even smaller. In 1976, Democratic nominee Jimmy Carter won thirty-five thousand votes in Iowa and New Hampshire, which as one account explains is "fewer than it takes to be elected city councilman in Cincinnati."[15] Carter's margin of victory in New Hampshire over second-place finisher Morris Udall was a mere 4,663 votes. That same year, Gerald Ford, the Republican nominee, received only 1,587 more votes than Ronald Reagan. In the New Hampshire primary, Al Gore defeated second-place finisher Bill Bradley by 6,395 votes.[16]

The Problem of Front-loading

The importance of New Hampshire and Iowa is related to the increasing number of states that schedule their primaries and caucuses earlier in the primary season.[17] This is referred to as front-loading. In 1968, New Hampshire was the only state that held its primary before the end of March. By 1988, twenty states did so, and by 2004, twenty-one primaries and nine caucuses were held before March 2. The primary season has become quite compressed. During the past few election cycles it has effectively lasted for approximately six weeks. For example, Robert Dole had the Republican nomination secured by March 13 of 1996. Al Gore and George W. Bush effectively secured the nomination in the third week of March by winning greater than 50 percent of the pledged delegates in 2000.[18] In 2004, John Kerry had the Democratic nomination secured by March 3.

In order to have a chance at securing the party nomination in a compressed primary season, one must organize, identify, and recruit volunteers and workers, campaign, and continue to raise money in several different states—simultaneously—within a very short period of time. This places a premium on raising a great deal of money early and doing well in early contests, especially Iowa and New Hampshire. These two factors are interrelated. Candidates who are less successful in the early contests find it difficult to raise the funds needed to compete effectively in subsequent races. This dynamic exacerbates the winnowing effect of Iowa and New Hampshire.

As the result, there has been an increase in early withdrawals during the primary season of presidential nominations. One account summarizes,

> In 1984, for example, eight major candidates sought the Democratic presidential nomination. By the middle of March, less than three weeks after the New Hampshire primary, five of the eight were already out of the race. In 1988 every one of George Bush's Republican opponents except Pat Robertson had dropped out by the end of March. In 1992 three of the five Democratic contenders had withdrawn by the end of the third week of March.[19]

John McCain and Bill Bradley, the only serious challengers remaining for their respective party's nomination of 2000, withdrew from the race on March 9, 2000. Although several candidates vied for the Democratic nomination in 2004, by February 19 it was essentially a two-man race between John Kerry and John Edwards.

Front-loading the primary season also results in a large number of state primaries and caucuses held after the nomination has effectively been decided. One analyst has divided states according to their role in the nominating process. "Kingmakers," the states holding the earliest primaries and caucuses, have the most influence. "Confirmers" come next, both chronologically and in terms of influence. In these states, leaders solidify their position. The final category, "rubber stamps," speaks for itself. These states are the last to hold primaries and caucuses, held after the nomination has in effect been decided.

In 2000, there were twenty-six states classified as rubber stamps since their delegate selection events were held after March 7. By 2004 there were only eighteen rubber stamp states but an additional twelve confirmers that held their events on the same day (March 2), although not all of these states had the same degree of influence.[20] In recent election cycles voters in as many as half of the states have no say whatever in the presidential nomination process. Rubber stamp state voters might participate in their state's nominating event, but the meaning of their participation is open to question.

The Nominating Electorate

Our final point about the representativeness of the nomination process deals with those individuals who actually vote and those who do not vote. Voter participation in primaries and caucuses is historically low, even in the states where participation has an effect on the outcome (New Hampshire is a notable exception). Because the primaries are held in the late winter–early spring, only a few people have given much thought to the presidential race. In addition, voting in a party primary is more challenging than in the general election, given that the general election presents a choice between two candidates from different parties. The choice in a primary is between candidates of the same party. In order to choose, voters have to take time to learn something about each one.[21] Participation in caucuses is even lower because caucus participation requires even more commitment than voting in a primary. Caucuses can take several hours, and participants typically spend more time acquainting themselves with candidates and issues.

Voter turnout in primaries actually hovers at about 15 percent of eligible voters. While this seems low, not all of these 15 percent actually influence the outcome. For example,

barely 4 million voters who participated in the Democratic and Republican presidential primaries in 2000 were "kingmakers." Almost 14 million were "confirmers," and nearly 14 million more voters were "rubber stamps."

Put another way, 12.9 percent of those who cast primary ballots in 2000 had a major role in affecting the Democratic and Republican contests; 43.6 percent had bit parts; and 43.5 percent had no part at all. They were little more than spectators.[22]

Only one in three general election voters in 2000 voted in a primary or participated in a caucus, and only one in six did so in the first six weeks, when their vote actually mattered. Only one in twenty-five could be considered kingmakers, and one in two hundred participated in the influential Iowa or New Hampshire delegate selection events.[23] In other words, very few voters, from very few states, have much of a say about who the presidential nominees will be.

In addition, citizens who vote in primaries and participate in caucuses are less representative of the general public. They are generally better educated, come from higher income brackets, are more politically knowledgeable and interested, and are slightly older than the broader electorate. Furthermore, these voters are generally more ideologically extreme than the average voter. Democratic primary voters tend to be more liberal than the average Democratic voter in the general election. Republican primary voters tend to be more conservative than the typical Republican general election voter.[24]

To summarize this section about the modern presidential nominating system, we face a conundrum. Greater desire for public participation in presidential nominations created the primary/caucus system. Even if "only" thirty million people vote in primaries or participate in caucuses, this is clearly many more than the several thousand that previously decided presidential nominations at the national party conventions. The process is clearly more open than it was previously.

However, full and equitable participation has not been attained. The influence of two states (Iowa and New Hampshire) on the outcomes is highly disproportionate to their population. After the delegate selection events in these two states, the nomination contest is effectively fixed such that a number of candidates cannot meaningfully compete. The compressed nominating season exacerbates this and dramatically reduces the number of states that actually have a voice in the process. Finally, of the citizens who do vote, few are actually participating in the decision of who will become the nominee, and even these are hardly representative of the electorate as a whole.

In the next section we take up the matter of the general election campaign. The focus here is on campaign strategy and organization. In particular, we examine how the logic of the electoral college skews the campaign, again, toward a few voters in a few states.

ELECTORAL COLLEGE STRATEGY

A presidential campaign, like a military campaign, relies on sound strategy.[25] The campaign must anticipate and account for a variety of factors, including paid and unpaid media (advertising and news coverage), campaign finance laws, technology (communications and transportation), political (the mood of the country), situational (current events), and even the candidate (style, background, etc.). One of the main elements of a sound campaign strategy is where to take the campaign and to whom. To what regions of the country should the campaign travel? What groups should the campaign attempt to persuade? At first, the answer might appear to be straightforward: to everyone. This, however, would be foolish.

Scholars and pundits know that campaigns group voters into three general categories. There is one group that will never vote for a particular candidate under any circumstances. These voters are typically hard-core or solid opposition partisans, people who strongly identify with the other party. Then there are the voters upon whose vote a candidate can likely depend. These are the people who strongly identify with the candidate's party. These "base" voters are unlikely to vote for the candidate of the other party. The third group, known variously as "swing" or moderate voters, is the group that campaigns try to persuade. How do these voting categories affect a campaign's strategy? A good part of the answer lies in understanding how the electoral college works.

Under the electoral college system, each state has the same number of electors (votes) as it has members of Congress. For example, as of 2004, North Carolina has thirteen members in the House of Representatives and two senators, giving North Carolina fifteen electoral college votes. The District of Columbia is awarded three electors, two for the senators and one for the member of the House that they *would* have, *if* they had congressional representation. Forty-eight states (and D.C.) award all of their electoral college votes to the candidate who wins (according to plurality winner rules) the popular vote in the state.[26] The candidate who wins the majority (not the plurality) of electoral college votes wins the presidency. There are a total of 538 electoral college votes, and a candidate must win 270 electoral college votes to win.

In terms of campaign strategy, it is not necessary to win the popular vote in every state or the popular vote in the country in order to win the election. In fact, a candidate can win the presidency by barely winning in eleven states, provided these are the states that have the largest number of electoral college votes. This means that a candidate can lose, and lose by a wide margin, in the other thirty-nine states (and D.C.).

Table 11.1.   Hypothetical Electoral College Outcome: Democrats Win, Losing Popular Vote in Forty States

	Democratic Candidate			Republican Candidate		
	Percent of Vote	Number of Votes*	E.C. Votes	Percent of Vote	Number of Votes*	E.C. Votes
The Big Eleven	50.01	33.38	271	49.99	33.37	0
The Other Forty	45.00	24.99	0	55.00	30.54	266
Total	47.73	58.37	271	52.27	63.91	267

*Popular vote is in millions of votes.
Note: The Big Eleven consist of California, Texas, New York, Florida, Illinois, Pennsylvania, Ohio, Michigan, Georgia, New Jersey, and North Carolina.

Table 11.1 is a hypothetical outcome of what this scenario might look like, using the actual number of votes cast in each state in 2004. Here the Democratic candidate received a bare majority (50.01 to 49.99 percent) of popular votes in the "Big Eleven," or the states with the most electoral college votes. This gave the Democratic candidate all of the electoral college votes in each of those states, while the Republican candidate received none. The Republican candidate got a larger margin of victory (55 to 45 percent) in the "Other Forty" electoral college units, giving the Republican candidate every electoral college vote in each of these forty. The net result, seen in the last row, is that the Democratic candidate wins the presidency with 271 electoral college votes, with a margin of victory of only 1/100 of 1 percent in each of only eleven states. However, the Democratic candidate loses the nationwide popular vote (47.7 to 52.3 percent).

Of course, it is not likely that the eleven states that are richest in electoral college votes would select the same candidate. The point is that a reasonable move by a campaign might be to craft an electoral college strategy that targets some states for more attention and others for less, based on how competitive they might be and how many electoral college votes are at stake. The history of how different states have voted in the past suggests that putting too much emphasis on certain states, depending on which party the nominee belongs to, is a potential waste of resources. Each party can typically count on certain states for consistent electoral support (for an electoral history of each of the fifty states and D.C., see table 11.2).

PRESIDENTIAL CAMPAIGN STRATEGY

In 1960, John Kennedy was the first presidential candidate to have access to an airplane for his campaign (arranged by his father), and he used it to bring the campaign to almost all fifty states. Since then, this has become the norm for presidential campaigns.[27] But the United States is a fairly

Table 11.2.   Electoral College Outcomes by Party, 1980–2004

State (E.C. Votes)	Rep. Wins*	Dem. Wins*	State (E.C. Votes)	Rep. Wins*	Dem. Wins*
Alabama (9)	7 (7)	0	Montana (3)	6 (3)	1
Alaska (3)	7 (7)	0	Nebraska (5)	7 (7)	0
Arizona (10)	6 (2)	1	Nevada (5)	5 (2)	2
Arkansas (6)	5 (2)	2	New Hampshire (4)	4	3 (1)
California (55)	3	4 (4)	New Jersey (15)	3	4 (4)
Colorado (9)	6 (3)	1	New Mexico (5)	4 (1)	3
Connecticut (7)	3	4 (4)	New York (31)	2	5 (5)
Delaware (3)	3	4 (4)	North Carolina (15)	7 (7)	0
D.C. (3)	0	7 (7)	North Dakota (3)	7 (7)	0
Florida (27)	6 (2)	1	Ohio (20)	5 (2)	2
Georgia (15)	5 (3)	2	Oklahoma (7)	7 (7)	0
Hawaii (4)	1	6 (5)	Oregon (7)	2	5 (5)
Idaho (4)	7 (7)	0	Pennsylvania (21)	3	4 (4)
Illinois (21)	3	4 (4)	Rhode Island (4)	1	6 (5)
Indiana (11)	7 (7)	0	South Carolina (8)	7 (7)	0
Iowa (7)	3 (1)	4	South Dakota (3)	7 (7)	0
Kansas (6)	7 (7)	0	Tennessee (11)	5 (2)	2
Kentucky (8)	5 (2)	2	Texas (34)	7 (7)	0
Louisiana (9)	5 (2)	2	Utah (5)	7 (7)	0
Maine (4)	3	4 (4)	Vermont (3)	3	4 (4)
Maryland (10)	2	5 (4)	Virginia (13)	7 (7)	0
Massachusetts (12)	2	5 (5)	Washington (11)	2	5 (5)
Michigan (17)	3	4 (4)	West Virginia (5)	3 (2)	4
Minnesota (10)	0	7 (7)	Wisconsin (10)	2	5 (5)
Mississippi (6)	7 (7)	0	Wyoming (3)	7 (7)	0
Missouri (11)	5 (2)	2			

*Numbers in parentheses are the number of consecutive wins in that sate for that party's presidential nominee.
Note: Data compiled by authors.

large country, and as such, it is impossible to campaign in every city and town. How much time should be spent in which locales? What regions, cities, and so forth, should be the focus? The question is a matter of degree.

Based on the electoral history of each state (both national and state), state polling data, conditions within the state, and other factors, campaign strategists make a determination of how likely it is that a particular state will vote for the candidate. These states are classified as "safe." Table 11.3 is a gauge of safe states for each party. It is derived by averaging the margin of victory for the winner (in all cases the same party) for the previous two presidential elections. If the margin of victory is greater than 10 percent, we classified the state as safe for that party.

Each party has an almost equal number of electoral college votes from safe states. One major difference is the number of states required to reach

Table 11.3.   Safe States, by Party

Republican States (E.C. Votes)	Democratic States (E.C. Votes)
Texas (34)	California (55)
Georgia (15)	New York (31)
North Carolina (15)	Illinois (21)
Indiana (11)	New Jersey (15)
Alabama (9)	Massachusetts (12)
Louisiana (9)	Maryland (10)
Kentucky (8)	Connecticut (7)
South Carolina (8)	Hawaii (4)
Oklahoma (7)	Rhode Island (4)
Kansas (6)	D.C. (3)
Mississippi (6)	Delaware (3)
Nebraska (5)	Vermont (3)
Utah (5)	Total Democratic: 168
Idaho (4)	
Alaska (3)	
Montana (3)	
North Dakota (3)	
South Dakota (3)	
Wyoming (3)	
Total Republican: 157	

Note: Compiled by authors.

that number, because only two states (California and New York) give the Democrats almost 32 percent of the 270 votes needed to win. Beyond understanding where the base (of safe states) is located, there are a few general rules that guide an electoral college strategy. First, small states, especially those in which the candidate has virtually no chance of winning, can be all but ignored. It makes little sense for a Democratic candidate to spend much time campaigning in Alaska, given that the state (1) has gone Republican in the past seven elections, and (2) there are only three electoral college votes at stake. Similarly, a Republican candidate could safely leave Delaware and Rhode Island out of their campaigning.

A second rule is that large states (California, Texas, New York, Florida, Illinois, Pennsylvania, Ohio) almost always get at least some attention from both party's candidates. For example, in 1976, Jimmy Carter and Gerald Ford targeted seven of the same eight states. Despite the fact that Bob Dole knew that he had no chance of winning in California in 1996, he spent a good deal of time (and approximately four million dollars) during the last three weeks of his campaign in the state.[28] Presidential candidates cannot afford to ignore large states completely. This is because of the large number of electoral college votes in these states and because there is a desire to ensure the party stays competitive in these states in the future.

However, it is generally pointless to much spend time in states where the candidate has little chance of winning. Although some time must be spent bolstering support in areas where the candidate is likely to do well, the central element of presidential campaign strategy consists of identifying states where the candidate has some chance of victory and focusing efforts there. In 1964, Barry Goldwater devoted most of his resources to campaign in the Midwest and West, while all but ignoring the Northeast. Richard Nixon, in 1968, focused on New Jersey, Wisconsin, and Missouri, where he thought he had a chance of defeating Hubert Humphrey, as well as in five border-South states to compete with George Wallace for the southern vote.

The decision on where to focus the campaign is more nuanced. Jimmy Carter's campaign manager, Hamilton Jordan, developed a complex formula that factored in state size, previous and existing Democratic support (based on control of elective offices), and state turnout. After identifying important states, each day of the campaign was scheduled according to state scores and the predetermined value of a Carter, Walter Mondale, or a family member visit.[29] According to one account, "Carter's scheduler Eliot Cutler, convinced that Ohio was the key to the race, scheduled 65% of vice-presidential candidate Mondale's time there in the last two weeks of the campaign (Carter won Ohio by 8,000 votes)."[30] In 1996, Clinton pollster Mark Penn devised a seven-variable model that he used to allocate television advertising dollars, including electoral history, advertising costs, number of persuadable voters, and impact of prospective ads on House and Senate races.[31]

Political scientist Daron Shaw examined the electoral strategies of both Democratic and Republican presidential candidates from 1988 through 1996. The first part of his analysis presented the states that campaign managers considered to be important to their effort (see table 11.4). Pure battleground states are those that both campaigns consider to be critical to their efforts. The mixed battleground–marginal states are those that were battleground states for one campaign and marginal opposition states for the other. There were roughly twenty states in total that were identified by both campaigns as being important to the campaign.

How exactly did this importance translate into the campaign effort? Using various data, Shaw shows that from September 1 through Election Day, the average amount of spending for campaign advertising in battleground states for three election cycles was more than quadruple that for each party's respective base states. Spending in marginal Democratic or Republican states was almost double that for spending in base states. Additionally, both Democratic and Republican candidates made more appearances in battleground or marginal states than in their base states. While the data show variation between election cycles and partisans, a

Chapter 11

Table 11.4. Geographic Focus, Presidential Campaigns, 1988–1996

Year	Pure Battleground States	Mixed Battleground–Marginal States
1988	California, Missouri, Ohio, Texas	Connecticut, Delaware, Illinois, Maine, Michigan, New York, New Jersey, Oregon, Pennsylvania, Vermont, Washington, Wisconsin
1992	Georgia, Michigan, Mississippi, New Jersey, Ohio	Colorado, Kentucky, Louisiana, Maine, Missouri, Montana, New Mexico, North Carolina, Pennsylvania, Wisconsin
1996	Louisiana, Nevada, New Mexico	Arizona, California, Colorado, Florida, Georgia, Kentucky, New Hampshire, New Jersey, Ohio, Tennessee

Source: Daron R. Shaw, "The Methods behind the Madness: Presidential Electoral College Strategies, 1988–1996," *Journal of Politics* 61 (1999): 899, 901, 903, tables 1A–1C.

pattern of resource allocation favoring battleground or marginal states is clear (see table 11.5).

A similar pattern emerges in 2000 and 2004 (see table 11.6). An index of battleground states in these two election cycles was created by using a simplified calculus. The criterion for inclusion was whether the average vote margin from 2000 and 2004 was under 10 percent. Data were then added tracking candidate visits to each state in 2000. These data represent the combined number of times that Bush, Dick Cheney, Gore, or Lieberman visited the state from October 18 through November 7, 2000. The data for candidate visits in 2004 are the total number of visits by Bush or Kerry to the state from March through November 2004. Finally, the last column indicates whether the state had one of the top ten media markets in terms of the money spent on campaign advertising.

Table 11.5. Resource Allocation in Presidential Campaigns, 1988–1996

Type of State	Rep. TV Advertising*	Dem. TV Advertising	Rep. Cand. Appearances	Dem. Cand. Appearances
Base Republican	1,646	1,200	0.7	0.7
Marginal Republican	5,577	1,797	3.5	1.5
Battleground	6,345	5,328	5.2	5.0
Marginal Democratic	3,232	3,501	4.4	2.5
Base Democratic	1,593	1,616	0.8	2.0

*TV advertising is the total number of gross ratings points (GRP) for all markets in each state. A GRP is a measure for audience reach and is an estimate of how many voters have seen an advertisement, for example, a score of one hundred GRPs would mean that 100 percent of voters would have seen an advertisement once.

Source: Daron R. Shaw, "The Methods behind the Madness: Presidential Electoral College Strategies, 1988–1996," *Journal of Politics* 61 (1999): 908, table 3.

Table 11.6.   Presidential Candidate Resource Allocation in Battleground States, 2000 and 2004

State (E.C. Votes)	Avg. Margin, 2000 and 2004	Cand. Visits, 2000	Cand. Visits, 2004	Top Media Market, 2004?
Florida (27)	2.5	13	29	Yes
Pennsylvania (21)	3.3	17	38	Yes
Ohio (20)	2.8	2	43	Yes
Michigan (17)	4.3	14	20	Yes
Virginia (13)	8.1	0	5	No
Missouri (11)	5.3	9	13	No
Washington (11)	6.4	6	4	No
Tennessee (11)	9.1	10	0	No
Wisconsin (10)	0.3	15	28	Yes
Minnesota (10)	2.9	6	15	Yes
Arizona (10)	8.4	0	7	No
Colorado (9)	6.5	0	10	Yes
Iowa (7)	0.5	9	25	Yes
Oregon (7)	2.3	6	5	No
Arkansas (6)	7.6	5	3	No
New Mexico (5)	0.4	7	12	Yes
Nevada (5)	3.1	5	10	Yes
West Virginia (5)	9.6	5	14	No
New Hampshire (4)	1.3	4	11	No
Maine (4)	7.1	4	0	No

Source: Strategic ranking calculated by authors. Media markets data for September 24 through October 7, 2004, from "Presidential TV Advertising Battle Narrows to Just Ten Battleground States," Nielsen Monitor-Plus and the University of Wisconsin Advertising Project, October 12, 2004, at www.nielsenmedia.com/monitor-plus/ in_the_news/releases/PoliticalReleaseOctober12_2004.htm. "Candidate visits 2000" data from David C. King and David Morehouse, "Moving Voters in the 2000 Presidential Campaign: Local Visits, Local Media," KSG Working Paper No. RWP04–003, January 14, 2004, at ssrn.com/abstract=489644, 11, table 1. "Candidate visits 2004" data from "The Fall Campaign: President Bush and Senator Kerry Visits by State," Democracy in Action, at www.gwu.edu/%7Eaction/2004/chrnfall.html.

Again, there is a fair amount of variation here with respect to battleground state status and resource allocation, especially in terms of major media market status. However, a similar pattern is clear: Of all of the states that received more than one candidate visit in 2000, only seven do not show up on this list (Illinois, six visits; New York, five visits; California, Louisiana, and New Jersey, four visits; Texas, three visits; and Indiana, two visits). All are fairly large states, and of those that received more than two visits in 2004, only four states are not on the battleground list (California, eight visits; Illinois and Louisiana, five visits; Georgia, four visits). In general, there is a maldistribution of resources in the fall campaign. The findings presented in this chapter correspond to other studies as well.[32] The fall campaign is not a true national campaign but rather an effort disproportionately targeted to a few voters in a small number of critical states.

CONCLUSION

To be clear, there are some truly national aspects of presidential campaigns worth acknowledging. First, news about the primary campaign is certainly national in its scope and reach. Second, reporting the results of national polls about presidential preferences likely has some impact on voters in the early primary states. Third, during the fall campaign, all Americans are aware of and can access information about what the presidential candidates are saying. By this point in the campaign, news stories about the campaign are ubiquitous.

Our point, however, is that some states are more equal than others with respect to the campaign. Attention and resources are maldistributed in the primary season and are heavily weighted toward the earliest delegate selection events. In the fall campaign, battleground states dominate. In short, while all citizens can participate, some have greater opportunities for *meaningful* participation.

FOR MORE READING

Baumgartner, Jody. *Modern Presidential Electioneering: An Organizational and Comparative Approach*. Westport, Conn.: Praeger, 2000.

Polsby, Nelson W., and Aaron Wildavsky. *Presidential Elections: Strategies and Structures of American Politics*. 11th ed. Lanham, Md.: Rowman & Littlefield, 2004.

Wayne, Stephen J. *The Road to the White House, 2004: The Politics of Presidential Elections*. Belmont, Calif.: Wadsworth, 2004.

Notes

PREFACE

1. Dave Montgomery, "Scare Tactics Make Ugliest Race in Years," *Pittsburgh Post-Gazette*, October 30, 2004, A6.

2. Robert Redford's character, Bill McKay, ran for a Senate seat in California in *The Candidate*; however, the movie's theme supports the popular notion that image matters most in American elections.

3. A 2000 Roper poll, for example, reported that 56 percent of Americans believe that a candidate's image matters a "great deal" in winning the White House. By comparison, the same poll showed that fewer Americans believe that a candidate's stand on foreign policy issues matters a "great deal" (46 percent); that a candidate's political experience matters a "great deal" (43 percent); or that a candidate's personal behavior matters a "great deal" (48 percent). Even the candidate's stand on social issues ranked the same in importance as image (56 percent). Figures were obtained from a LexisNexis Academic Reference Search of Polls and Surveys, Roper Center, "Public Opinion Online," February 16, 2000, Question Numbers 030–035.

CHAPTER 1

1. This includes polls conducted by the Harvard Institute of Politics and the Pew Research Center. See Joe Garofoli, "Youth Vote," November 3, 2004, at sfgate.com/cgi-bin/article.cgi.

2. John Della Volpe, "Campus Kids: The New Swing Voter," Harvard University Institute of Politics, May 21, 2003, at www.iop.harvard.edu/pdfs/survey/spring_2003.pdf.

175

3. Figures were obtained from a LexisNexis Academic Reference Search of Polls and Surveys, Roper Center, "Public Opinion Online," January 24, 2004, Question Number 073.

4. "Hillary Clinton tells P. Diddy 'Vote or Die' Slogan Hits Nail on the Head," MTV, August 5, 2004, at www.mtv.com/chooseorlose/headlines/news.jhtml?id =1489969.

5. Jose Antonio Vargas, "Vote or Die? Well, They Did Vote," *Washington Post*, November 9, 2004, C1.

6. Michael Hoover and Susan Orr, "Youth Political Engagement: Why Rock the Vote Hits the Wrong Note," in *Fountain of Youth: Strategies and Tactics for Mobilizing America's Young Voters*, ed. Daniel M. Shea and John C. Green (Lanham, Md.: Rowman & Littlefield, 2007), 141–62.

7. Figures were obtained from the Center for Information and Research on Civic Learning and Engagement (CIRCLE).

8. Stephen Watson, "Younger Voters Came Out at High Rate, but Percentage of Total Didn't Change," *Buffalo News*, November 9, 2004, B6.

9. Sarah Childress, "Not Slackers After All?" *Newsweek*, November 12, 2004, at www.msnbc.msn.com/id/6471283/site/newsweek.

10. Christina Nifong, "Candidates Court 'Twentysomethings,'" *Christian Science Monitor*, March 6, 1996, 4.

11. Figure was obtained from the Center for Information and Research on Civic Learning and Engagement (CIRCLE).

12. C. Frederick Risinger, "Encouraging Students to Participate in the Political Process," *Social Education* 67 (2003): 338–46.

13. *Oregon v. Mitchell*, 400 U.S. 112 (1970).

14. Analysts use several different measures to report voter turnout. The following two measures use the number of votes cast as the numerator in the equation. "Voting age population" (VAP) uses the number of citizens who are eighteen years or older as the denominator. Another method, "voting eligible population" (VEP), takes the number of citizens who are eligible to vote as the denominator. Since this number excludes illegal aliens, felons in many states, and some others, this number is smaller, leading to a higher percentage reported. The statistics reported in this chapter are derived by a method similar to deriving VEP statistics. See Mark Hugo Lopez, Emily Kirby, and Jared Sagoff, "The Youth Vote 2004, with a Historical Look at Youth Voting Patterns, 1972–2004," Working Paper 35, Center for Information and Research on Civic Learning and Engagement, July 2005.

15. Institute of Politics, "Attitudes towards Politics and Public Service: A National Survey of College Undergraduates," April 11–20, 2000, at www.iop .harvard.edu/pdfs/survey/2000.pdf.

16. Donald P. Green and Ron Shachar, "Habit Formation and Political Behaviour: Evidence of Consuetude in Voter Turnout," *British Journal of Political Science* 30:561–73.

17. Eric Plutzer, "Becoming a Habitual Voter: Inertia, Resources, and Growth in Young Adulthood," *American Political Science Review* 96 (2002): 41–56.

18. William H. Riker and Peter C. Ordeshook, "A Theory of the Calculus of Voting," *American Political Science Review* 62 (1968): 25–42; Anthony Downs, *An Economic Theory of Democracy* (New York: Harper, 1957).

19. See, for example, Angus Campbell, Philip E. Converse, Warren E. Miller, and Donald E. Stokes, *The American Voter* (New York: Wiley, 1960); Gregory A. Caldeira, Samuel C. Patterson, and Gregory A. Markko, "The Mobilization of Voters in Congressional Elections," *Journal of Politics* 47 (1985): 490–509; Samuel J. Eldersveld, "Experimental Propaganda Techniques and Voting Behavior," *American Political Science Review* 50 (1956): 154–65. For more on general reasons why people do not vote, see Nelson W. Polsby and Aaron Wildavsky, *Presidential Elections: Strategies and Structures of American Politics*, 11th ed. (Lanham, Md.: Rowman & Littlefield, 2004), chap. 1.

20. Raymond E. Wolfinger and Steven J. Rosenstone, *Who Votes?* (New Haven, Conn.: Yale University Press, 1980); G. Bingham Powell Jr., "American Voter Turnout in Comparative Perspective," *American Political Science Review* 80 (1986): 17–43.

21. Thomas E. Patterson, "Young Voters and the 2004 Election," Joan Shorenstein Center on the Press, Politics, and Public Policy, at www.ksg.harvard.edu/presspol/vanishvoter/Releases/Vanishing_Voter_Final_Report_2004_Election.pdf.

22. In almost all elections in the United States, the Australian ballot is used, which lists each office separately. Another balloting system is used in parliamentary elections, where citizens are presented with a list of party candidates, from which they choose one party list.

23. Robert D. Putnam, *Bowling Alone: The Collapse and Revival of American Community* (New York: Simon & Schuster, 2000).

24. Institute of Politics, "Attitudes towards Politics and Public Service."

25. John P. Katosh and Michael W. Traugott, "Costs and Values in the Calculus of Voting," *American Journal of Political Science* 26:361–76; for more information about trust in government, see Joseph S. Nye Jr., Philip D. Zelikow, and David C. King, ed., *Why People Don't Trust Government* (Cambridge, Mass.: Harvard University Press, 1997).

26. Steven J. Rosenstone and John Mark Hanson, *Mobilization, Participation, and Democracy in America* (New York: Macmillan, 1993); Cornelius P. Cotter, James L. Gibson, John F. Bibby, and Robert J. Huckshorn, *Party Organizations in American Politics* (New York: Praeger, 1984).

27. Ted Halstead, "A Politics for Generation X," *Atlantic Monthly*, August 1999.

28. Institute of Politics, "Attitudes towards Politics and Public Service."

29. Karon Reinboth Speckman, "Who Did a Better Job Informing Youth Voters in the 2000 Election—TV Network News or Online News?" *White House Studies* (Fall 2002).

30. Institute of Politics, "Attitudes towards Politics and Public Service."

31. Institute of Politics, "Attitudes towards Politics and Public Service."

32. John R. Hibbing and Elizabeth Theiss-Morse, *Stealth Democracy: Americans' Beliefs About How Government Should Work* (New York: Cambridge University Press, 2002).

33. George Will, "In Defense of Nonvoting," in *The Morning After*, ed. George Will (New York: Free Press, 1986).

34. This was an argument advanced by many classical political theorists including Aristotle and John Stuart Mill.

35. For an excellent discussion on these last two points, see Richard Hasen, "Voting Without Law," *University of Pennsylvania Law Review* 44 (1996): 2135–79.

36. Powell, "American Voter Turnout in Comparative Perspective"; Mark Franklin, "Electoral Engineering and Cross-National Differences: What Role for Compulsory Voting?" *British Journal of Political Science* 29 (1999).

37. Allie Shah, "The Young Head for the Polls," *Star Tribune*, October 26, 2004, A01.

38. Jo Becker, "Voters May Have Their Say before Election Day," *Washington Post*, August 26, 2004, A01.

39. Institute of Politics, "Attitudes towards Politics and Public Service."

40. Abby Goodnough and Jim Yardley, "In Florida, Early Voting Means Early Woes," *New York Times*, October 19, 2004, A19.

41. Robert M. Stein and Patricia A. Garcia-Monet, "Voting Early but Not Often," *Social Science Quarterly* 78 (1997): 657–71.

42. Institute of Politics, "Attitudes towards Politics and Public Service."

43. Diana Burgess, Beth Haney, Mark Snyder, John L. Sullivan, and John E. Transue, "Rocking the Vote: Using Personalized Messages to Motivate Voting among Young Adults," *Public Opinion Quarterly* 64 (2000): 29–52.

44. Alan Gerber and Donald Green, "The Effects of Canvassing, Telephone Calls, and Direct Mail on Voter Turnout: A Field Experiment," *American Political Science Review* 94 (2000): 653–63.

CHAPTER 2

1. Jill Lawrence, "Values, Votes, and Points of View Separate Towns—and Nation," *USA Today*, February 18, 2002, A10. See also E. J. Dionne Jr., "One Nation Deeply Divided," *Washington Post*, November 7, 2003, A31.

2. Scott Shepard, "Bush-Kerry Contest a Sharp Contrast in Charting America's Future," *Cox News Service*, March 6, 2004.

3. Quoted in James Q. Wilson, "How Divided Are We?" *Commentary Magazine* (February 2006), at www.commentarymagazine.com/cm/main/viewArticle.aip ?id=10023. The quotation does not reflect Wilson's own view of Republicans or Democrats but rather reflects what he believes are the extreme popular perceptions of them.

4. Quoted in E. J. Dionne Jr., "What Kind of Hater Are You?" *Washington Post*, March 15, 2006, A19. Again, to be clear, the quotation does not reflect Dionne's own view of Republicans or Democrats but rather reflects what he believes are the extreme popular perceptions of them.

5. Wilson, "How Divided Are We?"

6. Dionne, "What Kind of Hater Are You?" A19.

7. Karen M. Kaufmann, "The Gender Gap," *PS: Political Science & Politics* 39 (2006): 447–53.

8. James Davison Hunter, *Culture Wars: The Struggle to Define America* (New York: Basic Books, 1991).

9. Dick Meyer, "The Official Start of the Culture War," *CBS News*, July 22, 2004, at www.cbsnews.com/stories/2004/07/21/opinion/meyer/main631126.shtml.

10. Quoted in Linda Feldmann, "How Lines of the Culture War Have Been Redrawn," *Christian Science Monitor*, November 15, 2004, at www.csmonitor.com/2004/1115/p01s04-ussc.html.

11. E. J. Dionne Jr., "Why the Culture War Is the Wrong War," *Atlantic Monthly*, January/February 2006, at www.theatlantic.com/doc/prem/200601/culture-war.

12. Edward J. Larson, *Summer for the Gods: The Scopes Trial and America's Continuing Debate over Science and Religion* (Cambridge, Mass.: Harvard University Press, 1998).

13. Ellen Chesler, *Woman of Valor: Margaret Sanger and the Birth Control Movement in America* (New York: Simon and Schuster, 1992).

14. Dionne, "Why the Culture War Is the Wrong War."

15. Dionne, "Why the Culture War Is the Wrong War."

16. Meyer, "The Official Start of the Culture War."

17. Everett Carll Ladd, "The 1992 Vote for President Clinton: Another Brittle Mandate?" *Political Science Quarterly* 108 (1993): 1–28.

18. Alan I. Abramowitz, "It's Abortion Stupid: Policy Voting in the 1992 Presidential Election," *Journal of Politics* 57 (1995): 176–86.

19. Gary C. Jacobson, *A Divider, Not a Uniter: George W. Bush and the American People* (New York: Longman, 2007).

20. Peter L. Francia and Jody C. Baumgartner, "Victim or Victor of the 'Culture War'? How Cultural Issues Affect Support for George W. Bush in Rural America," *American Review of Politics* 26 (Fall/Winter 2005–2006): 349–67.

21. Figures were obtained from a LexisNexis Academic Reference Search of Polls and Surveys, Roper Center, "Public Opinion Online," November 19, 2006, Question Number 003.

22. Ruy Teixeira, "Lessons of the 2004 Election," November 3, 2004, at www.emergingdemocraticmajorityweblog.com/donkeyrising/archives/000923.php. For the most thorough and well-known account advancing this thesis, see Thomas Frank, *What's the Matter with Kansas? How Conservatives Won the Heart of America* (New York: Metropolitan Books, 2004).

23. Ronald M. Peter, "America in Red and Blue," *Extensions* (Fall 2005): 2.

24. Andrew Gelman, Boris Shor, Joseph Bafumi, and David Park, "Rich State, Poor State, Red State, Blue State: What's the Matter with Connecticut?" November 30, 2005, at www.stat.columbia.edu/~gelman/research/unpublished/redblue11.pdf.

25. Stephen Ansolabehere, Jonathan Rodden, and James M. Snyder Jr., "Purple America," February 6, 2006, at web.mit.edu/polisci/portl/material/papers/purple_final_feb6_061.pdf.

26. Morris P. Fiorina, Samuel J. Abrams, and Jeremy C. Pope, *Culture War? The Myth of a Polarized America* (New York: Longman, 2005).

27. Fiorina, Abrams, and Pope, *Culture War?*

28. James A. McCann, "Nomination Politics and Ideological Polarization: Assessing the Attitudinal Effects of Campaign Involvement," *Journal of Politics* 57 (1995): 101–20; John S. Jackson, Nathan S. Bigelow, and John C. Green, "The State of Party Elites: National Convention Delegates," in *The State of the Parties*, ed. John C. Green and Rick D. Farmer (Lanham, Md.: Rowman & Littlefield, 2003); Peter L. Francia, John C. Green, Paul S. Herrnson, Lynda W. Powell, and Clyde Wilcox, "Limousine Liberals and Corporate Conservatives: The Financial Constituencies of the Democratic and Republican Parties," *Social Science Quarterly* 86 (2005): 761–78.

29. Keith T. Poole and Howard Rosenthal, *Congress: A Political Economic History of Roll-Call Voting* (New York: Oxford University Press, 1997).

30. Alan Abramowitz and Kyle Saunders, "Why Can't We All Just Get Along? The Reality of a Polarized America," *Forum* 3 (2005): article 1, at www.bepress.com/forum/vol3/iss2/art1.

31. Abramowitz and Saunders, "Why Can't We All Just Get Along?"

32. Byron E. Shafer and Richard Johnston, *The End of Southern Exceptionalism* (Cambridge, Mass.: Harvard University Press, 2006).

33. Jonathan Kuckey, "A New Front in the Culture War? Moral Traditionalism and Voting Behavior in U.S. House Elections," *American Politics Research* 33 (2005): 645–71.

34. Abramowitz and Saunders, "Why Can't We All Just Get Along?"

35. Laura R. Olson and John C. Green, "The Religion Gap," *PS: Political Science and Politics* 39 (2006): 455–59.

36. Robert Wuthnow, *The Restructuring of American Religion: Society and Faith since World War II* (Princeton, N.J.: Princeton University Press, 1988).

37. Steven Waldman and John C. Green, "Tribal Relations," *Atlantic Monthly*, January/February 2006, at www.theatlantic.com/doc/prem/200601/tribal-relations.

38. Waldman and Green, "Tribal Relations."

39. Ann Coulter, *Godless: The Church of Liberalism* (New York: Crown Forum, 2006), 4, 21–22.

40. Waldman and Green, "Tribal Relations."

41. Waldman and Green, "Tribal Relations."

42. Ted G. Jelen, *The Political Mobilization of Religious Beliefs* (New York: Praeger, 1991); John C. Green, James L. Guth, and Kevin Hill, "Faith and Election: The Christian Right in Congressional Campaigns, 1978–1988," *Journal of Politics* 55 (1993): 80–91; Kuckey, "A New Front in the Culture War?; Clyde Wilcox and Carin Larson, *Onward Christian Soldiers? The Religious Right in American Politics*, 3rd ed. (Boulder, Colo.: Westview, 2006).

43. Feldmann, "How Lines of the Culture War Have Been Redrawn," at www.csmonitor.com/2004/1115/p01s04-ussc.html.

44. Fiorina, Abrams, and Pope, *Culture War?*

45. Jonathan Rauch, "The Widening Marriage Gap: America's New Class Divide," May 23, 2001, at www.theatlantic.com/politics/nj/rauch2001–05-23.htm.

46. Fred I. Greenstein and Raymond E. Wolfinger, "The Suburbs and Shifting Party Loyalties," *Public Opinion Quarterly* 22 (1958): 473–82.

47. Robin M. Wolpert and James G. Gimpel, "Self-Interest, Symbolic Politics, and Public Attitudes toward Gun Control," *Political Behavior* 20 (1998): 241–62.

48. Fiorina, Abrams, and Pope, *Culture War?* 5.

CHAPTER 3

1. We wish to acknowledge the contributions to this chapter made by Bruce Keith et al., *The Myth of the Independent Voter* (Berkeley: University of California Press, 1992), and Michael P. McDonald and Samuel Popkin, "The Myth of the Vanishing Voter," *American Political Science Review* 95 (2001): 963–74.

2. See, for example, Morris P. Fiorina, Paul E. Peterson, with Bertram Johnson, *The New American Democracy*, 3rd ed. (New York: Longman, 2003), 164–65.

3. John Dean, "Why Americans Don't Vote—and How That Might Change," WritLegal Commentary, CNN Interactive, November 8, 2000, at edition.cnn.com/2000/LAW/11/columns/fl.dean.voters.02.11.07/; "Voter Turnout May Slip Again," Pew Research Center for the People and the Press, July 13, 2000, at people-press.org/reports/print.php3?PageID=194; John Gray, "Trends in Increasing Voter Apathy Point to a Record Lack of Interest in Casting Ballots This Presidential Election," Toronto *Globe and Mail*, October 28, 2000, at www.commondreams.org/headlines/102800–03.htm.

4. See Bryan Mercurio, "Democracy in Decline: Can Internet Voting Save the Electoral Process?" *John Marshall Journal of Computer & Information Law* 22 (2) (2004).

5. Ruy A. Teixeira, *Why Americans Don't Vote: Turnout Decline in the United States, 1960–1984* (Westport, Conn.: Greenwood, 1987); Ruy A. Teixeira, *The Disappearing American Voter* (Washington, D.C.: Brookings Institution, 1992); Frances Fox Piven and Richard A. Cloward, *Why Americans Don't Vote* (New York: Pantheon, 1988); Frances Fox Piven and Richard A. Cloward, *Why Americans Still Don't Vote: And Why Politicians Want It That Way* (Boston: Beacon, 2000); Mark Lawrence Kornbluh, *Why America Stopped Voting: The Decline of Participatory Democracy and the Emergence of Modern American Politics* (New York: New York University, 2000); Martin P. Wattenberg, *Where Have All the Voters Gone?* (Cambridge, Mass.: Harvard University Press, 2002).

6. Raymond E. Wolfinger and Steven J. Rosenstone, *Who Votes?* (New Haven, Conn.: Yale University Press, 1980); Walter Dean Burnham, "The Turnout Problem," in *Elections American Style*, ed. A. James Reichley (Washington, D.C.: Brookings Institution, 1987); Mark N. Franklin, *Voter Turnout and the Dynamics of Electoral Competition in Established Democracies since 1945* (New York: Cambridge University Press, 2004); and David Lee Hill, *American Voter Turnout: An Institutional Approach* (Boulder, Colo.: Westview, 2006); Lisa Hill, "Low Voter Turnout in the United States: Is Compulsory Voting a Viable Solution?" *Journal of Theoretical Politics* 18(2) (April 2006); Arend Lijphart, "Unequal Participation: Democracy's Unresolved Dilemma," *American Political Science Review* 91 (1997): 1–14.

7. "About the Project," Vanishing Voter Project, at www.vanishingvoter.org/about.shtml.

8. See G. Bingham Powell Jr., "American Voter Turnout in Comparative Perspective," *American Political Science Review* 80 (1986): 17–43.

9. Earlier theorists posited that full participation might make compromise and accommodation less possible (Bernard Berelson, Paul Lazarsfeld, and William McPhee, *Voting* [Chicago: University of Chicago Press, 1954], 314). Several empirical studies suggest that nonvoters are not significantly different in their political attitudes than are voters (Austin Ranney, "Nonvoting Is Not a Social Disease," in *Points of View: Readings in American Government and Politics*, ed. Robert DiClerico and Allan Hammock, 8th ed. [Boston: McGraw-Hill, 2000]), that increased levels of nonvoting does mean increased citizen alienation (Warren E. Miller, "Disinterest, Disaffection, and Participation in Presidential Politics," *Political Behavior* 2 [1980]:

7–32), and that full participation would not dramatically alter the results of most elections (Ruy A. Teixeira, "Just How Much Difference Does Turnout Really Make?" *The American Enterprise* [July/August 1992]: 52–59).

10. This section draws on Elizabeth M. Yang, "History of Voting in the United States," in *The U.S. Election System*, ed. Paul McCaffrey (New York: H. W. Wilson, 2004); William H. Flanigan and Nancy H. Zingale, *Political Behavior of the American Electorate*, 11th ed. (Washington D.C.: CQ Press, 2005), 35–40; and Alexander Keyssar, *The Right to Vote: The Contested History of Democracy in the United States* (New York: Basic Books, 2001).

11. Flanigan and Zingale, *Political Behavior of the American Electorate*, 41.

12. Flanigan and Zingale, *Political Behavior of the American Electorate*, 41.

13. McDonald and Popkin, "The Myth of the Vanishing Voter."

14. Philip E. Converse, "Change in the American Electorate," in *The Human Meaning of Social Change*, ed. Angus Campbell and Philip E. Converse (New York: Russell Sage, 1972).

15. For an excellent review of voter fraud in the 1800s, see Peter H. Argersinger, "New Perspectives on Election Fraud in the Gilded Age," *Political Science Quarterly* 100 (Winter 1985–1986): 669–87.

16. McDonald and Popkin, "The Myth of the Vanishing Voter," 964.

17. Jerrold G. Rusk, "The Effect of the Australian Ballot Reform on Split Ticket Voting: 1876–1908," *American Political Science Review* 64 (1970): 1220–38.

18. Russell J. Dalton, *Citizen Politics: Public Opinion and Political Parties in Advanced Industrial Democracies*, 3rd ed. (New York: Chatham House, 2002).

19. John P. Avlon, "Independent Voters Burgeoning," *New York Sun*, April 28, 2006, at www.nysun.com/article/31852; Rhodes Cook, "Moving On: More Voters Are Steering Away from Party Labels," *Washington Post*, June 27, 2004, B01. See also David Lesher and Mark Baldassare, "California's Independent Streak," *Los Angeles Times*, February 19, 2006, M01; Greg Lucas, "Number of Independent Voters at Record High Statewide," *San Francisco Chronicle*, October 27, 2000, A06; Dave Denison, "State of Independents," *Boston Globe*, January 22, 2006, E01; Gary J. Andres, "Shrinking Center," *Washington Times*, April 27, 2006, A23.

20. "Polling Results: Independent Voters Hold Key to NJ Senate Race," January 25, 2006, Quinnipiac University Poll, at www.quinnipiac.edu/x1299.xml?ReleaseID=867.

21. George C. Edwards III, Martin P. Wattenberg, and Robert L. Lineberry, *Government in America: People, Politics, and Policy*, Study Edition, Brief Version (New York: Longman, 2002), emphasis in original. Among others, see also "The Election: Turbulence and Tranquility," in *The Elections of 1999*, ed. Michael Nelson (Washington, D.C.: CQ Press, 1997), 63–64.

22. David Broder, *The Party's Over: The Failure of Politics in America* (New York: Harper, 1972).

23. Paul Allen Beck and Marjorie Random Hershey, *Party Politics in America*, 9th ed. (New York: Longman, 2001), 118. To be fair, some parties, campaigns, and elections texts have not been taken with the notion of growing numbers of independents. See, for example, Nelson Polsby and Aaron Wildavsky, *Presidential Elections*, 10th ed. (Chatham, N.J.: Chatham House, 2000), 18; William J. Keefe and Marc J. Hetherington, *Parties, Politics, and Public Policy in America*, 9th ed. (Washington, D.C.: CQ Press, 2003), 173–76.

24. Barry C. Burden and Steven Greene, "Party Attachments and State Election Laws," *Political Research Quarterly* 53 (2000): 63–76; Steven E. Finkel and Howard A. Scarrow, "Party Identification and Party Enrollment: The Difference and the Consequences," *Journal of Politics* 47 (1985): 620–42.

25. See Russell J. Dalton, *Citizen Politics: Public Opinion and Political Parties in Advanced Industrial Democracies*, 3rd ed. (New York: Chatham House, 2002), 183–86.

26. For the classic formulation of this theory, see Martin P. Wattenberg, *The Decline of American Political Parties, 1952–1996* (Cambridge, Mass.: Harvard University Press, 1998).

27. See "The Origins of NES," at www.electionstudies.org/overview/origins .htm.

28. See "About ANES, 2006–2009," at www.electionstudies.org/overview/ overview.htm.

29. This question is variable VCF0301 in the current NES Cumulative Data File data set. See "Party Identification 7-Point Scale 1952–2004," at www.electionstudies .org/nesguide/toptable/tab2a_1.htm.

30. Angus Campbell, Gerald Gurin, and Warren E. Miller, *The Voter Decides* (Evanston, Ill.: Row, Peterson, 1954); Angus Campbell, Philip E. Converse, Warren E. Miller, and Donald E. Stokes, *The American Voter* (New York: Wiley, 1960).

31. Anthony Downs, in *An Economic Theory of Democracy* (New York: Harper, 1957), suggested that citizens select candidates or parties based on proximity to their own preferences. V. O. Key Jr., in *The Responsible Electorate: Rationality in Presidential Voting 1936–1960* (Cambridge, Mass.: Belknap, 1966), argued that voters are more rational than *The American Voter* suggests. Samuel L. Popkin, in *The Reasoning Voter: Communication and Persuasion in Presidential Campaigns* (Chicago: University of Chicago Press, 1991), updates Key's theory with particular attention to the effects of the media. Morris P. Fiorina argued in *Retrospective Voting in American National Elections* (New Haven, Conn.: Yale University Press, 1981) that citizens base their voting choices on the past performance of politicians and parties.

32. See Paul Allen Beck, "A Socialization Theory of Partisan Realignment," in *The Politics of Future Citizens*, ed. Richard G. Niemi (San Francisco: Jossey-Bass, 1974); Philip E. Converse, *The Dynamics of Party Support: Cohort-Analyzing Party Identification* (Beverly Hills, Calif.: Sage, 1976); Paul R. Abramson, "Developing Party Identification: A Further Examination of Life-cycle, Generational, and Period Effects," *American Journal of Political Science* 23 (1979): 78–96; and Paul Allen Beck and M. Kent Jennings, "Family Traditions, Political Periods, and the Development of Partisan Orientations," *Journal of Politics* 53 (1991): 742–63.

33. Barry C. Burden and Casey A. Klofstad, "Affect and Cognition in Party Identification," *Political Psychology* 26 (2005): 869–86.

34. See, for example, Gary C. Jacobson, "The Bush Presidency and the American Electorate," *Presidential Studies Quarterly* 33 (2003): 701–29; Marc D. Weiner, "Responsible Mass Partisanship in the 2004 Election," prepared for presentation at The State of the Parties: 2004 and Beyond, Bliss Institute, University of Akron, October 2005; Geoffrey C. Layman, Thomas M. Carsey, and Juliana Menasce Horowitz, "Party Polarization in American Politics: Characteristics, Causes, and Consequences," *Annual Review of Political Science* 9:83–110.

35. Martin P. Wattenberg, "Turnout Decline in the U.S. and Other Advanced Industrial Democracies," Center for the Study of Democracy, University of California, Irvine, 1998, at www.democ.uci.edu/publications/papersseriespre2001/marty.html.

CHAPTER 4

1. Evan I. Schwartz, "Are you ready for the Democracy Channel?" *Wired*, 2.01, January 1994, at www.wirednews.com/wired/archive/2.01/e.dem.html; Edwin Diamond, Martha Mckay, and Robert Silverman, "Pop Goes Politics New Media, Interactive Formats, and the 1992 Presidential Campaign," *American Behavioral Scientist* 37 (1993): 257–61.

2. Tracy Westen, "Can Technology Save Democracy?" *National Civic Review* 87 (1) (1998): 47–56; Stephen Coleman, "Can the New Media Invigorate Democracy?" *Political Quarterly* 70 (1999): 16–22; Richard Morris, *VOTE.com* (Los Angeles: Renaissance Books, 1999); Kelley Beaucar Vlahos, "Internet Campaigns Generate Buzz for 2004," Fox News, June 26, 2003, at www.foxnews.com/story/0,2933,90307,00.html; Adam Nagourney, "Internet Injects Sweeping Change into U.S. Politics," *New York Times*, April 2, 2006, A1; Martin Walker, "Howard Dean's Revolution," United Press International, November 12, 2003; Joe Trippi, *The Revolution Will Not Be Televised: Democracy, the Internet, and the Overthrow of Everything* (New York: Regan Books, 2004); Everett Ehrlich, "What Will Happen When a National Political Machine Can Fit on a Laptop?" *Washington Post*, December 14, 2003, B1.

3. See Jody Baumgartner and Carmine Scavo, "World Wide Web Site Design and Use in Public Management," in *Public Information Technology: Policy and Management Issues*, ed. G. David Garson, 3rd ed. (Hershey, Pa.: Idea Group Publishing, 2007).

4. This section draws heavily on the discussion in Michael Cornfield, *Politics Moves Online: Campaigning and the Internet* (New York: Century Foundation Press, 2004), 3–5, and Philip N. Howard, *New Media Campaigns and the Managed Citizen* (Cambridge, UK: Cambridge University Press, 2006), 8–17.

5. Cornfield, *Politics Moves Online*, 3.

6. This information is in the public domain and can be found by typing in the domain name at www.nwtools.com/.

7. Michael Margolis, David Resnick, and Jonathan Levy, "Major Parties Dominate, Minor Parties Struggle: US Elections and the Internet," in *Political Parties on the Internet: Net Gain?* ed. Rachel Gibson, Paul Nixon, and Stephen Ward (London: Routledge, 2003), 54.

8. Cornfield, *Politics Moves Online*, 3.

9. Cornfield, *Politics Moves Online*, 67–68.

10. Cornfield, *Politics Moves Online*, 68.

11. Cornfield, *Politics Moves Online*, 73–74.

12. Howard, *New Media Campaigns and the Managed Citizen*, 13–14.

13. Trippi, *The Revolution Will Not Be Televised*; Howard, *New Media Campaigns and the Managed Citizen*, 16–17.

14. Lee Rainie, John Horrigan, and Michael Cornfield, "The Internet and Campaign 2004," Washington, D.C.: Pew Internet and American Life Project, March 6, 2005, at www.pewinternet.org/pdfs/PIP_2004_Campaign.pdf.

15. TNS Media Intelligence, "U.S. Political Advertising Spending Reaches $1.45 Billion," November 1, 2004, at www.tns-mi.com/news/11012004.htm.

16. Cornfield, *Politics Moves Online*, 23.

17. Cornfield, *Politics Moves Online*, 24.

18. Figures were obtained from a LexisNexis Academic Reference Search of Polls and Surveys, Roper Center, "Public Opinion Online," October 29, 2006, Question Numbers 297, 299.

19. This section draws heavily on Lynda Lee Kaid, "Political Web Wars: The Use of the Internet for Political Advertising," in *The Internet Campaign: Perspectives on the Web in Campaign 2004*, ed. Andrew Paul Williams and John C. Tedesco (Lanham, Md.: Rowman & Littlefield, 2006).

20. Banner ads are small rectangular advertisements that appear on a web page; clicking on the ad will take the user to the advertiser's website.

21. Figures were obtained from a LexisNexis Academic Reference Search of Polls and Surveys, Roper Center, "Public Opinion Online," October 29, 2006, Question Number 295.

22. Michael Cornfield, "Presidential Campaign Advertising on the Internet," Pew Internet and American Life Project, October 2004, at www.pewinternet.org/pdfs/PIP_Pres_Online_Ads_Report.pdf.

23. Cornfield, "Presidential Campaign Advertising on the Internet."

24. Susannah Fox, "Digital Divisions," Pew Internet and American Life Project, October 5, 2005, at www.pewinternet.org/pdfs/PIP_Digital_Divisions_Oct_5_2005.pdf; Pew Research Center, "Cable and Internet Loom Large in Fragmented Political News Universe," January 11, 2004, at www.people-press.org/.

25. In spite of the fact that the 2000 and 2004 websites have now been taken down, those who are interested may view these older pages by visiting web.archive.org/, an online archive of old websites.

26. Monica Postelnicu, Justin D. Martin, and Kristen D. Landreville, "The Role of Candidate Web Sites in Promoting Candidates and Attracting Campaign Resources," in *The Internet Campaign: Perspectives on the Web in Campaign 2004*, ed. Williams and Tedesco.

27. Cornfield, *Politics Moves Online*, 66–67.

28. Postelnicu, Martin, and Landreville, "The Role of Candidate Web Sites," 105.

29. James Taranto, "Handicapping the Democrats," *Opinion Journal*, June 30, 2003, at www.opinionjournal.com/extra/?id=110003689.

30. Todd R. Weiss, "Dean's Online Campaign Dubbed Noteworthy," *PCWorld*, July 4, 2003, at www.pcworld.com/article/111457–1/article.html.

31. Jennifer Strommer-Galley and Andrea B. Baker, "Joy and Sorrow of Interactivity on the Campaign Trail: Blogs in the Primary Campaign of Howard Dean," in *The Internet Campaign: Perspectives on the Web in Campaign 2004*, ed. Williams and Tedesco.

32. Farhad Manjoo, "Blogland's Man of the People," Salon, July 3, 2003, at archive.salon.com/tech/feature/2003/07/03/dean_web/index_np.html; Farhad

Manjoo, "Howard Dean's Fatal System Error," Salon, January 21, 2004, at dir.salon.com/story/tech/feature/2004/01/21/dean_internet/index.html.

33. Kaye D. Trammell, "The Blogging of the President," in *The Internet Campaign: Perspectives on the Web in Campaign 2004*, ed. Williams and Tedesco.

34. G. Simms Jenkins, "Email Marketing and the 2004 Election," iMedia Connection, November 1, 2004, at www.imediaconnection.com/content/4499.asp.

35. Cornfield, *Politics Moves Online*, 67–68.

36. Cornfield, *Politics Moves Online*, 69.

37. Cornfield, *Politics Moves Online*, 70.

38. Clifford A. Jones, "Campaign Finance Reform and the Internet: Regulating Web Messages in the 2004 Election and Beyond," in *The Internet Campaign: Perspectives on the Web in Campaign 2004*, ed. Williams and Tedesco.

39. Jenkins, "Email Marketing and the 2004 Election."

40. See Ashli Quesinberry Stokes, "Discrediting Teresa: Wounded by Whispers on the Web," in *The Internet Campaign: Perspectives on the Web in Campaign 2004*, ed. Williams and Tedesco.

41. Rainie, Horrigan, and Cornfield, "The Internet and Campaign 2004."

42. Jenkins, "Email Marketing and the 2004 Election."

43. Cornfield, *Politics Moves Online*, 14–19.

44. Carol Darr and Julie Barko, "Under the Radar and over the Top: Independently Produced Political Videos in the 2004 Presidential Election," Washington, D.C.: Institute for Politics, Democracy and the Internet, October 20, 2004, at www.ipdi.org/UploadedFiles/web_videos.pdf.

CHAPTER 5

1. Dave Montgomery, "Scare Tactics Make Ugliest Race in Years," *Pittsburgh Post-Gazette*, October 30, 2004, A6.

2. Swift Boat Veterans and POWs for Truth, "Any Questions," August 4, 2004, at horse.he.net/~swiftpow/index.php? topic=Ads.

3. Kathleen Hall Jamieson, *Dirty Politics: Deception, Distraction, and Democracy* (New York: Oxford University Press, 1992), 43.

4. Jamieson, *Dirty Politics*, 43.

5. See, for example, Stephen Ansolabehere, Shanto Iyengar, Adam Simon, and Nicholas Valentino, "Does Attack Advertising Demobilize the Electorate?" *American Political Science Review* 88 (1994): 829–38; William G. Mayer, "In Defense of Negative Campaigning," *Political Science Quarterly* 111 (1996): 437–55; Richard R. Lau and Gerald M. Pomper, *Negative Campaigning: An Analysis of U.S. Senate Elections* (Lanham, Md.: Rowman & Littlefield, 2004); David Mark, *Going Dirty: The Art of Negative Campaigning* (Lanham, Md.: Rowman & Littlefield, 2006).

6. Ansolabehere et al., "Does Attack Advertising Demobilize the Electorate?"; Stephen Ansolabehere and Shanto Iyengar, *Going Negative* (New York: Free Press, 1995); Stephen Ansolabehere, Shanto Iyengar, and Adam Simon, "The Case of Negative Advertising and Turnout," *American Political Science Review* 93 (1999): 901–33.

7. Gina M. Garramone, Charles T. Atkin, Bruce E. Pinkleton, and Richard T. Cole, "Effects of Negative Political Advertising on the Political Process," *Journal of Broadcasting and Electronic Media* 34 (1990): 299–311; Craig L. Brians and Martin P. Wattenberg, "Campaign Issue Knowledge and Salience: Comparing Reception from TV Commercials, TV News, and Newspapers," *American Journal of Political Science* 40 (1996): 172–93; Mayer, "In Defense of Negative Campaigning"; Steven E. Finkel and John Geer, "A Spot Check: Casting Doubt on the Demobilizing Effect of Attack Advertising," *American Journal of Political Science* 42 (1998): 573–95; Kim Fridkin Kahn and Patrick J. Kenney, "Do Negative Campaigns Mobilize or Suppress Turnout? Clarifying the Relationship between Negativity and Participation," *American Political Science Review* 93 (1999): 877–89.

8. Mark, *Going Dirty*, chap. 1.

9. Paul Goodman, "The First American Party System," in *American Party Systems*, ed. William Nisbet Chambers and Walter Dean Burnham (New York: Oxford University Press, 1967).

10. Paul F. Boller Jr., *Presidential Campaigns: From George Washington to George W. Bush* (New York: Oxford University Press, 2004), 11. See also Charles O. Lerche Jr., "Jefferson and the Election of 1800: A Case Study in the Political Smear," *The William and Mary Quarterly* 5 (1948): 467–91.

11. Victor Kamber, *Poison Politics: Are Negative Campaigns Destroying Democracy?* (New York: Basic Books, 1997), 15.

12. Boller, *Presidential Campaigns*, 12.

13. Jamieson, *Dirty Politics*, 31.

14. Boller, *Presidential Campaigns*, 12.

15. Kerwin C. Swint, *Mudslingers: The Top 25 Negative Political Campaigns of All Time* (Westport, Conn.: Praeger, 2006), 184.

16. Swint, *Mudslingers*, 185.

17. For more information about the election of 1800, see Susan Dunn, *Jefferson's Second Revolution: The Election Crisis of 1800 and the Triumph of Republicanism* (New York: Houghton Mifflin, 2004). For more information about election results and totals for the election of 1800 and others covered in this chapter, see Jerrold G. Rusk, *A Statistical History of the American Electorate* (Washington, D.C.: CQ Press, 2001).

18. Aaron Burr, who became the Vice President after the election of 1800, later shot and killed Alexander Hamilton in a duel, at least in part because of the political attacks and opposition he endured from Hamilton. See Buckner F. Melton Jr., *Aaron Burr: Conspiracy to Treason* (New York: John Wiley & Sons, 2002, 23–24).

19. Swint, *Mudslingers*, 213–21.

20. Totals from Rusk, *Statistical History of the American Electorate*.

21. Swint, *Mudslingers*, 213.

22. Jeffrey A. Jenkins and Brian R. Sala, "The Spatial Theory of Voting and the Presidential Election of 1824," *American Journal of Political Science* 42 (1998): 1157–79.

23. Boller, *Presidential Campaigns*, 44.

24. Boller, *Presidential Campaigns*, 44.

25. Swint, *Mudslingers*, 217.

26. Swint, *Mudslingers*, 217.

27. Norma Basch, "Marriage, Morals, and Politics in the Election of 1828," *The Journal of American History* 80 (1993): 890–918. See also Boller, *Presidential Campaigns*, 45.

28. Boller, *Presidential Campaigns*, 46.

29. Basch, "Marriage, Morals, and Politics in the Election of 1828."

30. Boller, *Presidential Campaigns*, 46.

31. Swint, *Mudslingers*.

32. Swint, *Mudslingers*, 194.

33. Boller, *Presidential Campaigns*, 118–19.

34. Ward Hill Lamon, *Recollections of Abraham Lincoln, 1847–1865* (Chicago: A.C. McClurg, 1895), 143–48; Boller, *Presidential Campaigns*, 120.

35. Boller, *Presidential Campaigns*, 121–22.

36. Boller, *Presidential Campaigns*, 121–22.

37. John C. Waugh, *Reelecting Lincoln: The Battle of the 1864 Presidency* (New York: Perseus Books, 2001).

38. Swint, *Mudslingers*, 174.

39. Swint, *Mudslingers*, 174.

40. For information about the Liberal Republican convention, see Matthew T. Downey, "Horace Greeley and the Politicians: The Liberal Republican Convention in 1872," *The Journal of American History* 53 (1967): 727–50; See also Boller, *Presidential Campaigns*, chap. 22.

41. Boller, *Presidential Campaigns*, chap. 22.

42. Boller, *Presidential Campaigns*, chap. 22.

43. Swint, *Mudslingers*, 179.

44. Justus D. Doenecke, *The Presidencies of James A. Garfield and Chester A. Arthur* (Lawrence: University Press of Kansas, 1981), 80; Boller, *Presidential Campaigns*, chap. 25.

45. Kerwin Swint in *Mudslingers* rates the 1884 election between Cleveland and Blaine as the third most negative political campaign in American history.

46. Swint, *Mudslingers*, 211. See also Boller, *Presidential Campaigns*, chap. 25.

47. Lance Morrow, "Lance Morrow: Aaah! When Campaigns Were Really Dirty," CNN, June 12, 2000, at archives.cnn.com/2000/ALLPOLITICS/stories/06/12/morrow6_12.a.tm/index.html.

48. Boller, *Presidential Campaigns*, 149.

49. Boller, *Presidential Campaigns*, 152.

50. Thomas C. Reeves, "Chester A. Arthur and the Campaign of 1880," *Political Science Quarterly* 84 (1969): 628–37; see also Boller, *Presidential Campaigns*, chaps. 23–24.

51. Swint, *Mudslingers*, chap. 22.

52. Boller, *Presidential Campaigns*, 339.

53. CNN ad archive, at www.cnn.com/ALLPOLITICS/1996/candidates/ad.archive/humphrey.mov.

54. CNN ad archive, at www.cnn.com/ALLPOLITICS/1996/candidates/ad.archive/horton.mov.

55. Jamieson, *Dirty Politics*, 17.

CHAPTER 6

1. Humphrey Taylor, "Myth and Reality in Reporting Sampling Error: How the Media Confuse and Mislead Readers and Viewers," *Polling Report*, May 4, 1998, at www.pollingreport.com/sampling.htm.

2. Figures were obtained from a LexisNexis Academic Reference Search of Polls and Surveys, Roper Center, "Public Opinion Online," June 2, 2000, Question Number 185.

3. In this sense our objective is similar to Herbert Asher's, whose text (*Polling and the Public: What Every Citizen Should Know*, 6th ed. [Washington, D.C.: CQ Press, 2004]) is not only one of the leading textbooks in the field but also was an invaluable source of material for this chapter.

4. Tom W. Smith, "The First Straw? A Study of the Origins of Election Polls," *Public Opinion Quarterly* 54 (1990): 21–36.

5. See Susan Herbst, "Election Polling in Historical Perspective," in *Presidential Polls and the News Media*, ed. Paul J. Lavrakas, Michael W. Traugott, and Peter V. Miller (Boulder, Colo.: Westview, 1995).

6. From Herbst, "Election Polling in Historical Perspective," 26.

7. Robert S. Erikson and Kent L. Tedin, *American Public Opinion: Its Origins, Content, and Impact*, 7th ed. (New York: Longman, 2005).

8. Peverill Squire, "Why the 1936 Literary Digest Poll Failed," *Public Opinion Quarterly* 52 (1988): 125–33.

9. Olav Kallenberg, *Foundations of Modern Probability*, 2nd ed. (New York: Springer, 2002).

10. Herbert F. Weisberg, Jon A. Krosnik, and Bruce D. Bowen, *An Introduction to Survey Research, Polling, and Data Analysis*, 3rd ed. (Thousand Oaks, Calif.: Sage, 1996), 33.

11. Squire, "Why the 1936 Literary Digest Poll Failed."

12. Asher, *Polling and the Public*, 13.

13. Asher, *Polling and the Public*, 10–11.

14. Asher, *Polling and the Public*, 10–14.

15. Kelly Holder, "Voting and Registration in the Election of November 2004: Population Characteristics," U.S. Census Bureau, Current Population Reports, March 2006, at www.census.gov/prod/2006pubs/p20-556.pdf.

16. Erikson and Tedin, *American Public Opinion*, 45.

17. Asher, *Polling and the Public*, 151–54; Erikson and Tedin, *American Public Opinion*, 45–46.

18. "Bush Leads by Eight Points—or Two—Depending on Definition of Likely Voters," PRNewswire, October 20, 2004, at www.prnewswire.com/cgi-bin/stories.pl?ACCT=105&STORY=/www/story/10–20-2004/0002289475. See also Robert S. Erikson, Costas Panagopoulos, and Christopher Wlezien, "Likely (and Unlikely) Voters and the Assessment of Campaign Dynamics," *Public Opinion Quarterly* 68 (2004): 588–601, for an in-depth exploration of the methods of measuring likely voters by the Gallup Organization. The authors conclude that the variations in the measurement of candidate strength produced by these different methods are greater than actual shifting voter preferences and effects.

19. Richard Morin and Dan Balz, "Convention Gives Kerry Slight Lead over Bush," *Washington Post*, August 3, 2004, A1; Bill Nichols and Susan Page, "Poll: Bush Lead over Kerry among Likely Voters Narrows a Bit," *USA Today*, October 26, 2004, 2A.

20. Erikson and Tedin, *American Public Opinion*, 43.

21. Irving Crespi, *Pre-Election Polling: Sources of Accuracy and Error* (New York: Russell Sage, 1988).

22. Erikson and Tedin, *American Public Opinion*, 43.

23. William G. Mayer, "Forecasting Presidential Nominations, or My Model Worked Just Fine, Thank you," *PS: Political Science & Politics* 36 (2003): 153–57.

24. See the various polls at "White House 2004: Democratic Nomination," Polling Report, 2004, at www.pollingreport.com/wh04dem.htm.

25. Asher, *Polling and the Public*, 128.

26. "Clark Bows Out after Kerry Wins in South," CNN, February 13, 2004, at www.cnn.com/2004/ALLPOLITICS/02/11/elec04.prez.main/index.html.

27. Thomas Holbrook, "Campaign Dynamics and the 2004 Presidential Election," American Political Science Association, at www.apsanet.org/content _5167.cfm.

28. Asher, *Polling and the Public*, 145.

29. See, respectively, "Newsweek Poll: First Presidential Debate," PRNewswire, October 2, 2004, at www.prnewswire.com/cgi-bin/stories.pl?ACCT=109&STORY =/www/story/10–02-2004/0002263797; "Kerry Wins Debate, but Little Change in Candidate Images," Pew Research Center for the People and the Press, October 4, 2004, at people-press.org/reports/display.php3?ReportID=227; "Kerry Holds Edge over Bush Following First Debate," *USA Today*, at www.usatoday.com/ news/politicselections/nation/polls/2004–09-30-debate-poll.htm.

30. See, for example, "Kerry Wins Debate."

31. Stephen J. Wayne, *The Road to the White House, 2004: The Politics of Presidential Elections* (Belmont, Calif.: Wadsworth, 2004).

32. The range of possibilities includes values between forty and sixty, or specifically, 40.2 and 59.8). This assumes a confidence interval of 95 percent; see Erikson and Tedin, *American Public Opinion*, 27.

33. Asher, *Polling and the Public*, 78–80.

34. Gary Langer, "Poll: Last Presidential Debate Is a Draw: Equal Numbers Call Bush, Kerry the Winner," ABC News, October 13, 2004, at abcnews.go.com/ Politics/print?id=163784.

35. Some stories do not report the margin of error at all. See, for example, Carla Marinucci's ("Poll Boosts Bush into a Slim Lead," *San Francisco Chronicle*, September 28, 2000, A3) story about Bush's six-point lead. Although not reported, the margin of error must have been at least three points, perhaps more.

36. Humphrey Taylor, "Bush Leads Gore by Five Points," Harris Poll #65, October 28, 2000, at www.harrisinteractive.com/harris_poll/index.asp?PID=127.

37. "Gore Edges Bush in CBS News Poll," CBS News, October 17, 2000, at www.cbsnews.com/stories/2000/10/18/politics/main242058.shtml.

38. Asher, *Polling and the Public*, 79–80.

39. See the various polls at "White House 2000: Trial Heats," Polling Report, at www.pollingreport.com/wh2gen1.htm.

40. For just two, see the Rasmussen Reports, at www.rasmussenreports .com/election_2004.htm, or Real Clear Politics, at www.realclearpolitics.com/ bush_vs_kerry_sbys.html.

CHAPTER 7

1. "Strong Opposition to Media Cross-Ownership Emerges," Pew Research Center for the People and the Press, July 13, 2003, at people-press.org/reports/ print.php3?PageID=719.

2. "Fewer Favor Media Scrutiny of Political Leaders," Pew Research Center for the People and the Press, March 21, 1997, at people-press.org/reports/print .php3?PageID=530.

3. "Journalism Credibility Project, 1998, the Findings in Brief," American Society of Newspaper Editors, August 4, 1999, at www.asne.org/kiosk/reports/ 99reports/1999examiningourcredibility/p5–6_findings.html.

4. Rachel Smolkin, "A Source of Encouragement," *American Journalism Review* (August/September 2005), at www.ajr.org/article_printable.asp?id=3909. See also David Niven, *Tilt? The Search for Media Bias* (Westport, Conn.: Praeger, 2002), chap. 2.

5. "Strong Opposition to Media Cross-Ownership Emerges."

6. "Journalism Credibility Project, 1998, the Findings in Brief."

7. Doris Graber, *Mass Media and American Politics*, 7th ed. (Washington, D.C.: CQ Press, 2006).

8. Peter Humphreys, *Mass Media and Media Policy in Western Europe* (Manchester, UK: Manchester University Press, 1996).

9. Michael Schudson, "The Objectivity Norm in American Journalism," *Journalism* 2 (2001): 149–70. See also Michael Emery, Edwin Emery, and Nancy L. Roberts, *The Press and America: An Interpretive History of the Mass Media*, 9th Edition (Boston: Allyn & Bacon, 1999).

10. Jody Baumgartner, "Hunker Democrats (1848)," in *Encyclopedia of American Third Parties*, ed. Ronald Hayduk, Immanuel Ness, and James Ciment (Armonk, N.Y.: M. E. Sharpe, 2000).

11. Jody C. Baumgartner, *Modern Presidential Electioneering* (Westport, Conn.: Praeger, 2000), chap. 2.

12. Schudson, "The Objectivity Norm in American Journalism."

13. Stephen J. Wayne, *The Road to the White House, 2004* (Belmont, Calif.: Wadsworth, 2004), 226.

14. Schudson, "The Objectivity Norm in American Journalism," 156, 158, 163.

15. "Newspaper Guild," *Wikipedia*, at en.wikipedia.org/wiki/Newspaper_Guild.

16. Wayne, *Road to the White House*, 226.

17. Schudson, "The Objectivity Norm in American Journalism," 150.

18. "Strong Opposition to Media Cross-Ownership Emerges"; Chicago Tribune Poll, June 23–27, 2004, cited in "Journalism," Polling Report, at www.pollingreport .com/media.htm.

19. "Bottom-Line Pressures Now Hurting Coverage, Say Journalists," Pew Research Center for the People and the Press, May 23, 2004, at people-press.org/ reports/display.php3?PageID=825; "The Newspaper Journalists of the '90's,"

American Society of Newspaper Editors, October 31, 1997, at www.asne.org/index.cfm?ID=2480; Niven, *Tilt?* 13–14.

20. S. Robert Lichter, Stanley Rothman, and Linda S. Lichter, *The Media Elite* (Bethesda, Md.: Adler & Adler, 1986).

21. Eric Alterman, *What Liberal Media? The Truth About Bias and the News* (New York: Basic Books, 2003); Ben H. Bagkidian, *The New Media Monopoly* (Boston: Beacon Press, 2004); David Brock, *The Republican Noise Machine: Right Wing Media and How It Corrupts Democracy* (New York: Crown, 2004). For information about newspaper endorsements, see Harold W. Stanley and Richard G. Niemi, *Vital Statistics of American Politics, 2001–2002* (Washington, D.C.: CQ Press, 2001).

22. Robert S. Lichter and Richard E. Noyes, *Good Intentions Make Bad News: Why Americans Hate Campaign Journalism* (New York: Rowman & Littlefield, 1995); Dennis T. Lowry and Jon A. Shidler, "The Sound Bites, the Biters, and the Bitten: An Analysis of Network TV News Bias in Campaign '92," *Journalism and Mass Communication Quarterly* 72 (1995): 33–44; Paul J. Maurer, "Media Feeding Frenzies: Press Behavior during Two Clinton Scandals," *Presidential Studies Quarterly* 29 (1999): 65–79.

23. Eric Alterman, "The Not Obviously Insane Network," *The Nation*, September 13, 2001, at www.thenation.com/doc/20011001/alterman.

24. Dave D'Alessio and Mike Allen, "Media Bias in Presidential Elections: A Meta-Analysis," *Journal of Communication* 50 (2000): 133–56. See also Niven, *Tilt?* especially chap. 1.

25. Timothy Crouse, *Boys on the Bus* (New York: Ballantine Books, 1973), 355–56.

26. Robert W. McChesney, *Rich Media, Poor Democracy: Communication Politics in Dubious Times* (New York: New Press, 2000).

27. Thomas E. Patterson, *The Mass Media Election: How Americans Choose Their President* (New York: Praeger, 1980).

28. Thomas E. Patterson, *Out of Order: An Incisive and Boldly Original Critique of the News Media's Domination of America's Political Process* (New York: Vintage Books, 1994).

29. Center for Media and Public Affairs, "Campaign 2004—The Primaries," *Media Monitor* 18 (March/April 2004), at www.cmpa.com/mediaMonitor/documents/marapr04.pdf.

30. Howard Kurtz, "Embedded Reporters See What Makes Candidates Tick," *Milwaukee Journal Sentinel*, January 21, 2004.

31. "ABC Recalls Producers from Three Campaigns," *Boston Globe*, December 11, 2003, at www.boston.com/news/nation/articles/2003/12/11/abc_recalls_producers_from_three_campaigns.

32. Graber, *Mass Media and American Politics*, 221–22.

33. Graber, *Mass Media and American Politics*, 221.

34. Center for Media and Public Affairs, "Campaign 2004—The Primaries."

35. Center for Media and Public Affairs, "Campaign 2000—The Primaries," *Media Monitor* 14 (March/April 2000): 2.

36. Jacqueline Bacon, "Weeding the Field: The Lowest Circle," *Extra!* (September/October 2003), at www.fair.org/index.php?page=1153.

37. Howard Kurtz, "Ted Koppel, Anchor Provocateur," *Washington Post*, December 10, 2003, C1.

38. Ian Christopher McCaleb, "Gore, McCain Tops in Nation's First Election 2000 Primary," CNN, February 2, 2000, at archives.cnn.com/2000/ALLPOLITICS/stories/02/01/nh.primary.

39. Graber, *Mass Media and American Politics*, 222.

40. Kiku Adatto, "The Incredible Shrinking Soundbite," *New Republic*, May 28, 1990.

41. Graber, *Mass Media and American Politics*, 222.

42. Larry J. Sabato, *Feeding Frenzy* (New York: Free Press, 1993).

43. Adatto, "The Incredible Shrinking Soundbite," 22.

44. David R. Runkel, ed., *Campaign for President: The Managers Look at '88* (Dover, Mass.: Auburn House, 1989), 136.

45. Timothy Crouse, *The Boys on the Bus* (New York: Random House, 1973).

46. W. Lance Bennett, *News: The Politics of Illusion*, 7th ed. (New York: Longman, 2007), 171–73.

47. Center for Media and Public Affairs, "Campaign 2004—The Primaries."

48. Wayne, *Road to the White House*, 230; "Campaign 2000 Final," *Media Monitor* 14 (November/December 2000); "Campaign 2004 Final," *Media Monitor* 18 (November/December 2004).

CHAPTER 8

1. William J. Keefe and Marc J. Hetherington, *Parties, Politics, and Public Policy in America*, 9th ed. (Washington, D.C.: CQ Press, 2003), 49.

2. Alexander Cockburn and Jeffrey St. Clair, eds., *Dime's Worth of Difference: Beyond the Lesser of Two Evils* (Oakland, Calif.: AK Press, 2004).

3. Eric Boehlert, "Nader's Nadir," *Salon*, February 21, 2004, at archive.salon.com/news/feature/2004/02/21/nader/index_np.html.

4. Eric Alterman, "Bush's Useful Idiot," *Nation*, October 4, 2004, at www.thenation.com/doc/20041004/alterman.

5. Larry J. Sabato and Bruce Larson, *The Party's Just Begun: Shaping Political Parties for America's Future*, 2nd ed. (New York: Longman, 2002), 127.

6. See the American National Election Study, 2004, at www.electionstudies.org/.

7. Great Britain's Labour Party and Germany's Social Democratic Party, however, have received significant attention recently for adopting what some call "third way" positions that defy traditional left-wing policy prescriptions. See Knut Roder, *Social Democracy and Labour Market Policy: Developments in Britain and Germany* (New York: Routledge, 2003).

8. Alan Ware, *Political Parties and Party Systems* (New York: Oxford University Press, 1996).

9. Larry Smith, "The Party Platforms as Institutional Discourse: The Democrats and Republicans of 1988," *Presidential Studies Quarterly* 22(3) (1992): 531.

10. See James D. Hunter, *Culture Wars* (New York: Basic Books, 1991), for one of the first treatments of the culture war phenomenon.

11. Gerald M. Pomper, "Parliamentary Government in the United States: A New Regime for a New Century?" in *The State of the Parties: The Changing Role of*

Contemporary American Parties, ed. John C. Green and Rick Farmer, 4th ed. (Lanham, Md.: Rowman & Littlefield, 2003), 267–86.

12. Individual electors in Maine and Nebraska are awarded based on the winner of the presidential vote in each House district. In practice, all typically end up being allocated to the winner of the popular vote. See Stephen J. Wayne, *The Road to the White House 2004: The Politics of Presidential Elections* (Belmont, Calif.: Wadsworth, 2004), 323.

13. "City Council Election Methods," FairVote: The Center for Voting and Democracy, at www.fairvote.org/media/documents/City_Council_Manual.pdf.

14. Examples include stipulating that a party must receive a minimum percentage of votes (say, 5 percent) to receive any seats, or accounting for partial seats.

15. V. O. Key Jr., *Politics, Parties, and Pressure Groups*, 5th ed. (New York: Crowell, 1964).

16. Louis Hartz, *The Liberal Tradition in America* (New York: Harcourt, Brace, and World, 1955).

17. Maurice Duverger, *Political Parties: Their Organization and Activity in the Modern State*, trans. Barbara North and Robert North, 2nd ed. (New York: Wiley, 1965). See also Arend Lijphart, *Electoral Systems and Party Systems: A Study of Twenty-seven Democracies, 1945–1990* (Oxford: Oxford University Press, 1994).

18. William H. Riker, *The Theory of Political Coalitions* (New Haven, Conn.: Yale University Press, 1962).

19. Morris P. Fiorina, Samuel J. Abrams, and Jeremy C. Pope, *Culture War? The Myth of a Polarized America* (New York: Longman, 2005).

20. Fiorina, Abrams, and Pope, *Culture War?*

21. Duncan Black, "On the Rationale of Group Decision-Making," *Journal of Political Economy* 56 (1948): 23–34; Anthony Downs, *An Economic Theory of Democracy* (New York: Harper, 1957).

22. James A. McCann, "Nomination Politics and Ideological Polarization: Assessing the Attitudinal Effects of Campaign Involvement," *Journal of Politics* 57 (1995): 101–20.

23. Judith Parris, *The Convention Problem: Issues in Reform of Presidential Nominating Procedures* (Washington, D.C.: Brookings Institution, 1972).

24. Terri Fine, "Lobbying from Within: Government Elites and the Framing of the 1988 Democratic and Republican Party Platforms," *Presidential Studies Quarterly* 24(4) (1994): 855; see also L. Sandy Maisel, "The Platform-Writing Process: Candidate-Centered Platforms in 1992," in Robert Shapiro, *Understanding Presidential Elections: Trends and New Developments* (New York: Academy of Political Science, 1996).

25. Ronald Elving, "Party Platforms Helped Shape Fall Campaigns," *Congressional Quarterly Weekly Report*, October 22, 1988, 3041; Beth Donovan, "Abortion: Will the Big Tent Hold All?" *Congressional Quarterly Weekly Report*, Supplement: The Republican Convention, August 8, 1992, 19; Deborah Kalb, "Building with Broad Planks," *Congressional Quarterly Weekly Report*, Supplement: The Democratic Convention, August 17, 1996, 34; Alan Greenblatt, "The Platform Dance," *Congressional Quarterly Weekly Report*, Supplement: The Republican Convention, August 3, 1996, 14.

26. "Republicans: Convention Notes," *Time*, August 26, 1996, 21.

27. Jody C. Baumgartner, *Modern Presidential Electioneering* (Westport, Conn.: Praeger, 2000).

28. Keith T. Poole, "The Decline and Rise of Party Polarization in Congress during the Twentieth Century," *Extensions* (Fall 2005): 9. See also Keith T. Poole and Howard Rosenthal, *Congress: A Political Economic History of Roll-Call Voting* (New York: Oxford University Press, 1997).

29. See also Edward G. Carmines and James A. Stimson, *Issue Evolution: Race and the Transformation of American Politics* (Princeton, N.J.: Princeton University Press, 1989).

30. For work on this subject in the recent Republican-led Congress, see Jacob S. Hacker and Paul Pierson, *Off Center: The Republican Revolution and the Erosion of American Democracy* (New Haven, Conn.: Yale University Press, 2006). See also Geoffrey Layman, *The Great Divide: Religious and Cultural Conflict in American Party Politics* (New York: Columbia University Press, 2001).

31. Thomas E. Mann, "Redistricting Reform: What Is Desirable? Possible?" in *Party Lines: Competition, Partisanship, and Congressional Redistricting*, ed. Thomas E. Mann and Bruce E. Cain (Washington, D.C.: Brookings Institution Press, 2005), 92–114. See also Fiorina, Abrams, and Pope, *Culture War?* 108–111.

32. Poole, "The Decline and Rise of Party Polarization in Congress during the Twentieth Century," 9.

33. Poole, "The Decline and Rise of Party Polarization in Congress during the Twentieth Century," 9.

34. Nolan McCarty, Keith T. Poole, and Howard Rosenthal, *Polarized America: The Dance of Ideology and Unequal Riches* (Cambridge, Mass.: MIT Press, 2006).

35. Mathew I. Pinzur, "Nader Mounts Attack at UNF on Major 'Look-Alike' Parties," *Florida Times Union*, October 13, 2000, A09.

36. Laura Billings, "Candidates' Appearance Tonight Far from 'Debate,'" *St. Paul Pioneer Press*, September 30, 2004; Mike Glover, "Gore, Bush Debate Records," Associated Press, October 11, 2004.

CHAPTER 9

1. Joe McGinniss, *The Selling of the President* (New York: Trident, 1969).

2. Theodore White, *The Making of the President, 1960* (New York: Atheneum, 1961).

3. Jack W. Germond and Jules Witcover, *Blue Smoke and Mirrors: How Reagan Won and Why Carter Lost the Election of 1980* (New York: Viking, 1981).

4. Charles Lewis, *The Buying of the President 2004: Who's Really Bankrolling Bush and His Democratic Challengers—and What They Expect in Return* (New York: Harper, 2004).

5. Kathleen Hall Jamieson, *Packaging the Presidency: A History and Criticism of Presidential Campaign Advertising*, 3rd ed. (New York: Oxford University Press, 1996).

6. Kenneth L. Hacker, ed., *Presidential Candidate Images* (Lanham, Md.: Rowman & Littlefield, 2004); Shaun Bowler and David Farrell, *Electoral Strategies and Political Marketing* (New York: St. Martin's, 1992); Nicholas O'Shaughnessy, *The Phenomenon of Political Marketing* (New York: St. Martin's, 1990); Darrell M. West, *Air*

Wars: Television Advertising in Election Campaigns, 1952–2004, 4th ed. (Washington, D.C.: CQ Press, 2005).

7. Walter Troy Spencer, "The Agency Knack of Political Packaging," in *The New Style in Election Campaigns*, ed. Robert Agranoff (Boston: Holbrook, 1972), 78–95; Gene Wyckoff, "Adventure of an Image Specialist," in *The New Style in Election Campaigns*, ed. Agranoff, 341–49; Leslie Chester, Godfrey Hodson, and Bruce Page, "The Handling of the Candidate: Nixon's TV Campaign," in *The New Style in Election Campaigns*, ed. Agranoff, 312–29.

8. Larry J. Sabato, *The Rise of Political Consultants: New Ways of Winning Elections* (New York: Basic Books, 1981), 115.

9. Erika Tyner Allen, "The Kennedy-Nixon Presidential Debate, 1960," Museum of Broadcast Communications, at www.museum.tv/archives/etv/K/htmlK/kennedy-nixon/kennedy-nixon.htm.

10. O'Shaughnessy, *The Phenomenon of Political Marketing*, 231.

11. Jody C. Baumgartner, *Modern Presidential Electioneering* (Westport, Conn.: Praeger, 2000), 79.

12. Roger Simon, "Backstage at the Opening," *U.S. News and World Report*, June 28, 1999, 20–21.

13. See Keith Melder, *Hail to the Candidate: Presidential Campaigns from Banners to Broadcasts* (Washington, D.C.: Smithsonian Institution Press, 1992); Gil Troy, *See How They Ran: The Changing Role of the Presidential Candidate* (Cambridge, Mass.: Harvard University Press, 1996).

14. Baumgartner, *Modern Presidential Electioneering*, chap. 2.

15. Robert J. Dinkin, *Campaigning in America: A History of Election Practices* (New York: Greenwood, 1989), 67.

16. Dinkin, *Campaigning in America*, 68.

17. Allan Peskin, *Garfield* (Kent, Ohio: Kent State University Press, 1978), 482.

18. Noble E. Cunningham Jr., "John Beckley: An Early American Party Manager," *William and Mary Quarterly* 13 (1956): 40–52.

19. Robert V. Remini, *Martin Van Buren and the Making of the Democratic Party* (New York: Columbia University Press, 1959).

20. Willard King, *Lincoln's Manager: David Davis* (Cambridge, Mass.: Harvard University Press, 1960).

21. Paul W. Glad, *McKinley, Bryan, and the People* (Philadelphia: Lippincott, 1964).

22. Harry M. Daugherty and Thomas Dixon, *The Inside Story of the Harding Tragedy* (New York: Churchill Company, 1932).

23. James A. Farley, *Behind the Ballots: The Personal History of a Politician* (New York: Harcourt, Brace, 1939); James MacGregor Burns and Susan Dunn, *The Three Roosevelts: Patrician Leaders Who Transformed America* (New York: Grove, 2002).

24. Melder, *Hail to the Candidate*.

25. Paul F. Boller Jr., *Presidential Campaigns: From George Washington to George W. Bush* (New York: Oxford University Press, 2004), 67.

26. Boller, *Presidential Campaigns*, 112.

27. Baumgartner, *Modern Presidential Electioneering*, 25.

28. Stephen J. Wayne, *Road to the White House, 2004* (Belmont, Calif.: Wadsworth, 2004), 204–6.

29. David L. Rosenbloom, *The Election Men: Professional Campaign Managers and American Democracy* (Chicago: Quadrangle Books, 1973).

30. Quoted in Dinkin, *Campaigning in America*, 161.

31. Baumgartner, *Modern Presidential Electioneering*, 77; see also David A. Dulio, *For Better or Worse? How Political Consultants Are Changing Elections in the United States* (Albany, N.Y.: State University of New York Press, 2004), chap. 2.

32. Nelson W. Polsby and Aaron Wildavsky, *Presidential Elections: Strategies and Structures of American Politics*, 11th ed. (Lanham, Md.: Rowman & Littlefield, 2004), 143–47; see also Baumgartner, *Modern Presidential Electioneering*, 78.

33. Dennis W. Johnson, "The Business of Political Consulting," in *Campaign Warriors: Political Consultants in Elections*, ed. James A. Thurber and Candice J. Nelson (Washington, D.C.: Brookings Institution, 2000), 37–52.

34. Ruth Marcus and Ira Chinoy, "Lack of Primary Season Foe Leaves Clinton in the Money; President Saved for August Spending Spree," *Washington Post*, August 24, 1996, A1; see also John Harris, "Clinton's Campaign Consultants Reaped Millions from TV Ads," *Washington Post*, January 4, 1998, A4.

35. Sandy Bergo, with data analysis by Agustín Armendariz and John Perry, "A Wealth of Advice," Center for Public Integrity, September 26, 2006, at www.publici.org/consultants/report.aspx?aid=533#.

36. West, *Air Wars*.

37. Dinkin, *Campaigning in America*.

38. James Bryce, *The American Commonwealth*, vol. 2 (Indianapolis: Liberty Fund, 1995), 868–69.

39. Dinkin, *Campaigning in America*, 64.

40. Baumgartner, *Modern Presidential Electioneering*, 23.

41. Peskin, *Garfield*, 495.

42. See Bryce, *American Commonwealth*, 872.

43. Peskin, *Garfield*, 504.

44. Dinkin, *Campaigning in America*, 74.

45. Peskin, *Garfield*, 504.

46. Paul R. Abramson, John H. Aldrich, and David W. Rohde, *Change and Continuity in the 2004 Elections* (Washington, D.C.: CQ Press, 2006), 100–101.

47. Peter L. Francia, *The Future of Organized Labor in American Politics* (New York: Columbia University Press, 2006).

48. Evan Thomas, *Election 2004: How Bush Won and What You Can Expect in the Future* (New York: PublicAffairs, 2004), 168.

49. Wayne, *Road to the White House*, 216–17.

50. Wayne, *Road to the White House*, 217.

51. James W. Ceaser and Andrew E. Busch, *Red over Blue: The 2004 Elections and American Politics* (Lanham, Md.: Rowman & Littlefield, 2005), 133.

52. Richard Lowry, "Bush's Well-Mapped Road to Victory: How Rove et al. Pulled It Off," *National Review*, November 29, 2004, 40–45; Ceaser and Busch, *Red over Blue*, 133–34.

53. Rhodes Cook, "Voter Turnout and Congressional Change," Pew Research Center, November 1, 2006, at pewresearch.org/pubs/83/voter-turnout-and-congressional-change.

54. Thomas, *Election 2004*, 168.

55. "Reggie the Registration Rig Ready to Rock with MTV's 'TRL,'" Republican National Committee, at www.gop.com/News/Read.aspx?ID=4040.

56. William Saletan, "Conclusion," in *Divided States of America: The Slash and Burn Politics of the 2004 Presidential Election*, ed. Larry J. Sabato (New York: Longman, 2006), 269–78.

57. Lowry, "Bush's Well-Mapped Road to Victory, 40–45.

58. Abramson, Aldrich, and Rohde, *Change and Continuity in the 2004 Elections*, 45.

59. David D. Kirkpatrick, "Bush Campaign Seeks Help from Congregations," *New York Times*, June 3, 2004, at www.nytimes.com/2004/06/03/politics/campaign/03CHUR.html?ex=1401595200&election=18d9ee321823ad73&ei=5007&partner=USERLAND.

60. Ceaser and Busch, *Red over Blue*, 133–34.

61. Lowry, "Bush's Well-Mapped Road to Victory."

62. Ryan Lizza, "Head Count: How the GOP Learned Voter Turnout," *New Republic*, November 18, 2002, 14.

63. Lowry, "Bush's Well-Mapped Road to Victory."

64. Abramson, Aldrich, and Rohde, *Change and Continuity in the 2004 Elections*, 100–101.

65. For a thorough discussion on campaign effects, see Thomas M. Holbrook, *Do Campaigns Matter?* (Thousand Oaks, Calif.: Sage, 1996).

CHAPTER 10

1. David R. Mayhew, *Congress: The Electoral Connection* (New Haven, Conn.: Yale University Press, 1974), 81–82.

2. Joseph A. Schumpeter, *Capitalism, Socialism and Democracy* (New York: Harper, 1942); Robert A. Dahl, *A Preface to Democratic Theory* (Chicago: University of Chicago Press, 1956).

3. Figures were obtained from a LexisNexis Academic Reference Search of Polls and Surveys, Roper Center, "Public Opinion Online," October 27, 2006, Question Number 263.

4. James C. Miller III, "Incumbents Advantage," Citizens for a Sound Economy Foundation, at economics.gmu.edu/working/WPE_98/98_05.pdf.

5. Samuel Kernell, "Toward Understanding 19th Century Congressional Careers: Ambition, Competition, and Rotation," *American Journal of Political Science* 21 (1977): 669–93.

6. David Brady, Kara Buckley, and Douglas Rivers, "The Roots of Careerism in the U. S. House of Representatives," *Legislative Studies Quarterly* 24 (1999): 489–510.

7. Gary C. Jacobson, *The Politics of Congressional Elections*, 6th ed. (New York: Longman, 2004), 25.

8. David R. Mayhew, "Congressional Elections: The Case of the Vanishing Marginals," *Polity* 6 (1974): 295–317.

9. See also Jacobson, *Politics of Congressional Elections*, 26–31.

10. Jacobson, *Politics of Congressional Elections*, 31.

11. Janet M. Box-Steffensmeier, "A Dynamic Analysis of the Role of War Chests in Campaign Strategy," *American Journal of Political Science* 40 (1996): 352–71.

12. Roger H. Davidson and Walter J. Oleszek, *Congress and Its Members*, 9th ed. (Washington, D.C.: CQ Press, 2003), 143–44.

13. Jacobson, *Politics of Congressional Elections*, 33.

14. Jacobson, *Politics of Congressional Elections*, 35.

15. Davidson and Oleszek, *Congress and Its Members*, 143.

16. Davidson and Oleszek, *Congress and Its Members*, 145.

17. Stephen Hess, *Live from Capitol Hill: Studies of Congress and the Media* (Washington, D.C.: Brookings Institution, 1991); Timothy E. Cook, *Making Laws and Making News: Media Strategies in the U.S. House of Representatives* (Washington, D.C.: Brookings Institution, 1990).

18. "In addition to senators and representatives, the president, cabinet secretaries, and certain executive branch officials [are also] granted the frank." See "January 22, 1873: Senate Ends Franked Mail Privilege," U.S. Senate, Historical Minutes, 1851–1877, at www.senate.gov/artandhistory/history/minute/Senate_Ends_Franked_Mail_Priviledge.htm.

19. Morris P. Fiorina, "The Case of the Vanishing Marginals: The Bureaucracy Did It," *American Political Science Review* 71 (1977): 177.

20. Davidson and Oleszek, *Congress and Its Members*, 145.

21. Davidson and Oleszek, *Congress and Its Members*, 141–43; Morris P. Fiorina, *Congress: Keystone of the Washington Establishment* (New Haven, Conn.: Yale University Press, 1977).

22. For Senate members, see www.senate.gov/general/contact_information/senators_cfm.cfm; for members of the House, see www.house.gov/house/MemberWWW.shtml.

23. Michael J. Robinson, "Three Faces of Congressional Media," in *The New Congress*, ed. Thomas E. Mann and Norman J. Ornstein (Washington, D.C.: American Enterprise Institute, 1981).

24. Davidson and Oleszek, *Congress and Its Members*, 147–49.

25. For the classic treatment of this, and other legislative norms geared toward the goal of reelection, see Mayhew, *Congress*.

26. "Center for Responsive Politics Predicts '06 Election Will Cost $2.6 Billion," Center for Responsive Politics, October 25, 2006, at www.opensecrets.org/pressreleases/2006/PreElection.10.25.asp.

27. See, for example, any of the quadrennial "Financing the [Year] Election" books, the first of which was by Herbert E. Alexander, *Financing the 1960 Election* (Princeton, N.J.: Citizens Research Foundation, 1962), the latest of which is David B. Magleby, Anthony Corrado, and Kelly D. Patterson, eds., *Financing the 2004 Election* (Washington D.C.: Brookings Institution, 2006). See also Peter L. Francia, John C. Green, Paul S. Herrnson, Lynda W. Powell, and Clyde Wilcox, *The Financiers of Congressional Elections: Investors, Ideologues, and Intimates* (New York: Columbia University, 2003).

28. Herbert E. Alexander, *Financing Politics: Money, Elections, and Political Reform*, 4th ed. (Washington, D.C.: CQ Press, 1992).

29. Davidson and Oleszek, *Congress and Its Members*, 69.

30. Anthony King, *Running Scared: Why American's Politicians Campaign Too Much and Govern Too Little* (New York: Martin Kessler, 1997).

31. Davidson and Oleszek, *Congress and Its Members*, 74.

32. Paul S. Herrnson, *Congressional Elections: Campaigning at Home and in Washington*, 4th ed. (Washington, D.C.: CQ Press, 2003), 40–48; Davidson and Oleszek, *Congress and Its Members*, 62–64.

33. Gary W. Cox and Jonathan N. Katz, "Why Did the Incumbency Advantage in U.S. House Elections Grow?" *American Journal of Political Science* 40 (1996): 478–97.

34. Herrnson, *Congressional Elections*, 41.

35. Figures were obtained from a LexisNexis Academic Reference Search of Polls and Surveys, Roper Center, "Public Opinion Online," October 27, 2006, Question Number 269.

36. This example was taken from Michael D. Robbins, "Gerrymander and the Need for Redistricting Reform," October 25, 2006, at www.fraudfactor.com/ffgerrymander.html.

37. For a fairly comprehensive look at how different states deal with redistricting, see the "Voting and Democracy Research Center" ("Redistricting") section at the FairVote website, at www.fairvote.org.

38. David Lublin, *The Paradox of Representation: Racial Gerrymandering and Minority Interests in Congress* (Princeton, N.J.: Princeton University Press, 1997). See also Davidson and Oleszek, *Congress and Its Members*, 47–50.

39. Jacobson, *Politics of Congressional Elections*, 122–27.

40. Statistics from the U.S. Election Assistance Commission, at www.eac.gov/election_resources.asp.

41. "Ticket-Splitting Ebbs: The Increasing Congruency in Presidential, House Voting," *Rhodes Cook Letter* 6 (4) (July 2005), www.bepress.com/rhodescook/rcl34.pdf.

42. Richard F. Fenno Jr., *Home Style: House Members in Their Districts* (New York: Longman, 2003).

43. Jay Goodliffe, "The Effect of War Chests on Challenger Entry in U.S. House Elections," *American Journal of Political Science* 45 (2001): 830–44.

44. More recently, see James E. Campbell and Steve J. Jurek, "The Decline of Competition and Change in Congressional Elections," in *The United States Congress: A Century of Change*, ed. Sunil Ahuja and Robert Dewhirst (Columbus: Ohio State University, 2003).

CHAPTER 11

1. This section draws heavily on Jody Baumgartner, "Primary," and "Caucus," in *Encyclopedia of American Parties and Elections*, ed. Larry J. Sabato and Howard R. Ernst (New York: Facts on File, 2006). See also Rhodes Cook, *Race for the Presidency: Winning the 2004 Nomination* (Washington, D.C.: CQ Press, 2004); William G. Mayer, ed., *In Pursuit of the White House* (Chatham, N.J.: Chatham House, 1996); William G. Mayer, ed., *In Pursuit of the White House 2000: How We Choose Our Presidential Nominees* (Chatham, N.J.: Chatham House, 2000); William G. Mayer, ed., *The Making of the Presidential Candidates 2004* (Lanham, Md.: Rowman & Littlefield, 2004).

2. Kennedy was only the second Catholic to win his party's nomination (Al Smith, a Democrat, was the first, in 1928). This is the result of a long history in the

United States of anti-Catholicism and anti-papism, specifically, a fear that a Catholic president would take direction from the pope.

3. For the role of the media in the presidential nomination process, see Thomas E. Patterson, *Out of Order: An Incisive and Boldly Original Critique of the News Media's Domination of America's Political Process* (New York: Vintage Books, 1994) and his *The Mass Media Election: How Americans Choose Their President* (New York: Praeger, 1980). For the role of interest groups in financing presidential nominations, see Clifford Brown, Lynda Powell, and Clyde Wilcox, *Serious Money: Fundraising and Contributing in Presidential Nomination Campaigns* (Cambridge, UK: Cambridge University Press, 1995).

4. Cook, *Race for the Presidency*, vii–ix.

5. There is a fair amount of variation in how different analysts classify types of primaries, but the finer points of these classification schemes are not important to this analysis. We rely on the typology offered by Cook, *Race for the Presidency*, vii–ix.

6. Beyond the question of who may participate, there are other differences in state primaries and caucuses as well. One is the issue of what to print on the ballot: delegate names, candidate names, or both. Another is how closely the "pledged" delegates are tied to voter preferences. Although generally delegates follow voter preferences, in some states the vote is technically advisory only, while in others they are formally tied to the preferred candidate for one ballot or more ballots at the convention. A final difference is the formula used to allocate delegates to the winners. Republicans generally award all of a state's delegates to the plurality winner, while Democrats use a proportional representation system (Democrats also mandate that a certain percentage of delegates be women and minorities).

7. Baumgartner, *Modern Presidential Electioneering*, 127.

8. Polsby and Wildavsky, *Presidential Elections*, 11th ed., 101, table 4.2.

9. Baumgartner, "Primary."

10. Baumgartner, "Caucus."

11. Baumgartner, "Caucus," and "Primary."

12. Rhodes Cook, *The Presidential Nominating Process: A Place for Us?* (Lanham, Md.: Rowman & Littlefield, 2004), 100.

13. Stephen J. Wayne, *The Road to the White House, 2004: The Politics of Presidential Elections* (Belmont, Calif.: Wadsworth, 2004).

14. Baumgartner, "Primary."

15. Quoted in Cook, *Presidential Nominating Process*, 99.

16. Cook, *Presidential Nominating Process*, 99.

17. William G. Mayer and Andrew E. Busch, *The Front-Loading Problem in Presidential Nominations* (Washington, D.C.: Brookings Institution, 2003).

18. Barbara Norrander, "The End Game in Post-Reform Presidential Nominations," *Journal of Politics* 62 (2000): 999–1013.

19. Mayer and Busch, *Front-Loading Problem*, 41–42.

20. Cook, *Presidential Nominating Process*, 105.

21. Baumgartner, "Primary."

22. Cook, *Presidential Nominating Process*, 3.

23. Cook, *Presidential Nominating Process*, 107.

24. Baumgartner, "Caucus," and "Primary."

25. Baumgartner, *Modern Presidential Electioneering*, 134.

26. Maine and Nebraska have legal provisions that allow for the possibility of electors to be awarded to more than one candidate.

27. Baumgartner, *Modern Presidential Electioneering*, 134.

28. Wayne, *Road to the White House*, 225; Nathan W. Polsby and Aaron Wildavsky, *Presidential Elections*, 11th ed. (Lanham, Md.: Rowman & Littlefield, 2004), 66.

29. Judith Trent and Robert Friedenberg, *Political Campaign Communication: Principles and Practices* (Westport, Conn.: Praeger, 1995), 220; Robert J. Dinkin, *Campaigning in America: A History of Election Practices* (New York: Greenwood, 1989), 171.

30. Baumgartner, *Modern Presidential Electioneering*, 136.

31. Daron R. Shaw, "The Methods behind the Madness: Presidential Electoral College Strategies, 1988–1996," *Journal of Politics* 61 (1999): 902.

32. Steven J. Brams and Morton D. Davis, "The 3/2's Rule in Presidential Campaigning," *American Political Science Review* 68 (1974): 113–34; Larry M. Bartels, "Resource Allocation in a Presidential Campaign," *Journal of Politics* 47 (1985): 928–36; William G. Mayer, Emmett H. Buell Jr., James E. Campbell, and Mark Joslyn, "The Electoral College and Campaign Strategy," in *Choosing a President*, ed. Paul D. Schumaker and Burdett A. Loomis (New York: Chatham House, 2002), 102–12.

Index

About the Authors

Jody C. Baumgartner received his PhD from Miami University in 1998 and is assistant professor of political science at East Carolina University. His first book, *Modern Presidential Electioneering* (2000), dealt with presidential campaigns in the United States, France, and Russia. He also has an edited book dealing with presidential impeachment from a comparative perspective and an article about presidential pardon power. He has several other articles dealing with the effects of political humor on political behavior, including one that received a great deal of national media attention. His latest publications, *The American Vice Presidency Reconsidered* (2006) and "The Second-Best Choice? Vice-Presidential Candidate Qualifications in the Traditional and Modern Eras" (*White House Studies*, 2007), make the case that the classic view of vice presidents as mediocrities is outdated.

Peter L. Francia is assistant professor in the Department of Political Science at East Carolina University. He is author of the book *The Future of Organized Labor in American Politics* (2006) and coauthor of the book *The Financiers of Congressional Elections: Investors, Ideologues, and Intimates* (2003). Francia has written more than thirty articles and book chapters that have been published on subjects such as American national elections, campaign finance, election reform, political parties, political action committees, and interest groups. He teaches courses on American national government, the U.S. Congress, the American presidency, and social and protest movements in the United States. Francia holds a doctorate in government and politics from the University of Maryland, College Park.